My Life, Your Life

Steps to heal the heart

by Michelle Friedman

tokoloshe books

tokoloshe books

First Published 2002 by Tokoloshe Books
an imprint of STE Publishers
Apple Place 110 Sivewright Ave
New Doornfontein

First published in November 2002

Printed and bound in South Africa by Colours Print

ISBN 1-919855-13-0

Designed by Christian Stephen of Mad Cow Studio

Cover illustration by Ilse Pahl

Back cover photograph by Emil Wessels

Set in 11pt Garamond

About the author

Michelle Friedman, daughter of a Catholic opera singer and a Jewish stockbroker, was born in Johannesburg. Her early childhood years were straddled between a mother in England and a father in South Africa. At 12, under her father's guidance, she was converted to Judaism. After matriculating from Hyde Park High in Johannesburg in 1963, she completed her BA in English at Wits University.

Then began a lifelong search for belonging, identity and authenticity. She spent a year as an actor with the Performing Arts Council of the Transvaal. After a visit to Padre Pio the stigmatist, in Italy, Michelle worked in London as a teacher before returning to Johannesburg in 1969 where she entered the Holy Cross teaching sisters in Aliwal North.

Ten years later she left the convent and started Khula Business Communication in the 1980s working with black graduates and matriculants. To recover from an attempted rape, Michelle studied healing through macrobiotics in Switzerland. A year later she left South Africa for Israel where she returned to her Jewish roots and began her recovery from child sexual abuse. Four more years of healing and working in the United States prepared her for a return to South Africa in 1995.

Michelle has an English Honours degree, a teaching diploma and is completing a Masters in Adult Education. She continues to work in the fields of personal and spiritual growth, healing, conflict-resolution and community building.

To the reader

Hello
Welcome to *My life, your life: Steps to heal the heart.*

There are many ways to use this book.
I have written it in the hope that it will be like a match
rekindling the life of each person who reads it.

As you read, write what your experience has been
either in the pages at the end of each chapter entitled: "My life"
or in your own journal

At the end of each chapter are steps to heal the heart:
They develop some of the themes of each chapter.
Respond to those your heart draws you to.

You may choose to share your responses with a friend,
keep them to yourself
or read the book with a group of friends.

If you'd like to contact me
please call me on 0828930050
or you can write to me at Box 702, Auckland Park, Johannesburg, 2006

This book will be available in Zulu, Pedi and Afrikaans.
and we are available to spend time with you, your friends, community or
organisation accompanying you on your journey

May this book contribute towards your lasting happiness,
may you discover all of who you are and
may peace abide in you through sun and storm.

In your willingness to take this ride
remember you take us all with you.
Thank you for your courage.

Love

Michelle

Table of Contents

Part 1

Michelle Friedman/Hepburn/Charles

Chapter 1 *Small to Medium*

*I*t is the night sky and a five-year-old face presses against the window of a comet, en-route to London from Johannesburg. London — where Mother is. Millions of tiny lights stare back from the blank silence. "Where am I? Who am I?" Michelle closes her eyes tightly and the darkness is inside. Like the plane, she is going on into the nothingness forever. Her sister, asleep beside her, feels far away. Sucked into a vortex of neverendingness, Michelle knows no wall breaks her rush. "Forever. I go on forever." Panic knots her small stomach. "I am. I am forever." In terror she knows there is never an escape. She opens her eyes. Back in the seat she breathes quickly; the abyss closes behind her until, at another time, the blind is drawn back again.

Maybe it was all the movement, maybe it was the terror, but that feeling of neverendingness seemed to reinforce that I was alone, I was abandoned. No-one would ever come to be with me. I would go into eternity by myself, unheld, unprotected, unloved. There was no escape. How could I get away from my I-ness? "Who am I? What is this I?"

As I think back over my early years, these memories, like a swarm of broken bits of stained-glass windows dance like dervishes in the desert air around me, to fall in a puzzle at my feet. The pieces do not fit, and they are not clear.

I recall a honey-blonde child of five or six, with ringlets. She's playing at school, stuffing balls of brown mud into her small panties. How cool it feels; sticky sliding snails, wet warm wonders. Her skin, coated with earth, dries in scabs as it crumbles off like crushed cookies. Yummy!

To the right, there again she sits, but now in a steamy corridor with cold cement as a cushion for this still tiny bottom. Alongside her squat other small children, soap and towels in hand, are waiting for the next available bath at the Holy Family Convent boarding school. When numb-bum's turn comes, the child, too scared to miss her turn or speak her need, obediently enters the closet-like bathroom and, at once, drops two blobs of what once was breakfast and possibly lunch and had spent hours working its way down to this irresistible exit point — the floor. Double-plop! Relieved, she eyes the near-hysterical nun. "Your turn, Sister!"

My mother had become a Catholic after marrying my father, hence the convent boarding school for both her children — my sister Margot and me. Dad didn't seem to mind what religion mother had been or what she was. He was a Jew, forty, handsome, a sportsman, a wary gambler, a stock-broker, a mathematician. Mother was twenty, an actress, very beautiful, an opera singer enmeshed in the Arts. What did they have in common? Not enough to sustain a marriage. My mother moved away to live and work in England.

Dressing rooms in Dudley, deep in snow. In a too-long coat with her little head covered and her gloved hand held tightly in her mother's, the child is carried forward by grown-up-strides. It's Sunday, they're late for Mass. "Mummy," Michelle looks up as she flies, "you're not going to divorce daddy, are you?" Her mother looks down, keeping the pace. "Ofcoursenot-don'tbesilly-wheredidyougetthatfrom-whohaveyoubeentalkingto-what's-thisallabout-we'll be late" — and they rush to pray.

What's next? Yes, that piece. It's her school, Aida Foster's Theatrical School (her sixth school) where Michelle learns for a few hours in the morning, then sings, acts, mimes, dances tap, ballet and jazz till the day's done. Margot has chosen to attend the local grammar school. At Aida Foster's she is Michelle Hepburn, not Michelle Friedman.

Why was I "Hepburn" now? Because that was my mother's stage name. No explanations were necessary. "Friedman" was scratched off our luggage, defaced. Maybe it was too Jewish. Ironically I did not get my picture in *Spotlight,* the book of upcoming child actors. "Because," I was told, "you are not Jewish."

Ballet exam day. The dressing room and hallways steam in anticipation. Excitement oozes out of well-prepared nine-year-old bodies, preening, pointing, tip-toeing, bending, remembering. Lively chatter, all meaningless, floats about our heads like summer gnats circling. In this throng I stand, odd. Shoulders stooped slightly, I throb with anxiety, still clad in my black practice leotard and tights. My mother had sworn, promised, reiterated repeatedly that: "It will be there! Of course I'll bring your dress in plenty of time!" It's already two o'clock and the next name is called: "Sally Bennett".

My tummy knots. Why is this happening to me? What have I done wrong? Too vulnerable to be angry, I sweat in the terror of not being able to take this grade. It means all the world to me: a year's escape from the bewilderment of "life-with-mother-and-her-lover, not-now-her-lover, now-her-lover, here-a-move-there-a-move-everywhere-a-move-move". A year of safety within the structure of "1-2-3-4; 2-2-3-4; 3-2-3-4; 4-2-3-4" within the limits of a class where only the expected takes place. On this tantalising threshold into another year of peace I shiver with dread, tense in every pore. Where is she? 2.30. "Susan Greenstone."

My dress is white silk, fitted for my small, well-proportioned body. As I move the short skirt swirls a light wave. Made just for me. Where is it? You promised! My head feels as though someone is chopping away at it with a hatchet. I hardly dare breathe. Life has stopped in this waiting. Like a small animal knowing it will be slaughtered, I wait. All hope drains from my head down through my body, like blood oozing from a carcass. A coldness swims in its place. I twist my fingers, run again to the toilet, stifling the burning tears forming behind my eyes. I run back. It's 3pm. "Michelle Hepburn."

Her head appears around the door. Mother! Up shoots my energy high like a sudden volcanic eruption. You're here! I feel as though I'm going to vomit. She dangles the dress in my face, excuses pouring from her mouth in a green froth. I grab my ticket to freedom wordlessly and dash to change. I am alive again. Mother disappears. As I dress I try to wipe away the past few hours of desperation, of violence, of pain and concentrate on the long-awaited half-hour ahead.

Michelle Hepburn? Yes! I enter the classroom, stand in first position in the middle of the floor waiting for the music to soothe my soul. As it begins only the dance remains, only the present is in focus, only beauty exists. My dress dances with me gladly. The three adjudicators with their pencils and glasses are an audience of thousands, enraptured by my presence. I worship this moment and will live off it for the weeks ahead.

It was while I was at Aida Foster's that my mother threw her lover Rudolph out. "Who was he, this man? Was he my father?" He lived with us, he disciplined us, he was always there but he seemed like an outsider. Her rejection of him sent him spiralling into a nervous breakdown and I saw his haggard, unshaven face and slouched shoulders waiting for me after school.

"Are you alright Michelle?" he'd ask, helpless. "Do you need money? Food?" He cared, but now he was past tense as Mama moved on to new pastures.

I slipped into experimenting with sex as easily as opening my mouth to eat. In some way I was drawn to it and why not? Here was a place of comfort, of touch, of being held, maybe even of being wanted. My sexual experience began at Aida Foster's with a

9

kiss on the closed mouth of David Wilson; with touching the breasts and bodies of the other girls in the darkness of our bedrooms as we'd make-believe until the "real thing" came along. We were ten years old. In Scotland, while Mother was in a summer show, Margot and I tumbled and tossed with the McIntyre boys at the hotel where we were living — a touch, a kiss, holding hands — a starting point.

It's hot and hazy in the desert of my past. A mirage hovers to haunt me, till in time it shapes itself, firmly holding space. A curtain of concealment cloaks it from me until I am ready to receive it. I never thought to wonder why I couldn't remember much of my childhood. Wasn't everyone like that? I was too young to know that many memories had run, screaming, to a deep, dark corner inside my brain where they could huddle and hide, twist and writhe, protect me from their horror, allowing me to continue my life "as if" everything was just fine.

I was unable to remember that someone, someone close to me, someone I trusted — a male someone, hit me across the face, thrust his penis into my mouth, played with my clitoris, made me feel excited and terrified at the same time. In the darkness, when I was between three and five years old, he would come. No-one was there to help me. In the darkness he would invade my emotional and physical boundaries, probing, stimulating, using, taking and leaving me alone again. "What have I done to make this happen?"

My subconscious catches the cry and hoards it. "This is the way it will always be," my brain registers. "This is the way it has to be. A man has to be stronger than me, bigger, older. I have to not want this. He has to take it, and all the time he is betraying me. I can never expect to trust him, never expect to receive love unless it is taken from me, torn out of me." I feel the excitement, the stimulation and I do not want to feel that, but I like the feeling. How do I get the feeling? This way — all the time? This way — the rest of my life?

Unknown to us, Rudolph, my Mom's ex-lover had written to Dad. He was afraid for us and suggested Dad bring us back to Johannesburg. We had no schooling for almost a year, no clothes, no discipline. We played in Aberdeen, rode the boys' motor-bikes, picked strawberries in the long, light evenings and waited for mother to return from the theatre after her show. Dad sent for us. From Scotland we were put on a train to London and from there onto a plane to South Africa. "Tell your father the rest of your clothes are on the way!" whispered Mother before she stepped back to blow us a kiss, wave us goodbye.

Back to a country I had forgotten, a father I didn't know and felt nothing for. Back to a bleak. Filled with sub-conscious grief for my losses, I sat in my seat like a bundle of hay thrown onto any truckload. Soon a pitchfork would spew me onto the tarmac at Johannesburg International airport to begin another chapter. Our new life would be lived with Selma, my Dad's sister, her husband Jack and Patrick, Dad's son by his first marriage. His second son, Max, would appear only occasionally before he left South Africa permanently for London.

Dad had grown up as one of eight children of Jewish parents who had come from Lithuania. Poor, he had walked at least ten miles to school each day. Bored with class, he decided the racetrack was more fun and he began to bet. He won and gave tips to the teachers who also won. He could add and add fast, so he moved towards the stock market as a boy in his teens. He typed the prices all day and worked his way up to become a respected broker. Twice he lost all he had and twice he began again from nothing.

To me though, he was the man who sat in the large chair in our lounge, smoking a cigar and reading thrillers. He sat at the head of the table at dinner and was remote. He gave me pocket money in the mornings and brought sweets home in the afternoons. I felt I had to win his approval — I had to be clever, pretty, play tennis well, swim fast.

Then he was proud of me, then he'd come and watch me at school, as long as I was on show. It was my responsibility to make him happy.

There was one area of responsibility that Dad, Selma and Jack decided upon for us and that was that Margot and I were to be Jewish. It came like a thunderclap to me, pulling the one rug from under my feet that I had felt somewhat sure of. As a little Catholic, I felt safe. I had been baptised, confirmed — under the pencil-thin eyes of my grandmother — and Church was a place where there was quiet and order, a place to which I belonged. Besides which I had a feeling for Jesus and if I were Jewish, wouldn't I have to give him up? How could I give him up? Another person in my life who is leaving? Why? We were sent to a rabbi in Yeoville for instruction. I had to tell him of my anxieties.

"What about Jesus?" I asked, "Aren't I betraying Jesus?"

The rabbi was old; his long grey beard lay on the table like a duster. Behind his glasses his eyes were deep and he smelled of the sweetness of tobacco. He looked down for a few moments.

"My child," he offered, gently, "there is only one God."

If there is only one God, I thought, then it has to be alright.

For three years we took classes every week, learned Hebrew, the thirteen Principles of Faith, the *Shema*, and got ready to be tested by the *Beth Din*, the Board of Orthodox Rabbis. Dressed all in black with wide-brimmed hats and long dark beards, our judges appear menacing. No chewing gum here! We stand timidly, hardly daring to breathe. First we are asked a number of questions and have to read in Hebrew and recite the Shema. Heads nod, confer, and the judges rise. I look across at my sister. She is fifteen; I am fourteen. We never discussed how we felt about this. I wonder how she is feeling now.

We are led into what appears to me to be a small swimming pool. A woman with a scarf over her head tells us to undress in the cubicle. She hands us each a towel.

"Walk into the water by the steps at the corner. Leave your towels outside on the edge." Gingerly we tiptoe into the warm water.

From another cubicle a woman with grey streaks in her hair emerges. Naked and angry, she makes her way into the water. The assistant stoops to talk to her.

"Why?" she asks loudly, "why must I take off my wedding ring?"

In a hot rage she tugs at her ring to remove it.

"I've waited twenty years for this," she mutters to us between her clenched teeth, "twenty years. They didn't believe I'd stay married."

Clutching the side of the pool the three of us wait anxiously. Above our heads and slightly behind us, a door opens and at least three Rabbis come in and stand on a small ledge inside the door. Oh my God! My arms shoot up across my breasts. Higher than us and at a distance, the men can probably only see the top of our heads, or so we hope. One of the rabbis makes a motion with his hand.

"Go down," instructs our assistant.

We stare at her.

"Under the water," she insists.

We dip under quickly, rising with a bewildered look on our faces.

"Again," she directs, patting the air downwards with her hand.

We bob, obedient. We emerge, our hair covering our eyes.

"And again," she hisses.

Like ducks, we dive once more. I have no idea of the meaning of this.

The Rabbis pronounce words in Hebrew and disappear. We three clamber out in fast relief, grab the towels and dash for the cubicles. "Here," offers our assistant pushing a hair-drier into our hands. She beams, her eyes watering. The angry wife is in tears. I don't understand.

Dry and dressed we return to the main room where everyone congratulates us. Mazeltov! What have I done to merit such acclaim and approval? I understand that I am Jewish now. Orthodox. This will make me socially acceptable. Dad and his family can relax. I have a passport to marriage and a life happily ever after.

How did this change affect my everyday life? It hardly touched it, on the surface, except I wasn't allowed to date non-Jewish boys. I didn't go to Church and hadn't for three years, but we still celebrated Christmas with a tree and presents and dinner. I went with Dad to relatives for Passover and to synagogue on the High Holy Days of Rosh Hashanah and Yom Kippur.

That was a strange world for me. There was a lot of talking and movement. I couldn't follow what was happening. Why did everyone dress up so much? Why did we spend more time outside talking to the boys? It reminded me of the movies on a Saturday afternoon. On a deeper level this change threw me into a no-woman's land.

I didn't know how to contact God with sureness any more, and if God was gone, what was there?

Well, there was Patrick, my half-brother, son of my father. We called him Paddy. He wouldn't go away, would he? Paddy was gentle, tall, very thin, with brown eyes staring out of an almost gaunt face. I didn't know why he was living with us, what he did to make money, if anything, but I knew he was about forty. Dad, Selma and Jack were very considerate of Paddy. It seems he had "been sick in London" for some time. The nature of the sickness was vague, as if hidden. Paddy was a bit of a mystery.

He was also magic. He'd play with us, read to me before I slept, help me with my homework. He taught me to dance, to swim, to drive my Dad's car, to love the sound of words rhyming. He philosophised, read encyclopaedias and talked a whole lot about love and God. He seemed to know about that. I loved him.

Paddy had ideas of being an actor in America. He'd sing and act around the house. I found it a mite amusing but mostly it was embarrassing. He didn't have much of a voice and laughed loudly and often in high-pitched-bordering-on-hysteria shrieks at himself and his jokes. Sometimes I was so appalled I wished I could curl up into a small woollen ball and wriggle under the doormat. That was mostly when we had guests and Paddy pounced on the audience to entertain them. He had seen just about every musical ever made, knew all the songs, wrote his own, imitated actors and danced like Fred Astaire. There was no interval. We never had many repeat visitors. On the whole Paddy reminded me of Jesus — except when he was acting.

In his belief that his destiny lay in the States, he packed his bags and went to the airport expecting a ticket to be waiting for him. It would be a miracle. It wasn't. He had concocted a cock-and-bull story about a man who would give him what he needed.

"His sickness," muttered Selma to Jack, pursing her lips and shaking her head.

"Poor Jumbo," she murmured. Jack nodded. We all drove home in silence. I was secretly relieved he didn't go. What would I do without him?

Although the stab was stayed, the executioner's knife finally fell. Dad provided the miracle. He paid for Paddy to fly to America and seek his fortune there. After three years of his presence, Paddy's departure was traumatic for me. Going. Paddy is leaving me. There it was again. The same thing happening. Someone I loved was leaving and leaving me. What had I done to make this happen? Was I so bad? Was I not good enough for anyone to stay? What did I have to do or to be to make someone stay? I thought I would die without him. Who could I hold onto who wouldn't leave me?

Steps to Heal the Heart

Being a child

Sit where you can be quiet. If you are at home and have some privacy, you might like to light a candle or play a piece of music that makes you feel good. Perhaps you'd rather sit outside on the grass or under a tree. Some people find it easy to go to a café and find privacy in being alone there.

Wherever you chose, take a few deep breaths and ask yourself the question:

"What do I remember as a child? What part of my childhood needs my attention now?"

Close your eyes and rest in the dark, fertile, earthy silence. The question will go into your subconscious and when the answer is ready, it will appear. Your memory may be eager to speak or she may still be a little shy. Trust her. When you hear her, listen and write. If you feel like it you might begin to write now. Write whatever comes into your head or your heart about what it was like for you as a child. Stay with the feelings that rise.

Stay with yourself until you are ready to go back to be with other people. You might want to share your writing with a friend, or you might want to keep it to yourself for a little while or forever. It is your life and it is precious.

Father and Mother

What thoughts and feelings arose as you read this chapter? Can you remember the relationship between your mother and father? How would you describe it? Can you give examples? Did your parents bring you up or did you grow up with your grandmother? Who did you grow up with? Perhaps you lived with one of your parents? What was that like for you? What does it still feel like? Are you close to your mother? Your father? Is your grandmother/grandfather still alive? Is there a particular incident you remember in your early childhood connected to your parents or one of them? Would you like to write about it? Or would you like to tell somebody you trust? Begin to write what you want to.

Your name

How do you feel about your name? What is the meaning of your name? Are you named after anyone else in the family? Who named you? Do you have more than one name?

What was it like for you at school — having your name? If your class list was arranged alphabetically, how did you like where your name sat? How did the other children and the teachers react to your name? Would you prefer to be called by another name? What would that be? Would you change your name?

If you are female and you decide to marry, would you take your husband's name? If you are male, would you expect your wife to drop her surname? If you are a gay couple, what are your plans around name-retainment or name-change if you marry? If you have children whose surname will they take?

Sisters and brothers

Which child were you? First? Middle? Baby? Describe your siblings. Did you like them? All of them? Who was more important for you? If you were an only child, what was that

my life

like? Where are your brothers and sisters today? Do they have any influence on your life? Have you drifted apart? Do you feel that the friends you have now are more like brothers and sisters to you? Would you like your family to be bigger? Smaller? Why? What did you gain by the size of your family? What did you lose? Draw your family and allow the colours you choose to tell you how you feel about them. Write about your sisters and brothers, or maybe even write to them. Tell them now what you have never told them.

Female or male

When did you realise you were female, not a male; or male, not a female? What was that like for you? Do you remember noticing that the other sex had to do different things from you? That as a girl, you had to be home early? That boys could play rough games, but you couldn't? What were the messages you began to understand about your being a girl or a boy? Is there anything in particular you remember? Write a poem about being the sex that you are. What feelings arise for you as you think about this?

Your life at school

How would you describe that? Did you feel part of it all? What was your class like? Your teachers? Did they make any impact on you? If so, was it positive or negative? Does any particular experience stand out for you? Did you go to more than one school? What do you most want to write about now?

What about your friends at school? Who were they? Were they casual or close friends? Was there any one particular friend who meant a lot to you? Do you know where s/he is today? Would you like to? What would you say to that friend? Write it. Or say it out loud. Then sit opposite yourself and answer back as your friend. Continue the conversation in this way.

God

If ever you did, when did you first hear about God? Who told you? What did that word mean to you when you were small? Did you ever hear it in your home? What are your earliest memories about God or religion? What were your early feelings associated with God or religion? Did you go to Church or Synagogue or to the Mosque? Did your parent/s or caregivers believe in God/not believe in God and how did that affect your relationship with them?

Did you say prayers at night? What was that like for you? What about at school? Did you have a religious assembly each morning where you would sing and pray? What was that like? Did you have an early experience that there was something about life that you couldn't see but you could sense there was more to life than what you saw? Can you describe that? What is your stance now on God and on religion?

Whichever one or more of these questions gets to you, write a response. You could also write a letter to your parents or caregivers telling them how you felt about what they taught or didn't teach you about God and/or religion. You might prefer to write to a child of your own telling her or him what you wanted to hear about God or religion or the life of the spirit when you were a child.

Losing a family member

Did you lose a parent — either through death or because s/he was never there? Did any of your brothers or sisters disappear never to return? Did you experience a loss early in life?

my life

Take some time to write about the person you lost. Or write to that person and tell him or her how you feel. Tell your loved one everything you ever wanted to. That person may not be physically present but they are not gone. You just can't see them. Talk to them as though they were sitting with you. Listen for a reply. It may come in many ways — through a person, through a song on the radio, through something that happens. Another way to access a response is to use your non-writing hand to write a reply to yourself. You may be surprised. When your heart reaches out a response returns.

Your roots

Do you know your mother's or your father's background? Where did they originate? How far back can you trace your roots? What languages did your parents speak? Did you know your grandparents? Your aunts and uncles? What languages did you grow up speaking? How do you feel about your home language, your own language now? Is it important to you to preserve and use? If so, how can you ensure that?

A special person

Was there anyone who was there for you when you were growing up whom you could call a special friend? Someone you could turn to any time? Someone who would always understand you? Who was this person? Write about her or him or write to her or him.

Someone who is "funny"

When I was small I realised that people thought of Paddy as "strange". He had gone through some demanding experiences on an emotional and mental level. My family spoke about him in hushed tones. I learnt that these are the tones you use for someone who is "not like the rest of us". Is there anyone in your family or are you yourself physically, emotionally or mentally different to the so-called "able" majority? What is that like for you? What were the messages you got from society about children or people who were different in these ways? Imagine you are a person who is deaf or who has emotional challenges or who has been born with a cleft foot or has a spinal malfunction. Write what it is like for you to live in a world where you are treated as though you are not a human being. What advice would you give to those of us who need to understand you better? What advice would you give to other people like yourself? Write this now.

Chapter 2 *Medium to Matric*

*I*was fourteen, going on forty, and love was in the air. It came down to earth in the form and shape of Matt Kenton who looked like James Dean, only blonder and taller. Four years my senior and in Matric (the final year in South African schooling) Matt was "one of the okes, the main *manne*" at our school, Hyde Park High. We'd stand a short distance away from each other at the breaks. I'd be with my friends; he'd be with "the gang." He'd saunter over to me acting like he was passing, then he'd throw me a slow smile. My stomach swung into a vibrant rock 'n roll and I'd beam back at him. I'd excuse myself from class and walk past his classroom, trying to catch his attention. He'd do the same. Every day was a calculation. When and how could I see him? How many times could I see him? What were the words we'd say? I lived like a highly-strung violin, in a state of continuous readiness to play the mating game.

Matt drove a motorbike and had the use of a car. He was definitely a big deal. When, oh when, would we go out? How would this happen? We were part of a larger group and we'd all go to parties together. One evening Matt asked me if I'd like to be his partner at the farewell dance for his class. "Yes, oh yes." It was the most romantic date. We behaved impeccably. He drove me home and we walked down the driveway under the full moon. Halfway down he stopped and took me in his arms. He kissed me in a gentle, reassuring way. He knew what he was doing and I knew nothing except I was delirious with joy. That kiss lasted for hours in my mind. I swooned for days after, living in remembrance of the promise and comfort of that moment.

We were on our way. We were definitely dating. Parties abounded. Matt and I would dance well and wildly till about two hours before midnight, then we'd nip outside to hold and kiss each other. We'd start by holding hands and then we progressed to kissing "properly" with our mouths open. We developed a system. A kiss was Base One. Fondling my breasts was Base Two. My holding his penis was Base Three. He touching my clitoris was Base four. And so on. We moved slowly and cautiously over time from one base to the next — always agonising over our uncontrollable behaviour and promising to behave better next time. Next time was always worse.

We had no safe place to be together, so the car came in very handy, so to speak. The afternoon my uncle Jack came upon us kissing against the wall in the card room was a turning point, literally. Matt turned around to face Jack who was having a near-death experience. "Oh my God," spluttered Jack. The back door of the room led to the garden and could be reached within five seconds. Matt held the record. Jack, hardly breathing, stumbled up the stairs, "Selma, Selma!" he wheezed gasping the news to Selma who promptly hit all the ceilings in the house (and there were many). Dad, duly informed, obeyed Selma and agreed. "Michelle, you are not allowed to see, speak to, or have anything to do with Matt ever again!" Besides which he wasn't Jewish. That put the lid on it.

In Matt's car and at a party to which he wasn't going and to which my friend Diane's parents were taking me, Matt and I considered the situation carefully. We were almost at home base. Could we, should we, behave and obey my scandalised family? What would I get in exchange for giving him up? What was he giving me in my life? He was someone I was beginning to love, someone I could talk to, someone who was interested in me, who paid me attention, who touched and held me, who looked beautiful, who loved God and who filled the holes of my loneliness. I was in heaven. Why should I give him up? I would lie and deceive to get out of the house, but I would not let him go.

On my sixteenth birthday I lost my virginity. (Bass chords in the background). Matt planned it all (enter right, twirling moustache). On a Friday night he fetched me from Diane's house (an unpaid accomplice) and drove me on the back of his forbidden bike (Help! Help! He's got me!) to his home in Craighall Park, which was empty. His mother was away; she'd eat both of us alive if she found out.

It was winter. Only the tiger-eyed fire watched us from the grate as Matt deftly and gently laid me on the carpet and took off my jeans and panties. There was no discussion, no foreplay. This wasn't making love; this was breaking and entering only. The room was dark, warm and silent. We locked eyes as he inched inside me carefully. It was sore and uncomfortable. Matt placed a towel underneath us, just in case. There, we'd done it. A bloodless, calculating act. I was no longer government property; I was Matt's. Taken. The lust and the sperm would come later. This was enough for the first night. Matt biked me back and I crept into bed, waking no-one.

On Saturday morning, on the hockey field, I held my secret. Now I was a woman. A penis had pierced my vagina. I was home to someone now; one of two. I belonged. Separate from the foolish virgins flailing around the hockey field, I had graduated to graver responsibilities. I felt superior and sure. I had traded innocence for intimacy. My eyes veiled instead.

For the next three years of high school Matt and I met and made out wherever we could, however we could — in the car, at his home, in gardens, in elevators, rarely in peace. We were afraid of being caught, afraid of my falling pregnant, and soaked in guilt.

Towards the end of my final year I began to lose interest in Matt. I was bewildered. This was supposed to last forever; I had imagined us as an elderly couple groping our way into a darkened cinema, clutching onto each other for support, holding hands in the dark, dozing on each others' shoulders, then shuffling carefully out again to be driven home by one of our children. Breaking-up was anguish for both of us. We'd talk, I'd cry, we'd try again. Matt would plead, bargain, get angry and walk away cowed. I'd wonder if I were making a mistake, call him back, start the process again and again. Until the thread was so thin, the interest so fragile, the futility so clear.

At the time of our first parting, I was ill-equipped to deal with men. If I felt attracted to the man, then I sleep with him? Is this the pattern? Matt told me, matter-of-factly that I'd sleep with many men. I was horrified and pained.

"Of course I won't," I remonstrated, tears filling my eyes.

"You will," proclaimed his royal majesty sombrely, "you'll see."

I was on a slippery road with no skates, no ring to contain me, no instructions on how to chart my course, no one to hold my hand, just my pressing needs, my gaps of loneliness, my fear of abandonment, my losses adding up. The one difference here was that I had ended the relationship; I chose to leave Matt.

Dad decided to sell the house when I was sixteen. A woman who was clearly insane bought it and we all moved into The Hotel Quirinale, in Hillbrow. Margot and I shared a room again.

"Mickey, I don't want to stay at school." She was sitting on the edge of the bed.

"Why not? You're so popular, you could be head girl!" I was appalled.

"I don't want to be head girl, anyway, I would never be. They'd never vote for me."

"Who wouldn't?"

"The teachers. I'm not that clever."

"You are! That's not true, you'd easily make it, you know you would!" I insisted, now standing with my hands on my hips, determinedly.

"I hate school. I hate Afrikaans. I can't do it."

We had missed years of basic Afrikaans and it was a struggle to try to catch up.

"I hate sport ... can't bear the uniform ... don't like the boys and they don't like me ... so what the hell ... I'm going to speak to Daddy."

"What'll you do?" My voice was quiet, afraid.

"Don't know ... go to business college or something. Damelin."

"But you won't have a matric, Margot ... "

"I don't want one." She got up and walked to the bathroom. "I don't want to be there, Mickey, and I'm not going to stay."

I felt it was a drastic move and also very grand. My sister was leaving school, taking her life in her own hands.

Margot took charge of the situation as she had done in Scotland when she had written to Dad telling him about our life. She talked him into letting her leave school without a matriculation certificate. She went to a business college, left the hotel to stay with a friend and moved out of my life. I hardly felt her go, I was on the move myself. Both of us were desperately trying to survive in our own way; we were unable to help each other. We needed to feed from the same trough but the trough wasn't big enough for two. We went our own ways, walking into the distance, occasionally looking back, making eye-contact, wistfully wishing we could be sisters. That would come much, much later.

It was coming up to my final year in high school. Mr Marais, our Afrikaans teacher, called me out of class one morning.

"Michelle, how are you feeling about your final year?"

"Fine, I guess," I quipped, not sure what I had done wrong now.

"How is it at the hotel? Do you have time to study there?" he probed.

"Not really," I admitted.

"I think that if you want to get your matric you'd be better off living with a family. Isn't there anybody you know you could stay with for a year?"

Who could I ask?

"What about Mrs Harrington?"

"Who's that?"

"Julie's mother, the hockey coach. How well do you know Julie?"

"She's in Standard Seven. I only know her from hockey."

"Do you like her?"

"I guess ... I hardly know her."

"Well, why not ask her just the same?" He was kind, concerned. I will always be indebted to Mr Marais.

I spoke to Julie, who spoke to her mom, who thought it was a great idea. Dad saw the sense in it, Mrs Harrington's husband, James, approved and abracadabra I was in a house, in my own room in Melrose and Dad was a Saturday morning visitor armed with fruit and cake. Father Christmas was a role he loved playing.

This was my foster family. Julie was three years younger and generous towards me — a newcomer, almost an intruder. Emma taught children with learning difficulties, children who were often committed to institutions. She was a brilliant teacher, a woman of strong faith who loved and encouraged her students and often saw them enter the mainstream. Her relaxation was love-story-comic-books and hockey. James, an engineer, passionate about gardening, was an agnostic with a heart of gold and an irrepressible sense of humour. The three of us would argue for hours: philosophy, poetry, religion, morals, ethics ... we'd hit 'em all. I loved them, I felt loved and accepted.

Shadrack and Lizzie were the Harrington's servants. They moved in and out of the

20

house with ease. In "Casa de Paz", my first home in Saxonwold, we had servants of course, but they were like shadows. The kitchen was theirs. I'd seldom venture into their rooms in the courtyard without some sense of trespassing and unease. Their rooms were small and dark, places of mystery and secrecy, invaded spasmodically by the police. I took our servants for granted, expecting my food to be ready when I returned from school, my bed to be made, my dirty clothes returned within a couple of days, clean and pressed. Having been in South Africa now for at least three years, I was becoming blind, losing my sight. But Paddy saw clearly. He flicked the switch which set me a course of releasing myself from the complex coils of the apartheid chain.

One morning when I was thirteen, before I left for school and before I went to live with the Harringtons, I noticed Paddy was in tears.

"What's the matter?" I asked, stricken to see him so.

"Maria," he blew his nose, "Maria's baby is dead."

Maria? Our laundry-maid? I didn't even know she had a baby. She was a shadow who came in early on Monday and left late in the afternoon.

"If she were white," Paddy continued, looking at me through pain-filled eyes, "she would not have lost her child."

"What do you mean?"

"If she were white, she would have access to a doctor, she would be treated as a person, she would have the money to get her child to the hospital, but she is black. She is poor. She has no telephone in her home. She has no health insurance. She has no car. And nobody cares because she is black. It doesn't matter because she is black. What's another dead black baby?"

His voice was quiet and grim, his anger controlling it so that it pierced knife-like into me. I gasped, feeling his pain and beginning to glimpse the horror of the truth he might be showing me. He was standing at a window of revelation, his hand on a curtain, about to draw it back to allow me to see what gruesome truth lay on the other side.

"Have you looked into the faces of the black people you pass in the street?" he asked.

"No," I whispered, dropping my head, "I can't tell the difference."

"That's because you don't look," he said, gently lifting up my face in his hand. "You don't see a black person as a person. Today I want you to walk to school. Wheel your bicycle on the pavement and look into the faces you pass!"

Disturbed and shaken I did that. I walked slowly, looking into eyes. At first I saw only faces and then I began to distinguish eyes that were different in each face; noses that were not the same; cheekbone structures; height, weight, body shape, foot length, hair differences, mouth variations — these were people, just like me! It came as a shock. I had been living in a world of human beings who were white, and then shadows who were black. I sat stunned throughout class that day. What had I missed? Was it too late? Who were the people who lived in my home, who made my bed every day, who cooked my food? What was life like for people who slept in tiny rooms on the roof, who could not get jobs like "we" could, who could not travel around like "we" could, who could not use a toilet in a shop or any building because they were black? I remember seeing a woman in her fifties stop in the middle of the street and relieve herself. She had nowhere else to go.

I was faced with the enormity of a system so unjust and so omnipresent. It swarmed around me, in the streets, in my home, on the radio, among my friends. Like a malignant disease it seeped into all our pores, blinded our eyes, hardened our souls. What could I do about it? Who else knew how ill we were? Was I alone in this? I had to face it, that was my first step, face the facts and find a way to do something.

I didn't know then that my own feelings of powerlessness, of being a victim, made it easy for me to identify with the position of black people around me. My own sense of inadequacy found a home in the lack of self-worth held by many. All the repressed rage seething in me because I had been sexually and physically violated and abused between the ages of three and five, found a focus in the injustice of South African apartheid. I also had a heart that was compassionate. On a genuine level I cared. It was that level that propelled me to act, to do what I could to change the pain, to heal. In the reaching out to heal others, I learned to heal myself.

So there I was, my final year completed, sixteen going on seventeen. My father still lived in the hotel with his sister Selma and her husband Jack. Margot had gone to London to live with mother who, after the divorce, had left South Africa for Australia. What was unknown to us was that she had been refused permission by the court to have any contact with her children. The only communication I had from her between my twelfth and seventeenth birthday was when a set of photos arrived of her marriage to an Australian physicist. She had simply disappeared from my life, a misty memory, a cloud on the horizon. Now for some reason she was in London.

What was my next step? I wanted to be a singer but I wasn't clear how to do that. My English teacher, Rene Carson, suggested I try a teaching career. Why not? I'd take a government loan, live in residence (where would I live anyway?) and the next three years of my life would be tied up in a BA degree at the University of the Witwatersrand. I'd teach for three years to pay back the money. Simple.

Like a six-year-old wobbling out the front door in her mother's hat and high-heels, I headed for the student world. On the surface I appeared to be full of vitality and confidence. I weighed in at 125lbs, 34-22-34.

Underneath and largely unknown to me, stands the child alone on a wide road in a desert of nothingness. She has a vague sense of direction. Knotted inside her are cancers of loss, abandonment, of shame and guilt, of not being good enough, of not being worthy. Her little hand gropes in the air to feel for someone to take it, to hold her, to lead her, to love her. Ghosts file past: her mom, Margot, Paddy, Matt. Is there anybody out there? Yes, there are Emma, James and Julie waving from their front door and Dad disappearing into the hotel. There is nothing to do but to keep moving.

As Michelle Friedman, seventeen, white, not a virgin, just woken to the stench of apartheid, now a Jew, I signed in to Reith Hall residence on Hoofd Street, Braamfontein for the next leg of the journey.

steps to heal the heart

First love

Who was your first love? Or with whom did you have your first sexual experience? Go on a journey of remembering how you met; what happened after that; how your relationship developed; when it became physical and what that was like for you. How old were you and did you tell anyone? Do you still know that person? Is there one main feeling that has remained with you? If you had to create an object or a symbol of your first boy or girl friend what would it be? Can you draw it or use some play-doh and sculpt it. Then think about this question and write the answer: How has your first sexual experience affected other sexual relationships in your life?

When did you first become aware that you, as a girl, were sexually attracted to boys or that you were attracted to girls? When did you first become aware that you, as a boy, were sexually attracted to girls or to boys? Did you discuss your feelings with other boys or girls? If you, as a girl or a boy, were attracted to the same sex what were the messages you got about this? Who could you talk to? What was your process of claiming your right to be gay or lesbian?

Stepmothers and fathers, stepsisters and brothers

I had a step-father in London; a step-mother in Johannesburg; two half-brothers and in my final year at high school I lived with Mr and Mrs Harrington — they became my foster-parents. What about you? Did you, as a child, live with a woman who was not your mother, or a man who was not your father, but who took on the role of parent? What story could you write about what that was like for you?

Perhaps you are adopted. I met a young girl of sixteen who was going through a crisis. She discovered that she was adopted, and that both her parents had died in a car crash. She was sad and confused. She suddenly felt unloved and unwanted and angry that her "parents" had not told her. It came as a shock. Over time she began to realise that the people who took responsibility for her did love her. But it wasn't easy adjusting to the fact that they were not her real parents.

What about you? When did you find out you were adopted? Do you know who your biological parents are? Do you want to find out and do you know how to do this? Write how you feel about being you and about the people who are your parents now. Write a letter to the parent or parents who, for one reason or another, couldn't bring you up. Stay with the feelings that come up and if you have a close friend, share them with her or him.

Did your family structure change when you were growing up? Did your parents divorce or separate or were they never together? What was that like for you? Were you involved in the divorce? Was your opinion asked? Did you have any choice as to who you would live with? Were you separated from your brothers and sisters or from your parents? How did you cope with the change? How do you feel about this now? Respond in writing.

Apartheid

If you were alive in 1994 and more than a baby, you must have experienced what it

my life

was like to live under the apartheid system. At what point in your life did you become aware that you were treated differently than people of another skin colour? What was your first experience of seeing people abused because they were not white? What was your first experience of abuse because you were black or brown? What did you think and feel? What did you do? Think about this and translate it into a physical form — a poem, a drawing, a piece of music, a sculpture, a dance, a song, a dramatic scene or one-act play.

Or just write!

Choice of career

How far did you go at school? How do you feel about that? How did your being at school or not being at school affect your future? If you were unable to complete your schooling, is it too late now? What would you have chosen if you were free to make a choice? Would you have stayed at school? And then? What career path? What further study? Who helped you to make choices when you were a teenager? Were you pushed into your life after school? Or did you slip into it? Write a letter to yourself as a seventeen year old. Tell yourself everything you needed to hear from someone, like a parent or close adult friend who loved you, encouraged you, believed in you. Write this letter of appreciation to yourself now.

Chapter 3 *Student to Singer*

Wits campus was very Jewish and the pressure to find my place as part of that wedged in on me. I'd spend the Jewish holidays with Devorah Katz in Klerksdorp and mid-term Dev and I went home with Ariella Samuels to Durban. Although I had Jewish girl friends we never talked about being Jewish. It was just there. That wasn't enough for me. I wanted to know more. Perhaps if I went to Israel I'd have a better idea?

I asked my Dad to send me. Not only did he agree to my going — *Dayenu*! (And that would have been enough in itself!) Not only did he pay for the trip — *Dayenu*! But he also agreed to pay for me to go to Europe and visit my mother and Margot in London.

In November 1963 I flew to Israel alone and went straight to Kibbutz Tsorah not far from Jerusalem. I would meet up with the group a few weeks later. First I wanted to get the feel of Israel on my own. Tsorah was sandy, spartan and smelled of paraffin. I slept in a guest hut at the edge of the kibbutz. I was led to understand that to be accepted by the "sabras" (Israelis) I had to prove I could work well. No problem. For three weeks I could bluff anyone. I ironed shirts in the laundry (first time ever), cut cane in the fields and other back-breaking exercise, sliced tomatoes in the kitchen and lost all my table manners just like the Israelis. It was stretch or starve. I met with approval.

On December 25th I sat in a cane field cutting the long stalks into small segments. I was alone. Christmas was just another day here. It was as if Jesus never happened, no-one ever knew. But I knew. I knew that at this moment, people in Johannesburg were opening Christmas presents; they had been to midnight Mass. Carols were still being sung and the mistletoe was watching couples kissing. "It's Christmas day," I thought, "it is."

Tsorah was not without romance in the form of a young Kibbutznik, Avi, who raced me around the area on the back of his bike, and made love to me at night, deftly showing me all the international positions that a simple South African had no conception of. For this I was eternally grateful. My other beau was a married man who'd sneak down after dark and lie with me, gently. We never made love; we talked a lot.

After three weeks on Tsorah I was ready to join the group of forty Zionist students from Wits. Two cities were unforgettable. Tiberias we reached as the sun slipped undercover and the night lights flickered like fairies over the valley. Magic and mystery held me enthralled. Jerusalem pressed my heart like a hot iron sizzles silk. There was something about it that lingered, something I could never quite forget, nor shake off.

Smoke from the cigarette of someone at a nearby table wafts by me. Like a memory long-forgotten it returns to stir my soul. The whiff haunts, taunts tenderly. What is that smell, subtly sealed in the flimsy flight of smoke? Something about Jerusalem caught in my skin, nestled in my pores.

At the Mount of the Beatitudes I thought about Jesus, just as I had on Christmas Day. Here it was, I thought to myself, he talked on this spot. "Blessed are the pure in spirit." I felt something, a presence. I wanted to stay longer. How could I explain my feelings to my tour-mates?

I went to Israel to find out what it means to be Jewish. I didn't find that out then.

I got a sense of what it means to be Israeli, and I liked that. I felt comfortable running around the country, talking to strangers, taking risks that I shuddered about later, but at the time I felt as if a huge blanket of protection draped me loosely in its folds. I felt God-Who-Is-One with me. I could come to no harm. And I didn't.

In discussing my planned European tour with Barry Furman, our tour guide, I decided to act on his advice and go straight to London to spend more time with my mother. "Europe you can visit anytime. You're treating your mother like another tourist attraction." He had a point. But then, in a way, she was just another tourist attraction. Margot had been out of my life for at least two years and I had little contact with her. This was going to be an unusual reunion.

How do you act when you meet your Mother? I didn't know what to say, didn't know how I felt. It could have been anyone. I was numb. She was excited and anxious; there were tears in her eyes. What must that meeting have meant for her? How did she feel being torn from her children for seven years? I couldn't begin to think that through. It was too much for me. "I've cooked a special meal for you," she blurted out. "Chicken!" Guess what I had been eating every day for the past six weeks in Israel? Chicken!

Our apartment was on a railway line — well, it seemed as if it were. Every few minutes the distant rumbling of the monster would warn us that the next few sentences would be erased forever. Our conversations were punctuated with sentences stopped in mid-stream, punchlines obliterated, responses repeated and breath held. At the warning rumble we had a choice: we either rush the sentence or wait till the roar swallowed us up and spat us out again, carrying our unspoken words with it into the night. A combat zone.

Mummy (Mom? Mother? What can I say?) and I decided Israel and kibbutz life would be the ideal place for Margot to go for a while to "sort her out". I wasn't sure why she needed sorting out or what she really wanted to do anyway. It seemed as if she and my mother were having a great time in London, but let's try anyway! We outlined our plan to her as she was lounging in soapsuds, manicuring her long red nails.

She listened, stopped, placed the emery board on the edge of the bath, dropped her head just the right number of inches, arched her well-groomed eyebrows, pursed her lip-sticked lips and beamed her huge owl-eyes on us. "You must be joking," she said.

I dared not breathe. Mother and I exchanged a quick glance in the passing of which our plan evaporated into the steam-filled bathroom. We agreed instantly. Of course we were only joking. Margot and kibbutz was a relationship we were crazy to contemplate. Wrong! We laughed and shrieked at our temporary insanity, hoping Margot would forgive and forget our presumptuous blundering. She generously did.

Identity or Jewishness was not on Margot's list of priorities. She was attending the Stanislavsky school of acting, following in her mother's footsteps. An actress, at the very least. With mother murmuring something about coming to South Africa with her new husband who was then in Australia, I left London and returned to my studies.

So what was I at that point? A Jew who had been to Israel and enjoyed myself — and so? The only difference to my life was that I took Hebrew as a subject the following year. Mother returned to South Africa with her new husband — a dour man, no fun at all. I accepted her as part of my life; it felt good to have her around. There was no anger, no resentment, no blame in me. I was not fully in touch with all my emotions; they were buried deep. I was involved with life on campus and my own budding career as a singer.

At university I landed a job as a singer at a local restaurant-dance club, The Mozambique, where I sang on Friday and Saturday nights. Then a bandleader called Doug Laing called and asked if I'd do a few gigs with him. Sure. This started as the occasional wedding or barmitzvah and then a permanent offer for an engagement at a hotel on the Vaal River on weekends. I chose that.

I also chose Shaun Jenkins, the drummer of the band. Shaun was a lot older than me, balding, slightly podgy, easy-going. Shaun became my lover. Why? I didn't know at the time. He was married — which meant there was no chance of my establishing a long-term relationship with him. In my psyche this probably reassured me I could not get hurt. The relationship was doomed from the start. Instead of waiting for the man to leave, I chose one who could not stay anyway. Then there was his age. Why so much older? Was I looking for a father-figure or was he a reminder of some sexual experience I'd had with an older man? Was I repeating a pattern I didn't even know existed? It wasn't as if I found him physically irresistible. I wasn't that physically attracted to him. Which would make sense too. On the surface I felt safe with him. That's all I knew at the time.

By the end of my degree I was moving away from Shaun. He was moving closer. He planned to divorce his wife and marry me. I baulked. It was all too real now. I couldn't imagine being married to him. The break up was miserable and messy, again. Bewildered, confused, angry, Shaun forgave me only when he heard I was entering a convent. Second best to God was a position he could live with.

What effect did the campus have on my awareness of injustice? Wits University ran an African night school where I taught English one evening a week. Adult men and women sat bent over books after a gruelling day at work. I found it easy to teach. It satisfied me on a new level. I was able to give, to do something constructive. Sure I stood on street corners with placards, marched in protest, attended rallies and discussions, but I had no black friends, I was still safe in my white world.

One of my majors was Biblical Studies. Professor Geyser was our teacher. As a Dutch Reformed minister he had been asked by his Church (who also were Government) to prove from the Bible that apartheid was part of God's plan. He'd refused to do this, knowing that it was in no way part of God's plan unless Hendrik Verwoerd happened to be God and that was highly unlikely since he wasn't even Jewish to begin with! Geyser was thrown out, excommunicated, defrocked and we were lucky enough to be in his class and benefit from his knowledge, courage and integrity.

Another person who influenced me was Dave Adler, a friend who was passionately involved in the struggle against apartheid. Dave worked in education. He introduced me to the National Union of South African Students (NUSAS) and I attended a conference at Pietermaritzburg. I gained knowledge and grew more aware of the truth of what was happening. I couldn't but be affected when Dave was imprisoned for a number of years or when other people I knew disappeared or died. This was no game.

I was in no way proud of being a South African. My aim was to leave the country as soon as possible and live somewhere else, probably London again. Besides which, I really wanted to be on the stage. I responded to an advertisement in the paper for actors/singers/dancers for the Performing Arts Council of the Transvaal (PACT) Children's Theatre group. I went along, sang a few songs, jittered about somewhat in a manner faintly resembling an imitation of what might loosely be termed a dance routine; sprouted a few lines of a Shakespearean sonnet and smiled in my most exhuberant fashion. The combination of this approach served to blind Manuel de Sousa (the director) to the possibility of my not being Liza Minelli and he gave me the job immediately. He also gave me his private time and attention.

One foot firmly set on the ladder to stardom, the other one slightly off the ground, I was not the least perturbed when I told my father I would not be teaching for three years as I had promised, and would he please repay all the monies I owed to the government? Please? It was a lot of money. Dad agreed before he knew just how much and all he said to me later was, "I'll be paying this off for a long time". It didn't register with me. Not for a minute did I consider I was acting irresponsibly. He was there to pay for me. He never said no. Isn't that what dads are for? I was left to wind my way around life like a creeper covering a house. It goes where it wishes. But the route through PACT led me to Padre Pio and a turning point which would propel me into ten years of all the direction and discipline I so desperately craved.

PACT was based in Pretoria, the administrative capital of South Africa and thirty-five kilometres from Johannesburg. Ten actors comprised the cast. I changed my name. I found "Friedman" unglamorous. I chose "Charles" because of my Dad. At least I'd still be connected to the family in some way. Michelle Charles.

Ten of us comprised the company: Cheryl and her dog; Pierre and Jan — a couple; Stefan who thought he was Errol Flynn reincarnated (and nothing we could say or do could make him see the error of his daze); Magda, a real actress from Holland who became a lifelong friend; Hugh, a large sweetheart with a penchant for young, very young, men; Phillip, who had a great deal of difficulty in keeping his false teeth in his mouth; Michael, our stage manager with whom I struck up a light-hearted love affair on tour (well I mean it was so dreary in those small towns dahling!); and Paulette who left us alone once she had butchered all the texts as a producer. Marguerite and James made an interesting couple. She was six feet three inches, blonde with a reedy voice. She never washed. James was considerably smaller and British. Very pseudo-British. Nothing, but nothing, he constantly reminded us, could come anywhere near the quality of English theatre — and everything else. Maybe that was why she went unwashed — more British, what?

Thrown together, we'd philosophise for hours as we drove in the mini-bus on tour. Most of us wanted to pierce the mystery of life. The night of my twenty first we had a small party in Pierre's apartment. Pierre was laid-back and receptive. I'd left a note for my Dad in Johannesburg telling him I loved him and what he meant to me. Written on impulse, I didn't know what I was trying to say or do. Perhaps I felt guilty that I'd spent so little time with him over twenty one years; maybe I wanted to feel that love that I could only write about. Dad was touched by this; he drove thirty miles to Pretoria to be with me at the party. The impact of his action passed me by. I didn't spend much time with him at the party either. We never really talked to one another. I spoke to him only when I needed something. He must've been lonely. So was I. At the end of the evening, when everyone had left, including my father, I felt very depressed.

"What's it all about, Pierre?" I asked, sitting with him on the sofa in the early dawn, sipping coffee. There were answers I had to have. I wanted to find God and myself.

As we travelled I'd nip into small, empty churches and sit in the silence, waiting, not knowing what to say, what to ask for, or who to speak to. A friend gave me a book on an Italian priest called Padre Pio who bore the stigmata. Padre Pio had holes in his hands, his feet and a gash in his side. These wounds bled daily. He wore mittens over bandages on his hands and a sash around his waist. As I read that book I developed an irresistible compulsion to see him. Yes, I had to be in the presence of this man. He knew God. He didn't talk about God, he experienced God. That's what I wanted: to know and to touch and to be touched by God. I had to visit him in Italy. He lived and prayed in a small town called Foggia. As I had spent most of the year travelling, I was able to save money. I had enough to get me to Italy. Why only Italy? I had no patience with South Africa, and I wanted to be an actress, so why not leave? Everything seemed to fit so nicely. Manuel would meet me in Rome as he had a business trip planned. I'd spend a few days with him, catch the train to Foggia, see Padre Pio and go on to London, to sing, dance and act my way to fame and fortune.

I was twenty-one. I had no idea what life was like on a day-to-day basis. I'd lived as a student and an actress. I hardly ever cooked a meal for myself or washed my own clothes. I lived on intuition and on what felt right. That also included who felt right. Nothing and no-one was going to stop me getting to the top. Not that I was brittle and determined; no, I was naive and enthusiastically optimistic about life and people. I believed I'd be safe and there was nothing to fear. I also had a wonderful smile, a great body, was an intelligent and warm person. Underneath the bravado lurched the lonely child, the abused woman. In the shadows her grief, anger and fear hid. Over time the volcano would erupt. Now it was resting. In the year ahead I would face the best and the worst of myself.

steps to heal the heart

The group

Do you belong to a particular religious group? Or another kind of group? Are you part of a minority or a majority? How strongly do you identify with "your kind of people"? Do you feel under any pressure to behave in a certain way because you belong to this group? Would you prefer not to belong or does belonging to this group and therefore acting in a specific way help you? Is your choice to belong a conscious one? What led you to make this choice? What has this decision brought into your life? Have you sacrificed anything or anyone in the process? Write your responses to these questions or discuss them.

Away from home

When was the first time you went away, relatively far away, from your home as a child?

What was that like for you? Did you travel by taxi? By train? By plane? What were the reasons you had to leave? Did you go alone? Describe what it was like for you — in words or in writing. Or draw your feelings around leaving.

If you have children, how did you feel when your child left home for the first time? Maybe on holiday or to visit an aunt?

If you were the child of a migrant worker, you probably stayed at home and your parent or parents left you with a caretaker — a grandmother, an aunt or a close friend. Can you connect to those early memories and feelings? Can you describe them in some way? Are they still with you? Now write to the child — your inner child — who stayed at home. Talk to her or him as a loving parent who didn't want to be away; who never wanted to miss the opportunity of being there when you grew up. Explain to the small child who waited how difficult it was for you as an adult to make that decision — because you had to make some money to keep your child alive. Tell the little one how much you longed for her or for him. Ask your baby to forgive you and reassure her that you never stopped loving her.

Even if you know your parent may not have felt like this, write the letter because you are now the positive parent to your inner child.

Making a contribution

For me, teaching at African Night School was my first experience of sharing a skill. When did you first do something for another person or persons that benefited him or her? It could have been a small action — taking someone to hospital; teaching the alphabet; giving someone a ride in your car; binding a wound, showing someone how to light a fire. Can you now touch your feelings at that time?

If you have continued to be of service in some way, what has kept you at this? If you used to do things like this, but stopped, why did you stop? Which of these questions would you like to write about or respond to in some way?

First pay

What was the first work you got paid for? Did you look for it or did someone ask you to work or offer it to you? How did you find it? How long did you stay at your

my life

first job? Describe how you felt when you got paid for the first time. What difference did that make to you and to your family? What does money mean to you? If you didn't need the money, would you still do what you do now if you were not paid for it? What does your answer tell you? Share this with a friend. Compare your answers.

Questions about life

Do you have questions about life? What are they? When did first formulate them? Have you found answers for them? Any of them? Have the answers changed over the years? Have the questions changed? What do you most want to know about yourself, about life, and about the world? If a child asked you "Why are we here?" what would you say? Write a dialogue in which an inquiring young person asks you these questions and you reply. What do you notice?

Chapter 4 *Saints and Sinners*

Rome has to be the most romantic place in the world, especially when you're young and with someone you're fond of. Manuel arrived a couple of days after me. He was impressed with my apparent familiarity with the city and some of its people. I was relaxed and happy, on another adventure.

At my hotel the clerk looked from Manuel then back to me, put one and one together and came up with three.

"Same room?" he leered at us.

"Well, I have my room already," I explained, almost apologetically.

He tittered. "This is Rome, this is the city of love! I have a wonderful room, perfect for you, together?"

Manuel looked at me. "It's fine with me," he shrugged.

"Okay," I acquiesced reluctantly, not knowing how to say what I wanted, which was that I preferred my own space, my own room. "Okay" also meant that Manuel and I would probably make love for old times' sake. I didn't realise that I still had a choice.

After we'd spent the day together and as we lay in bed that night, the "ho-hum-this-is-expected-of-me-I-suppose" feeling was there in full. My heart was no longer involved. I liked Manuel but I was headed for London and he back to Africa. There was no future, a slight past and the present was hardly a passionate one. I had no condom, nor did he. I used nothing to protect myself. "It will never happen to me", I believed. Wasn't this the "great romantic moment"? Why spoil it worrying about realities like falling pregnant or whether I really wanted to be here with this man now. I chose to ignore the feeling inside me, the deeper feeling that was saying, "I don't really want this". Besides which I was on a spiritual quest and that guaranteed my safety, didn't it? So we made love or whatever it was, and said our goodbyes.

Sandwiched between four exuberant Italian families eating a continuous breakfast-lunch-supper meal I sat holding my breath for the six-hour ride from Rome to Foggia. Smells wove together like a tapestry, hanging in the thin slice of air trapped in the compartment. Suffocation awaited me. Aha! Nature's call.

A trip to the toilet necessitated first my exhaling. As the breath was released I shot out of my seat like a rocket off a launch pad. The vacuum left by my body was instantaneously closed by a natural shifting of ten bodies on one seat sliding over an inch or two. The now impenetrable mass made me question if I had ever sat there!

Twisting and shouldering, I elbowed and squeezed my way through a human-papered-passage, "*Scusi! Scusi!*" I muttered, smiling as I shoved. Edging the toilet door open I half expected dozens of bodies to come spilling out.

Ecstasy was in the release and I was tempted to remain in that small room for the rest of the ride. Regrettably I was not the only owner of a bladder. The journey back to what could euphemistically be termed "my seat" was as thick and as slow as the getting there, but without the urgency. It was like swimming upstream in a thick minestrone river.

With neither hope nor wish to re-enter the human seat, I stood in the crowded corridor breathing the wafts of wine-air above my head. How much further? "Foggia! Foggia!" the murmur passed from mouth to ear. This is it. I am about to meet God.

"Padre Pio! *Vene!* Padre Pio!" yelled a bus driver as I stumbled off the train.

"Wait for me!" I hurtled after the echo as it disappeared into a small, already bulging bus. Closer. I am closer now.

At the foot of the steep hill the bus halted. We rose as one, now respectfully quiet. The huge church at the top of the hill stood outlined against the sky. I recognised it from the photographs in the books I had read. From the darkness a small guest house emerged, dim yellow light glowing in the window. Timidly I knocked at the door.

"Senorita Michelle?" A round smiling woman beckoned me in, ushered me into a simple room where a bowl of steaming soup and fresh bread beamed at me from a white tablecloth. "*Domani* Padre Pio!" she squeezed my hand. I felt heat and stinging behind my eyes as tears collected. Yes, tomorrow I shall see him. I lay in bed awake. My last visit to a Catholic church was at twelve; now I am Jewish. What am I doing here?

5.30am. Already a crowd of women hovered at the huge doors of the church. Walking quickly in the cold morning air, I took my place behind them, warm, armed with expectation. Exactly on time the doors swept back as I was carried in on the wave of bustling bodies scuttling for space. Women in long dark skirts with scarves over their heads and rosary beads dangling from their hands made up a large percentage of the prayer-force. I landed in one of the pews towards the back. The church filled.

Padre Pio entered slowly. The scuffling stopped; silence shrouded the sanctuary and eyes stared in rapt, adoring attention. I sat through the Mass doing what everyone else did. I stood when they stood, sat when they sat, bowed when they bowed. Intense concentration caught the hour, holding it tightly by the neck, allowing nothing to escape, not a sigh, not a breath, not a whisper.

Padre Pio lifted the host and then became transfixed. Sunk into a place where no-one could go, he stared at the round communion wafer and we lost him. Jealous, a server tinkled a small bell after many minutes passed. This reminded Padre Pio that there were hundreds of people present and the Mass had to continue. Obediently, Padre re-entered the space in front of his eyes and the Mass went on.

I began to pour out my soul to him. I told him of my search, of my need for God, of my loneliness and of my emptiness. "Help me, Padre, help me please!" I begged with intensity. He lifted his head and stared across the row upon row of supplicators. For four rows in front of me women began to turn around, like a domino effect. They looked behind them, saw me and jabbed their fingers at me, barking "You! He's looking at you!" They smiled, nodded and pointed. "You!" I gazed back at him, believing them, certain that he had heard.

Something had opened in me, a space. I began to speak to God, to Jesus, to someone I couldn't see. The words came from somewhere soft and tender, a place where there was no protection, no pretence. Like a cable stretching across nothingness but reaching a safe spot, my speaking, my praying, wording, emoting was gripped in a sure contact which returned to me as a bonding. I was not alone. There was a connection. A switch had been turned. A current began. A direct relationship tripped. The cry: "Is there anybody out there?" came back to me. "Yes!" Comfort surged through my veins as I returned again and again to the church. I was beginning to understand what it meant to pray. I was feeding myself, sucking from the teats I had been blindly groping for all this while. Nourishment, at last.

Learning I was from South Africa, someone introduced me to Luciano Lucchesi, a South African Italian who'd been welding when an explosion had shot pieces of iron into his eyes. Instantly blinded, he'd called on Padre Pio to protect him. In hospital, the doctor removed the fragments of iron from his eyes. His eyesight was unblemished. He could see. His skin bore traces of the burn; his eyes were clear and shining.

Luciano took me to visit the grotto of St Michael, now my guardian angel.

"You have to confess and re-enter the Catholic Church," he informed me gravely. I didn't understand why I had to confess. I wanted to stay swimming in the stream I had just dipped into and if confession was part of this, well, "Let the good times roll!"

I waited my turn, entered the confessional and fell to my knees. Luciano hovered outside.

"Bless me Father, for I have sinned," I began hesitantly, searching for sins.

"Did you go to nightclubs?" the priest asked from the darkness.

"Of course. I sang in them!" I retorted. What's his problem?

"Did you succumb to the sins of flesh?" Did I what?

"How many times?" What's with this guy? Is he some sort of pervert that he wants to know number of times?

"Say an act of penance." Panic! What's an act of penance?

"Your sins are forgiven you. You can go my child."

I was a Catholic again, I guessed. I emerged from the booth feeling no different.

Luciano was beaming. "Now you have to see Padre Pio. Come, I will help you to get a ticket."

After the morning Mass, Padre Pio would shuffle slowly out of the sanctuary, through a narrow passageway and into a confessional where he'd remain all day. He called himself "a priest who prays". The ticket allowed me to stand in the line of people he would pass. This was a privilege. It was a way of being with Padre Pio if one was not able to go to him for confession. That you could do only if you spoke Italian. I was excited and apprehensive, having read how he could see through people and was often blunt. He didn't mince his words.

The atmosphere in the small passage shifted into silence as Padre emerged, bent. Slowly he padded down the line towards the far door. The woman on my left scurried away from his words. Then he was standing before me. I knelt, looking up at him, looking into his eyes, looking into two steady pools of brown. He rested his hand on my head and patted it gently, twice.

I search for words to communicate the expression in his eyes. Imagine someone loves you completely. This person knows everything about you: your secret fears, your hidden motives, your weaknesses, your strengths, your beauty. This person accepts you unconditionally. Not only that, but he or she radiates a positive energy towards you as if only the good exists in you. Such was the gaze of Padre Pio — non-judgemental, total acceptance, unlimited love. I felt firm, whole, innocent. Not only that. I experienced being vast as though I had no physical form. For that instant I did not exist as Michelle but as energy. I was everywhere. Accompanying this was a knowledge of myself as pure, innocent, free from blame. If this is God's gaze, I'll take God any day.

That moment was a turning point. Being so close to this feeling I could only term "love", being touched by it, began the healing process of my life. It was my first experience of wholeness, of completeness. In that instant I became what I inherently was, but was not aware of — in balance, integrated. The integration was a *fait accompli* on a profound level. Now I would begin to move towards this consciously

For two days following that meeting I had no need to eat. I prayed and felt a peace that satiated me. One afternoon, while walking in the garden outside the hospital Padre Pio had built, I watched a nun tilling the ground. As my eyes followed her movements, I heard the thought flicker in my mind like a camera lens clicking open and shut. "You're going to be a nun." I slapped my hand in front of my mouth as if to stifle a cry. "I can't!" I protested in a silent scream, "I could never live without a man!" Briskly brushing the thought away, I ran to the nearest restaurant and ate a hearty meal to regain my sanity. It's time to move, kid. Next stop, London!

Why had this thought penetrated? Why should I be drawn to this life? What did I see? I saw a peace I so badly wanted; a ceasing of struggle. I saw meaning and quietness. I saw a smaller world, one that might be controllable. Somewhere beyond my need for what I thought a man could give me — and that was a confused area anyway — was now a yearning for nurture, for safety, for refuge. None of this surfaced to my conscious mind. It just pushed and prodded and leaned on me from inside, urging, directing, throbbing me forward. I was like a blind puppy, pushing its way instinctively into the light. I was on a path to save myself from death, to find a life.

There is a moment when the wheel of death stops spinning; stops, and then starts again in the other direction. Where was I headed? For London, the stage, fame and fortune. For what? I didn't know! I was rushing to my death, lemming-like again. The meeting with Padre Pio stopped my perilous plunge. An intervention occurred. "Whoaaa!" The reining in of a runaway horse. Whose was the hand that checked me? I think it is the hand of life, the "that-ness" companion that acts on our soul-screech. That's why I'm telling you this. We do not grow alone, unseen, unheard, uncared for. That which Is acts in our lives, comes to our rescue. Sometimes It sweeps us swiftly onto a path or, for an instant, dusts a ledge for us to lie on in the sun. A bee is drowning in a pool. We cup our hands and toss the water carrying the lifeless form onto the ground. The bee lands on its back, wriggles, turns over and flies off. Like that. Who this woman is, why this man acts, why you go one way and I another, I cannot tell you. Ask yourself. Ask. At an everyday point-of-peril-moment as you race to a place which is a dead-end for you, you'll reach a subtle-possible-stop in the death plunge. Call from your soul, howl with your gut. Choose life in whatever vague or inarticulate groping way you can. Allow the process to begin.

I left for London, still keeping to my original plan to become an actress. In the process I would have to eat. The only way to do that was to apply for a teaching position. Pretoria Girls High on Durban Road in the East End of London, of all places, was my initiation into teaching. I came to the school knowing nothing about teaching, nothing about discipline, nothing about girls. In my class the students all but climbed the walls. They chased and swore at each other. Anything remotely like order was unimaginable. One day the headmistress, Miss Smith, a tiger of a woman, marched into this mêlée and, to my astonishment, the class calmed down immediately. Like lambs they sat in their places; like angels they raised their hands when she asked questions; like real people they listened and responded. How did she do it? I had to catch on quickly if I were to survive.

Miss Smith sent me on a training course to teach drama. That saved my job. I could teach and play at the same time. Over in the boys' school (a treacherous playground crossing had first to be navigated) was a hall which the girls were allowed to use for their drama classes.

"None of us teachers really knew what went on there, behind closed doors. We'd see Miss Friedman (She was from South Africa. No, not black. Yes, surprising isn't it?) trotting over to the hall with a small book on drama clasped in her hand. As if we needed any more! Once over the other side, I can't tell you too clearly what went on. I mean there was a lot of music and the girls seemed to be dancing. No, not what they do at clubs but miming and pretending to be statues. Acting out all kinds of fantasies, schemes and dreams. All a bit odd if you ask me, but it kept them all happy. Even the boys wanted those classes. Can you imagine?"

There were a number of Pakistani girls at the school. They had a difficult time. The locals couldn't accept that they were allowed to wear trousers to school. Of course the dress the girls wore was not trousers in the sense that the English understood. They were part of the Pakistani cultural dress and were covered with a skirt anyway. But the dark-skinned girls were different and many of the English girls were unable to appreciate those differences. They were afraid of people who looked different and dressed "funny" and didn't speak English — or the variation of English they spoke.

One of the students was particularly reclusive. Her long black hair all but covered her face and she hardly ever spoke. She was an eagle contained in fear. Over time I managed to befriend her, and one Saturday I took her to the London zoo. Meena was terrified of everything — of the underground, the noise, the people, the animals. She threw up along the way. In my naïvety I thought I was "opening the world up" to her. Instead she was opening up her insides to the world! I wanted to do something to ease her exile. I felt her pain and isolation. It was clearer to me than my own.

As the days passed I began to look forward to school and not be too keen on scanning the paper for auditions, running to rent a studio to practice singing or taking evening classes at Covent Garden in jazz-dance. Physically I wasn't taking these days in my stride. I never ate properly. I didn't know how to look after myself. As a spoiled South African I believed food mysteriously appeared at hungry-tummy times. When it didn't, I'd eat chocolate as I sat in the Underground on the way to or from school. Although there was a hot plate in my bedsitter in Hampstead, it didn't get used all that much. I was unprepared for the real world. I found teaching emotionally exhausting. I cared about the girls and would return spent, to a cold, foodless and empty bedsitter.

What also began to sap my energy was the nagging fear that I might be pregnant. My periods hadn't started. At first I thought it might be the change in country, but as the weeks passed I knew my flippant attitude to that night in Rome was bearing fruit, fruit that I could not consider as a reality. It had happened to me. I was in shock. The awareness that I was bearing a life fell on me with a panic. What do I do? How do I hide this? Take it away?

Max, my other half-brother and older than Paddy, had left South Africa to become an editor in London. He was my only hope. He lived with his wife Tessa and their two boys. On one of my Sunday visits I broke the news to him. He said he'd find out the name of someone and I should phone him the following week. He didn't blame or scold me or pass judgement. I wrote to Manual and told him. He agreed to send me money.

Tuesday night I phoned Max from an Underground station. He gave me the name and address of a woman and the cost. I left my umbrella in the telephone booth. A yellow umbrella. It was raining. Following his directions I found the house, rang the bell and a man silently showed me into an upstairs room. The woman motioned me to remove my pants and lie on my stomach on the bed. She then inserted what I thought to be a tube into my womb. It felt like an enema. I had no idea what to expect. A few minutes later she told me I could get up and go. Leaving her £30, I walked downstairs out into the street, bought a pear from a fruit vendor, caught the bus back to my bedsitter and waited. It had all been trance-like, as if I were an observer, separate from myself. Nothing happened. I phoned Tessa. "Come over right away," she insisted.

The bleeding began. I was due to move into another bedsitter but I couldn't. Max and Tessa drove over, packed my clothes and moved me. They hadn't asked any questions; didn't know who the father was. We hardly knew each other anyway — Max, Tessa and I.

I was dry-eyed and stone-faced. One afternoon as I sat on the toilet, a small lump slid into the bowl. "That's it," I thought watching it disappear. I was pale and losing blood. Tessa called her local doctor who came over and suggested I go into hospital to have my womb washed — a DNC. Still in a trance-like state, I agreed and spent two days under white sheets in a wide ward. I was visited by a priest. I couldn't talk to him. This was not happening. The following week I returned to school. I'd missed three or four days. I said I'd had flu.

One rainy evening, months later, when the downpour was determined, I took my raincoat and walked to the Catholic Church seven or eight blocks away. I was coiled in tension. I knelt in the confessional, now in a very different frame of mind from the Foggia confession. I spoke my sin.

"Yes," there was a pause, "and what else?" came the voice from behind the grid.

What else? How could there be a "what else"? Isn't this enough?

"Nothing else, Father," I whispered.

He set me some prayers to say and released me with absolution. I wasn't released. I stood outside the entrance to the church sheltered from the storm by the stone archway over the door and allowed the tears to flow down the streets of my cheeks. Both the sky and I were in harmony as together, it seemed, we spilled our souls. The rain was a curtain for my crime; it harboured me, held me, hid me as I let go. My anguish was minimised as Nature both nurtured me and reflected back to me creation's reverberation of the blow I had struck against life.

On another level what I had done reinforced the already clear message I had about myself. "I'm a bad girl. I'm bad enough for my mother to leave me; bad enough for my father not to be there for me; bad enough for Paddy to go to America; now bad enough to kill."

What could I ever do to make reparation for this hideous deed? Not only was there shame for the abuse I still did not know about, but there was this shame, this disgrace.

"I'm a slut! I'm a killer!" Underneath was the grief only slightly expressed by the outburst after confession; grief that I could have been a mother; grief that there could have been someone in my life I could love and who could love me; grief for my inability to do the right thing. Loss. Loss of my innocence, loss of my self-image, loss of life. All these feelings were sub-conscious. I was out of control. How could I stop this happening again? Who could help me?

I continued to drag myself to school, uncertain of what I was achieving in England.

I wrote a letter on impulse to my former English lecturer, Robert Lester, who happened to be in London, unknown to me. The letter was re-routed and we met. He was morose, brooding about his failed marriage.

"Why do you want to stay here?" he asked, finally tired of his own pain.

"I wanted to be an actress," I muttered, now not sure at all.

"Why don't you go home?" he suggested, seeing me from a distance of at least fourteen years. I didn't tell him about my dreadful deed. It lay like a living weight inside me. Still, inside me. He could sense I was fragile and comforted me and himself. I took what he offered — his body. I didn't know how to say what I really needed. I didn't know what I really needed. It felt less lonely to be under a body, within arms. For that moment.

I wrote a note to Foggia to be read to Padre Pio by Brother Bill who spoke English and Italian. Three weeks later I received the reply. "Go where it is best for you." Where is it best for me? In South Africa? In a convent? The thought of becoming a nun returned often. I'd see it, look at it, then put it aside. "I'm at the end of my tether," I told myself, "I'm going home."

At our final school assembly, Miss Smith read out the names of the teachers who were leaving. At the sound of my name an audible groan ascended from the girls.

"Wow!" I thought, "they really are sorry to see me go! It must have been all the dancing! I didn't know you cared." I realised teaching was probably not a bad choice for me as a career, but one I now chose to do in South Africa.

After a holiday in Wales with another teacher, I returned home by sea, docking in Cape Town. I took the Blue Train up to Johannesburg where I arrived with six pennies in my pocket. Dad collected me, of course, and we drove into town to see Margot who was working as a bookkeeper in a clothing outlet. Dad was still at the Stock Exchange with his sister Selma as his long-term secretary. Uncle Jack continued to sell carpets at Arma Carpet House and they all still lived in the Quirinale Hotel. Little had changed in the year I had been away, except that Mom had divorced her Australian husband. She lived in Killarney, in a block called Hampshire House, a couple of streets away from Dad and Margot who were in Greenhills. I joined them. I was twenty-two.

Within a month I'd secured a teaching position at an all-boys Catholic school in Observatory where I taught Standard Four to ten year olds. It was close to heaven on earth. We were crazy about each other, the class and I. The thought of becoming a nun grew firmer and firmer, especially in these surroundings.

It was becoming clear that I was in love with Jesus. None of the men I knew stood a chance against him. Jesus was understanding, compassionate, supportive, forgiving and would always be there, inside me. Jesus would not hurt me. Jesus would not leave me. Jesus could not make me pregnant. There could be no problems with Jesus. I was safe.

None of these thoughts rose into my rational mind. On the surface I felt overwhelmed by love. I'd slip out the kitchen door and drive to Mass in the mornings. Leaving my dressing gown in the car, I'd cover my street clothes with it on my return, so Dad wouldn't know I'd been to church. He had no idea what was brewing in my mind. I was dreading breaking the news to him. Going to Mass was enough to plunge him into confusion and bewilderment. Imagine if I told him I wanted to become a nun? Our maid Maggie knew everything.

"Miss Michelle," she'd say, "you are going to make the Master mad when he knows."

"Sssh, Maggie," I'd beg, "please don't say anything!"

She said nothing. Maggie lived upstairs, on the top of the building where the servants lived. "Soweto in the sky", it was called.

I'd heard of a convent in Rivonia where the Sisters lived in silence and were behind bars when you visited them. Was this because they were dangerous? Should I be with them on the other side? Was I, too, a potential danger to society?

Telling myself there could be no long-term side effects from asking, I drove up to The Wall, rang the bell, asked for an audience and was led into a room divided into what looked like cages. Seated on the safe side (or so I presumed) and seeing no labels which might identify the nature of the beast to appear, I waited for the curtain on the other side to be drawn back. A woman clothed in brown smiled out at me. Good. She looked harmless enough.

I cleared my throat. "I was thinking of the vague possibility that somewhere in the far distant future I might conceivably entertain the notion of changing my lifestyle in rather a radical manner and, it might not be beyond the bounds of propriety at this stage to make a few discreet inquiries, which of course could not commit me in any manner whatsoever, with regard to — er — taking the plunge? Donning the veil? Leaving the world? Becoming a Nun?" (There. I'd said it — the "N" word!)

"What kind of order were you thinking of joining?" the sister asked sweetly from behind the bars. (I had brought my banana.)

"I don't know." I replied wisely. (What's an order? One tuna mayo on wholewheat to go?)

"Tell me the names of some and I'll choose."

What an intelligent approach. Boggles the mind. The Sister disappeared momentarily, to reappear with a small booklet through which she thumbed. As she turned the pages, she read the names. Obviously I'd stumbled on the correct way of doing this.

"Holy Family, Holy Rosary, Sisters of Notre Dame, Holy Cross ..."

"Hold it right there!" I interjected, "Let's hear about them, the last one, the Holy Cross Sisters, please."

I leaned forward, my nose now definitely through the bars and on the other side.

"They're Franciscan. They teach and nurse and they are mainly found in mission stations and in education and nursing."

"Say no more! That's it!" I barked, "Take me to their leader!" Sister of the Sweet Smile smiled again and wrote down a name and phone number on a piece of paper she just happened to have at her side. The number was in Alexandra township, one of the poorest living areas for black people in Johannesburg. Excellent! I leapt to my feet.

"Thank you, Sister," I gushed. (Do I shake her hand?) Pulling myself together I added, "Of course, I have no intention of taking this any further. You understand that I'm a normal, well-balanced, run-of-the-mill individual with a great future and to lock myself away from humanity for any fixed period of time would surely impoverish the world." And lying thus through my teeth, I made my escape. As I scampered out I thought I heard a guffaw from behind the now-curtained bars. They laugh? My God, they're almost human!

The next step was to make arrangements to meet these Sisters without anyone in the world knowing. Alone at home I phoned "the number" and asked to speak to the Sister Superior. I mumbled something about being interested in meeting her and we arranged that she pick me up, no, not at the apartment, at the corner way down the road. What should I wear? Not slacks. A skirt, a quiet and simple skirt. Did I possess one?

"Please God, don't let anyone see me getting into the car, please God, let me be invisible as I stand here ... "

I tried not to look as though I was about to leap off a hundred-storey building. The car drew up with two habit-clad nuns in the front seats. I dived in at the back, ducked down and peered at them from half-way on the floor.

"Hello. I'm Michelle Friedman. Let's go!"

Not many whites drove into Alexandra township even though it was easily accessible from the road. Around the red brick school building lay the cluttered streets and shabby houses typical of a township. The position of the convent was not without danger. The sisters, in their simple lifestyle, continued to teach and live there, quietly convinced that they could contribute. I was impressed. The simplicity and poverty was just as I had anticipated. I wanted to be part of this. If I were to stay in South Africa, I had to be in the heart of it. This was more like it.

Sister Timothy, the Superior, was clothed in serenity. I found her easy to talk to as we sat in the small parlour sipping tea. Tall and stately, she sailed along the corridors like a swan on a lake. I was entranced, like Siegfried! She was also a friendly swan and full of humour. It wasn't surprising that she was eventually elected world leader of the Holy Cross swans, I mean Sisters. She was a role-model for me. "Yes! That's what I want to be like!" I knew I had to enter. Now, how and when do I tell my father?

Margot was engaged to Lester Greenberg, a nice Jewish man. We didn't talk much. She noticed how I was changing. One night before we fell asleep, she asked me.

"What's going on, Mickey?"

"I'm thinking of becoming a nun." I told her in the darkness.

"Why do you want to do that?"

"I just do."

"It'll kill Daddy," she warned.

I waited in the silence.

"If you go off and I go off at the same time ... "

I hadn't thought of that. Maybe I should wait. A year perhaps.

"What's in your hands?" she asked, hearing a rattle.

"A rosary." I felt on the edge of martyrdom.

"God, I've forgotten all about that. How does it go again?"

"Hail Mary, full of grace ... "

" ... the Lord is with thee ... " and we fell into the night.

I put it off for a year. Margot got married and I got the room to myself and continued to teach at Observatory. I found the older boys attractive. They'd come to my classroom and talk to me. They were seventeen or eighteen. I was twenty-three. It was dangerously exciting. All the while I was preparing for the convent. I didn't even try to examine the fact that I was hungry for the touch of one of the boys, and considering becoming a nun at the same time. "Just let me get there," I thought, "all this will pass. I'm not doing anything now, just flirting. Soon I'll be shrouded in purity, untouchable."

I'd go to Alexandra secretly, have tea with Sister Timothy, try on the dress they were making me. It was sexless, white and dowdy. It didn't put me off.

I told my mother. She felt a mixture of relief and pride. A searcher herself, she recognised that in me and wasn't surprised. She'd travelled to India, prayed at various sites, was a vegetarian and practised yoga. She had now returned to the Catholic Church.

I think she was grateful that I would be looked after.

I had to tell my father. I had arranged to leave for Aliwal North in December. One Sunday when Dad was sitting in the lounge, I sat next to him on the couch. What words I used I no longer know, but I told him of my intention to become a nun. He was stunned.

"Will they feed you?" was his first surprised response. And then, in exasperation: "Why didn't you tell me this before? Why did you let me convert you?" he accused.

What could I say? "You never asked me, Dad! You took me away from what was important to me. You never cared what I felt or what I was going through. Why didn't you ask me? How did I know at twelve what I would want at twenty-three? Don't be so ridiculous!"

I said nothing. I wasn't in touch with the withheld anger I felt towards him. I had no idea how to express my pain. I didn't know how much pain I had inside. I was numb and stubborn. I was going to be a nun. Nothing and no-one would prevent me. I was fighting for my life. I left him sitting there.

Over the next days he struggled with this knowledge. He was losing me and it was a death for him, a double death. He was losing me to Christianity. His wife had won in the end. I had rejected him and his efforts and longings to give me what he thought was best, the best opportunity for happiness. I had thrown it back at him. If I had married a man who wasn't Jewish that would have been nothing compared to this.

"Kalinka," he pleaded, "I'll send you to see Paddy in America if you give up this idea." He knew how much I loved him.

"No, Dad. Thanks, but no."

What did I want to say? "Bribe me, yes bribe me. Why didn't you send me to Paddy before? Do you think money can make me change my mind? Why don't you think of me? Why don't you ask me what I want, what makes me happy?"

"I'm going away," he muttered, crushed and bewildered under the blow. "I'm not staying here to see you go." And he flew to Durban before my departure.

My action was painful for him, a personal loss and a social disgrace. Selma and Jack were shocked and horrified. I was resolute and unyielding. "Get away!" I fumed inside, "this is my life." On the surface I was incredibly sure and serene. Unflustered. Impenetrable. Nothing was leaking out, no pain, no anger, nothing. My uncle Issy, head of Baragwanath Hospital, the largest black hospital in the southern hemisphere, was incensed.

"Do you know how religion killed one of the patients in my ward? One man was convinced if he went to Lourdes he'd be healed. The whole ward helped him get there as if their lives depended upon it. He got there and nothing happened and the whole ward full of people died with him! Is this what you want?"

I had no reply for him. I was going to a place where I would be safe. I wanted to live a life as close to God as was possible. I saw no other way. I wanted to teach and to be part of a South Africa I could be proud of. I wanted to be with black people as well as white. I longed for silence and solitude and prayer and spirituality. I felt I had found a way to have all this. I would belong to God, belong to Jesus, belong!

On another level, one I was unaware of, I was being prompted to do this as a survival course. I had to have a place which would offer me a routine; where day after day would be similar. I desperately needed to be part of a family, to feel I could contribute. The convent could provide this. Someone had to give me a code of ethics, a moral map I could hold on to. I wanted an identity. Here I would have it. Sister Michelle, nun.

Also, my guilt was screaming at me. Here was a way I could make up for being such a bad girl. Unlovable, I would spend my life loving others. And I would not leave. God would not go away. I was choosing a life sentence.

Underneath even this and far too buried for me to sense in the slightest, I was racing away from the complexity of men and sex. Intimacy was so scary. In the softness of my belly all the terror, the panic, the pain, the anger, the grief from abuse and abandonment was growing daily. It was too soft, too squelchy. I had to prepare a place for myself so that when this insisted on coming out I would be ready to meet it, ready to see it and allow it. I had to put myself together somehow and become a person. Some external covering was necessary if I wanted to survive in this world. I had to have a shell. I could not do this by myself. I needed help. The convent would help me. How I didn't know, but I had to go!

Perhaps this is something like a first marriage one leaps into convinced it will last forever and unaware of other forces inside which propel us. Thank God I didn't know all the reasons I had for entering the convent. I could never have dealt with any of them. This was a path that was completely right for me at the time. On the surface I was in love with God and ready to spend the remainder of my life in service through the Holy Cross sisters.

In December 1969 my mother and I drove down to Aliwal North where I was accepted into the order as a postulant. The healing cycle was well on its way.

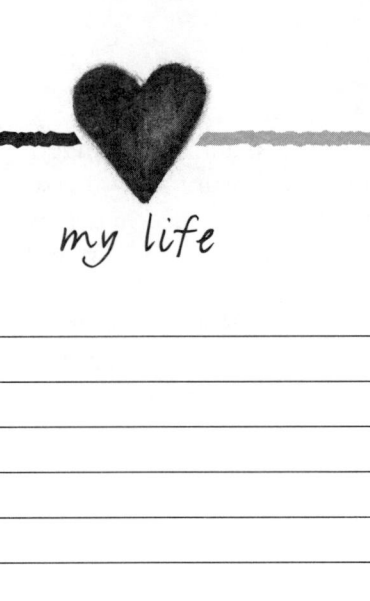

my life

steps to heal the heart

On saying yes when you didn't know what you wanted

That night in Rome I could have asked for a room of my own or insisted on taking the only available room. There were plenty of other hotels nearby. What is it that prevents some of us from saying no? It took me years to find out what stopped me from saying no. Can you remember a time in your life when you couldn't say no? Maybe you, too, didn't know what you wanted so you went along with whatever was happening. Maybe you couldn't say no because you were drugged; maybe you were afraid to say no because you would be punished or hurt in some way. Using an art form — writing or drawing — recreate your experience and then share it with a friend who you can trust. What would you like to have said to prevent the act taking place? What would you like to have said afterwards?

Destiny

What are you looking for? Are there times when you want to be alone? Or do you prefer never to be alone? Do you think there is a purpose to your life? What do you think it is?

Design a collage — a sheet of paper with all the questions you want answered. Put it where you can see it and then keep open for the answers to come. You may be surprised. They can come from a stranger, a friend, the radio, a movie, a song, anywhere. Be alert.

A hand that holds us? A hand that guides us?

"Whose was the hand that checked me? I think it is the hand of life, the 'that-ness' companion that acts on our soul-screech. We do not grow alone, unseen, unheard, uncared for. That which Is acts in our lives, comes to our rescue." What is your response to these lines? Do you believe there is a "hand that acts"? Why for some, but not for others? Does anyone hear us when we ask or cry for help?

Pregnancy

Have you ever been pregnant or did you make a woman pregnant and didn't want the baby? As the mother, what did you do? If you were the father, what did you do? Talk or write about your feelings in as much detail as possible — both then and now. I had the abortion when I was twenty-one. I have done a lot of healing work around my loss and my action. I remember doing voice therapy. I talked to my child and then I took her place and replied to myself. She was very gentle and loving. I still miss her. Recently I talked to a therapist about how I still feel about losing the child. She told me the child has grown up on another plane and is connected to me and cares about me. It's hard for me to come to complete peace. But that's me; what about you? How is it for you?

Being unable to conceive your own child

Have you ever desperately wanted a baby and not been able to conceive or father a child? Have you sought medical help? Would you consider adopting a child? Draw a picture of the child you would like to have or write your feelings about this.

My child is pregnant!

Has your child fallen pregnant or did your son make a girl pregnant? What was that like for you? How did you decide what to do? Did you tell anyone or did you carry this alone? Is there any way you can heal the wound that this might have caused — for yourself,

my life

between you and your child, or between you and your family? Or did the pregnancy have an entirely different effect? What happened?

Sex

Think about your sex life. What's important to you in the sexual act? Do you know all there is to know about love-making? Do you believe it just comes naturally? There are many ways to enhance your expression of love for your partner. This includes using incense in the room; making love in different rooms; dressing for the occasion; taking the initiative; experimenting; using music as a background. The list is endless. Do you know what you like? Have you told your partner? Do you talk about sex?

A first marriage

For me entering the convent was rather like a first marriage or first long-term committed relationship. It was necessary. How about you? What was your first marriage or long-term relationship like? What attracted you to the other person? How did your relationship develop? What led you to move on? Are you glad you did? Or did your partner choose to leave? How was that for you? Have you resolved that relationship? Can you draw your relationship? Then talk about your drawing with someone you trust. What did you learn about yourself from those years? What qualities emerged? How did that relationship prepare you for the next one or for another stage in your life?

A name change

I expected to be given another name as a nun and was pleasantly surprised when I found I could keep my own name. Often when one moves into another way of life one changes one's name — a symbolic gesture. In marriage it is the woman who takes the man's surname. That is partly about possession, but it also signifies a change in status. (We have not yet designed a name change for men that reflects they are husbands.) Have you experienced a spiritual change, the intensity of which makes you realise your previous name does not fully encompass who you are now? If so, what name did you release and what name have you chosen?

Saying goodbye

Can you recall a time when you had to tell someone you loved that you were taking a path he or she could not feel happy about? Like when I had to tell my Jewish father I was becoming a Catholic nun. How did you tell the person? How did you make it as easy as possible for the person to understand? Or was that impossible? Were you ever given news about a loved one's choice that shocked or disappointed you? How did you heal yourself from the blow? Or is it still sore for you? Write a letter to the person you told or to the person who told you. You don't need to send it; just write what you want to say now.

Padre Pio

I draw on the memory of my experience with Padre Pio if I tend to forget who I really am — unlimited, part of being, innocent and most of all, deeply loved, if not love itself. There are a number of books written about Padre Pio. He is still close through prayer. Do you have an experience that was a "mountain top" for you? One that altered the course of your life or led you to reconsider your choices? How has this experience sustained you or changed you? Who knows about this? How do you honour the positive outcome of this experience in your life today? Write about it now. You never know whose life you can touch as a result.

Part 2

Sister Michelle

Chapter 1 *Struggle and Strangeness*

Aliwal North was not the friendliest of places. Situated on a flat piece of countryside, it was desert-like in its sparseness and barrenness. The convent itself was a huge old house with high ceilings and corridors wide enough for two-way traffic plus cyclists. I would hesitate to describe it as cosy. Aliwal North qualifies easily as a small town. Not only was it resistant to change but many of the sisters who lived in Aliwal had a hard time remembering that there was a world beyond it.

The "Mother House" was so named because it was the first station to be developed by the Holy Cross sisters in Africa. Mother Bernarda Heimgartner, the Swiss founder of the order, lived from 1822 to 1863. At the time Aliwal was founded, the sisters believed it would be the centre of development in South Africa. The original idea was to have a "Mother House" where all the action was, rather than stuck away in what became the back of beyond.

On our arrival my mother and I were given tea and a snack and I was led into a room by Amanda, a young girl who had recently joined the Order. She was to cut my hair. This reminded me of all I had heard about convents. First thing to go is hair! My hair wasn't very long and I would be wearing a type of veil which allowed the top portion of it to show. For me, shedding my hair was a symbolic gesture of my "leaving the world" and I wasn't too perturbed whether Amanda was adept at the art of shearing. It didn't seem to matter any more. Who would see my hair anyway? While she cut she chatted away non-stop.

My mother sat waiting uneasily for me in an adjacent room. She had mixed feelings. Part of her felt proud that her daughter had been "chosen" as a bride of Christ. Part of her felt that the convent would save me from myself. Much of her felt terrible pain at losing me, again. It wasn't easy to say goodbye to her because there was so much, if not everything, we had never said. She would break into tears when we touched subjects related to our relationship, to the past. I sensed what she had gone through. I was not angry with her, never blamed her, made it clear that what was past was gone. I also never allowed myself to feel my own pain, anger and resentment. I blocked it all. The sisters gave us a room together. I was glad they had not separated us.

The next morning after we had been shown around the convent and the grounds, I walked her to the car wearing the white dress made for me by the Alexandra Sisters. It had a Peter Pan collar, three buttons down the front, long sleeves, a belt around the gathered waist and fell in an ample amount of material almost to the floor. I felt quite saintly already! I looked plump and neutral. I was concerned that she would drive all the way back alone but I had to trust she would be all right. "Goodbye, darling," she whispered as she held me in a hug and I could hear the tears in her voice. "Goodbye, Mom," I said, half of me ready to see her go so I could get on with my life, the other half terrified of losing her. She could not show how she really felt and certainly not in front of the few sisters who stood around waving goodbye. "I'll write," she reassured me as she looked out the window and tried to raise a smile. She looked away quickly and drove out. I was on my own.

I was not alone, however. There were a number of us who wanted to "take the veil". Of the initial eight or ten, two or three became nuns and took their final vows. In the meantime our motley crew got on as best we could. One of the most entertaining of the new entrants was Jo-Ann, the daughter of a champion boxer. Her entire family drove her down and took over the convent for a few hours. After copious hugging and weeping and goodbying, they left her with a couple of pairs of boxing gloves. Of course we tried them out. Jo-Ann beat me in the sixteenth round on a technicality.

Our first sleeping abode was a giant dormitory at the top of the building opposite the student bedrooms. Each of us had a cubicle large enough to hold a small bed, a bedside table and a chair. The "walls" were of light board and the lights were controlled by one main switch. To get out of one's cubicle and to the toilet in the night was a feat demanding dexterity, perseverance, unbridled bravery, and an unmitigated desire for relief. The boards all creaked, and tip-toeing out was rather like firing a machine-gun in slow-motion. Everyone awoke at every shot. If one managed to untangle the maze of cubicles and not inadvertently land up in someone else's cubicle, opening the door was enough to quick-start the comatose.

Then began the long, eerie shuffle in a flapping sheet of a night-gown down the shadowy passage in the most chocolate of darkness with only the thin trail of a torchlight as guide. The creak of the toilet door magnified the terror of opening it and perhaps finding some long-departed sister standing shrouded in the silence begging you to pray for her tortured soul (shiver!). The longing for bed sent you, like a pin-ball, ricocheting back praying not to make yet another mistake and turn the knob on the opposite door which action would wake the sleeping ninja teenagers. Then, indeed, it would be *Apocalypse Now*!

On the surface I fell into the daily routine. We'd rise, make our way downstairs for the morning prayer lauds, followed by mass, then breakfast. Aliwal housed at least thirty-five to fifty sisters and we'd all meet at meals. As a postulant I had various duties at meals. They included fetching the food from the kitchen and placing it on the tables, or, at the end of the meal, I'd collect the small washing basins, fill them with water and place them on each table with a small towel. Each of us would wash our cutlery, dry it, wind our serviette over the knife, fork and spoon then slide our own holder over it. We'd collect the plates and return them to the kitchen where the black servants would wash them.

Even though I was new to the religious life, I was not new to teaching and I was immediately assigned to teach Standard One. These were seven- to eight-year-olds. I was way out of my depth. I wasn't trained to teach such young children and I hated it. There was preparation, then teaching, lunch, maybe a rest, more preparation, a walk, late afternoon prayer which was vespers, time to sit together and talk, then night prayer and the silence. I'd cry in chapel at the mass just because it was such a relief to be there, or because I'd feel overcome by the feeling of oneness with God. I had no way to contain that feeling, so I'd cry. At other times I'd cry from frustration but I couldn't explain what I was frustrated about.

On the next layer, underneath the surface, I felt as if I were being shrunk into another shape and size. Everything happened on time, the same time every day, the same way, the same. Although I'd been used to the routine of teaching, I'd still had the remainder of the day for myself. Now I didn't have that. I didn't allow myself space for the adjustment. I thought I'd just "fit in" and be a good girl. It was sore.

At times the five of us postulants would giggle and clown around. What did we have to worry about? Everything was taken care of — our clothes, our food, our time. So we could relax, gleefully regressing into infantile behaviour and moods. We'd swim in the walled pool nestled in the huge orchard. I was surprised we were permitted to swim! My swimsuit was very modest, a far cry from the bikini I gave away back home. Often I'd sit in the orchard, on a bench, reciting the rosary, feeling exquisitely at peace. One late afternoon I saw a man standing on the other side of the fence staring at me like a grazing horse raises its head to a passer-by. But with a difference. This man had his fly open and was waving a white cock at me. He probably thought I'd never seen one. Up from my now ruined place of refuge I leapt and fled as fast as I could to the house, eager to report my experience. Everyone was shocked and sympathetic. The police were told and the sisters were warned. I recognised the culprit some months later as I stood on the platform of the train station waiting the arrival of a sister. He was a post office clerk. "That's him!" I wanted to shriek. Instead, I said nothing.

How was I dealing with no men in my life? I wasn't thinking about them. Although no-one ever suggested that the life of a nun is a natural one, we were told that as we had been called by God to lead this life, we would be given the means to do so. I felt loved by Jesus. I would be filled with His love and closeness. Did I miss being held? Probably, but I never admitted it. Did I find it difficult to change the way I acted around men? Yes. I had to remember I was no longer sexually available. At this time the only men I was exposed to were a couple of priests. One was very shy and distant; the other was chatty and a little strange.

I had contact with the older girls when I taught the higher classes. One of the girls and I became friends. She came from divorced parents, was noisy and demanding. She was also quite boyish and as I look back I realise I was attracted to her. She had a crush on me. I thought it was okay. I didn't see the sexual implications — that I might be repressing my own sexuality and it was leaking out here. Also I didn't dream of thinking that sexual attraction is not necessarily confined to one sex and that we put ourselves in boxes and limit ourselves at that level as well.

I had no means of dealing with conflict either. I avoided it. I so badly wanted to be accepted, to be "nice". I was terrified of Sister Mary-Theresa who looked like an owl and swished along the corridors with a "don't-stop-me-now" rhythm. I had to pluck up courage to speak to her and it was necessary because I took over her History and English classes when she went away. The girls were as scared and they told me. I was much closer to them age-wise and it was only natural they'd be drawn to me. I felt guilty, as though I was in competition with her.

Sister Germain was German, large and never looked happy. I couldn't get to her at all. I avoided her as much as possible. She'd express her feelings, her ideas, her indignation — loudly and regularly. The waves parted when she walked. One evening I landed up in the car with her. She was driving. I was trying to be as attentive and polite as possible. As I listened to her, I saw a shadow leap out from the sidewalk, felt a thwack on the left side of the car where I was sitting and said nothing. I didn't want to interrupt her. There was blood on the car when we got out. She was shocked.

"Yes," I murmured, "I think we hit an animal."

"Why didn't you tell me?" she glared at me. Sister Germain always glared. What could I tell her? I wanted to say: "You are loud. You have no gentleness in your face. You are abrasive. I am scared of you." For me it was peace at any price.

Sister Gertrude was the choir mistress. She'd get irritated and moody, spitting and fuming in anger. I was on red alert in her presence. But she had a great sense of humour.

"You never know someone until you've eaten a bag of salt with her, Sister Michelle," she'd say, her hand on my shoulder.

"Please God," I thought, "never put me in that position!"

One Saturday morning I helped a sister clean one of the guest cottages.

"I remember cleaning the room of one of our old sisters, Clare, the day after she died. Clare had a hard time," she told me.

"What do you mean?" I asked.

"Well, she was a difficult person."

"Difficult?"

"Yes, she had a terrible temper and she'd say the most horrible things and make people cry. As I was cleaning her room I was thinking how with a temper and a tongue like that, Sister Clare must be paying for her words now and she probably deserved it! Just as I thought this I saw Sister Clare with a radiant smile on her face holding a number of gladioli. There she was, large as life, smiling at me. I nearly fainted!"

My cleaning companion pointed out to me that there is a vast difference between what we perceive a person to be, the judgements we make about her, and how God knows her. I was an idealist, full of expectations, quick to judge. I wanted the sisters to be "the real thing" which I presumed was some form of enlightened being like a yogi or a guru. It was disappointing to realise they were ordinary people. Like me? But I didn't see myself as ordinary. I was "special" so I had to be nice and polite and keep all the "bad stuff" hidden as far as I could.

Every town had its township. Aliwal North was no exception. On its outskirts lay the black ghetto. We had a school there. I was asked to help out for a few terms. I was delighted. At last my dream was coming true. Or so I thought. Here I would be faced with apartheid in Africa and apartheid in the convent; with Michelle as a nun and Michelle as a woman. The dream versus the reality — of both religious life and myself.

my life

steps to heal the heart

It was funny
Do you remember when you laughed so much you got a pain in your side? When was this? Where were you? Who were you with? What made it so hilarious?

Mother-in-law
In some customs, women are expected to spend some time in the home of their husband's mother. If you experienced this, write about it or express what that was like for you in a creative way, maybe draw or paint or tell a story. Describe the home; tell about your mother-in-law and what she was like; how you and she got on or didn't get on. How did the community receive you? What difference did your new home make to your relationship with your husband? How did you feel as the days passed?

   If you are a mother-in-law, how did you feel about your new daughter- or son-in-law at first? Did that change over time? How did your relationship with her or him affect your relationship with your child? What is your relationship to both of them now?

   As a husband, what was it like for you to take your new wife into the home of your mother? What were the positive and negative aspects? Did your relationship with your mother or your wife change in any way?

Strange attraction
Sometimes we think that because we have committed ourselves to one person as a life partner, we will never be attracted to anyone else. Have you experienced being married or being in a committed relationship and finding that you are attracted to another person? How did you react? How did you feel? Have you ever found yourself attracted to a person of the same sex? Write your experience.

Making a judgement
Can you recall judging someone favourably or unfavourably because of something they did or said and then you found out the person was completely different from how you judged them to be? Write this as a conversation between yourself and your thoughts. Tell the story of what you saw, what you believed and how you caught yourself out.

Servants and sisters
I remarked in this chapter that the servants, who were black, washed our dishes. Did that strike you in any way as incongruous, as not fitting into the picture? Why do you think it was strange that servants washed dishes for women who had dedicated their lives to the service of others? Why do you think this happened? Do you think it still happens today?

   Another aspect of this is the fact that both servants and sisters, for the most part, were women. If you are a woman, what is your relationship with and attitude to women from other race groups who are of the same economic status as yourself? What is your relationship and attitude to women who, today, are your servants? Where do you situate yourself in the Women's Movement? Are you a feminist? What does that mean?
Do you think all women relate regardless of class or race?

my life

Mothers and daughters; mothers and sons

At this point, my relationship with my mother was careful and somewhat superficial. We were scared of upsetting one another. What was your relationship with your mother like when you were in your twenties? Make a few notes on this. Thoughts and feelings may arise as you write. Notice them. Write them down too. Do you think your relationship with your mother was more complicated than your relationship with your father? How did those relationships differ?

Hair

What is it about hair? Women have to cover their hair or cut it off if they are committed either to God or to a husband. This is the case in many a religion. Hair makes a woman beautiful, we are taught. So in order not to be attractive to men (and we are taught that this is our role) we cut off our hair, shave it off or cover it up. It seems it is a turn-on and we bear the responsibility (or so we are taught) if men get turned on.

What do you think about this? How do you feel about your hair — as a woman? About hair on your legs or under your arms? How is hair related to the way you feel about yourself? Talk to another woman about this. Compare notes.

Fitting in

Have you ever felt you were under pressure to behave like everyone around you or not be yourself? Did you try to be accepted for what you thought people wanted you to be? This sometimes happens when you start a new job or a new relationship. If there was a camera following your every move, what would the film look like? Describe yourself in this situation through the lens of a camera.

A man out of balance

When you read the part where a post office clerk exposed himself, what was your immediate reaction? Write that down. Imagine you were asked to talk to the man. What would you most want to know from him? What would you want to tell him? Let him answer you. Don't think about his answer or what you expect. Let the writing lead you. If you, as a man, ever found yourself in this situation, write a letter of understanding and forgiveness to yourself. You might also like to write to the woman you frightened. Try to do this exercise with no judgement.

Chapter 2 *Classrooms and Conflict*

St Francis Mission was the name of our school and hospital in the township. Both facilities were small. A large and simply constructed church sat alongside the convent house within arid, treeless, dusty and poor ground on which a few teachers lived. Square plots on which older students attempted to garden, dotted the back of the church.

The children were the flowers in this desert. Full of enthusiasm and spurts of vitality, they packed the classroom sixty at a time. Between ten and fourteen years old, they'd sit bunched on the benches in my classroom like flocks of birds on telegraph wires, their eyes rapt, their attention span challenged by the lack of writing or reading materials and no breakfast. Swelling stomachs slowly sprouted plenty of open space for food that would never be enough. Crowded classrooms offered extreme heat, intense cold, and yet another language — English. The class sat quietly, brimming over with eagerness to learn. Sometimes a child, losing the fight, would rest her small head on her inch of the table, while her baby brother lay sprawled on his back sleeping soundly on the floor in apparent absolute contentment.

One experience remains a highlight in all my years of teaching for sheer serendipity. The class next door, Standard Three, held seventy-five children. I had no direct contact with them. One day as I was leaving my class, Sister Gerda, the school principal, yelled at me in her German accent as she walked back towards the convent.

"Sister Michelle!"

"Yes?"

"Oh, please take the standard threes for an hour or so — next door. Their teacher's sick. Do anything!" she sang into the dust, lisping slightly, "just keep them awake!" and she disappeared into the house, her laughter wobbling in the heat.

From the windows the children watched me walk towards their door. There was silence as I entered. In the centre of the clear space at the front of the classroom I stood looking at them. Slowly I looked into the eyes of each child and each child looked back at me. The minutes moved second by second, stare by stare. Then, as if rehearsed and as if a hidden signal had been sent, we all burst out laughing together. Love at first sight.

Sister Gerda appeared as a dragon, belching fire and smoke as she marched around with her loud voice and threatening stick. I had met her before at Aliwal where I had seen how enthusiastic she was, how much she cared about the students. Her large heart lay on her sleeve. Although wary around her, the children knew the dragon was friendly.

I was naïve enough to think that religious life in South Africa would be free of servants. Some sisters who came to South Africa from Europe arrived with open minds, but over time they bought into the apartheid doctrines as the "we-they" syndrome sucked yet another victim into its unquenchable trench. There were black servants in the kitchen at St Francis. They'd clean the floors, wash dishes, set the table and so on. One evening at dinner, tea was spilt on the floor. A young black woman came in, dropped to her knees and wiped up the mess. I was horrified. Here was I, a "madam" again, posing as a nun. We had become part of the system. My mind was full of St Francis of Assisi, of a life of poverty and prayer, of washing lepers, of serving, not being served. I said nothing about this. I didn't challenge Sister Gerda or any of the other six sisters. I held it in, afraid of confrontation. What could I do about it? I felt guilty about keeping quiet and guilty about accepting it but I still wanted to be a nun. I began to look out for sisters who were aware of this discrepancy. It was like searching for a secret clan. Who saw it the way it was and wanted it to be different? These sisters would be my support group. Maybe we could change it all.

It dawned on me that all the sisters were not, in fact, one happy family. We dressed somewhat alike, said the same prayers in public, ate at the same table, followed the same rules, but some of us hurt one another, misunderstood each other, were angry, resentful, jealous. It was all there. Many of us didn't know how to deal with our feelings, how to resolve the pain, how to confront each other, how to heal. I was part of this group. Most of us bottled our emotions up. As the years passed we grew ill and died from holding in. I was neither in touch with my own anger and pain, nor of the gulf of loneliness within.

I saw myself as being such a cheerful, outgoing, fun person. Why wasn't everyone like me? To find a friend was solace. Someone you could really talk to and open up to. It was rare. If you found it with another sister, good. If you found it with someone outside the Order, it would be more difficult. If you found it with a man, you were in a dilemma.

I believed once I became a nun, once I donned the white robe, all my sexual desires would be spirited away. Whoosh! Gone! Themba Ndamane taught History and Maths. In his twenties, handsome, darkly brown, he drew me. He was the second black male I had befriended. At Marist Brothers where I had taught, the school carpenter, Jacob Mogawa, and I used to chat regularly. But Themba was physically attractive to me. I wasn't supposed to feel this.

I learnt that in black schools children were beaten with a stick. I wondered if Sister Gerda ever used hers? How could she? Jesus didn't go around beating students! Themba, however, did. One afternoon I walked in upon him whipping a teenage girl with a long, snakelike whip which curled around her bare legs as she screamed and slapped her thighs and calves in an effort to dull the pain. I fled into the empty church shaking and sobbing. Sister Gerda found me there and tried to explain it was "their way". I was simply not facing a cultural difference. The student had been staying away from school. This was her punishment, an attempt to bring her back.

Some weeks later Themba and I were talking in his classroom.

"I was really upset when I saw you beating Lindiwe," I ventured, after we'd been talking about Martin Luther King and non-violence.

"I know," he replied, watching me carefully. "I saw your face as you left."

We looked at each other. Neither of us dropped our gaze.

"What's the point?" I asked playing with a pencil.

"It's her punishment. She knew that."

What did he want to say?

"Mind your own business. What do you know? You come in here and think you know it all, have all the answers, can tell us how to run our schools, teach our kids. Get out of here, white woman!"

What did I want to say?

"Themba, how could you? We talk about history and philosophy and suddenly you turn into a savage and beat a girl! Did you get a kick out of that? I think you're vile!"

Instead, I told him how much it hurt me, how I had cried, how I didn't understand. I was in pain again. I sat on the desk. He stood leaning against the cupboard. His eyes drank in the pain on my face. I felt my cheeks burning as the blush began.

"He must know," I thought, "he must know how I lie awake at night and think of his body on mine, his brown-black hands on my pink-white breasts." I looked away.

"I must go," I excused myself, "I'll see you tomorrow."

"*Tsamaya hantle*, sister," Themba courteously responded. "See you tomorrow." His eyes never left my face.

"How can you," I berated myself as I made for my room, "how can you want to be a nun and want to have sex with Themba? What's the matter with you? Why doesn't it go away? I don't want to feel like this! What can I do?"

The school term was about to end. Sister Gerda was holding the final assembly. This was nothing short of a chaotic celebration where she'd call out the names of those who passed and each child would give a wild whoop of delight, leap onto the stage and jig about hysterically with the whole school egging her on. The failures waited for a name never called.

Themba and I were in a nearby classroom hurriedly totalling the final scores of the last few students.

"Fifty-six plus forty-five plus forty-two ... "

He'd write the answer on a chart.

We were almost through. I looked up to see if he'd finished writing. He was looking at me, his mouth slightly open, his eyes wide and I saw reflected in them what was smouldering in me — the desire. All my hormones were at the ready. There sat my libido, her napkin tucked in like a bib, knife and fork poised in each fist resting on the table, licking her lips. I stared back at him, feeling my belly pulse, aware of my breasts pushing against my clothing. I wanted to tear my habit off, to rush at him, pull him onto the floor. He couldn't do it: This was South Africa, and I was a nun. It was up to me. I dropped my eyes, feeling a cold stab of reality burst my sexual bubble. I wouldn't do it. I was afraid. We completed our work quickly, avoiding eye contact and joined the frenzied ritual where we could hide.

I couldn't do it. Themba was married. I was a nun. He was black. I was white. I had broken a barrier. I could be attracted to a black man. I was okay. Who could I talk to about this? Who could I tell? I wondered what was worse, entering the convent as a virgin, having never known a man, or having sweated with the mingling of flesh and lusty excitement and then never doing it again?

I remembered what it was like to pocket a penis in my inner purse; to pulse with the pounding thrusts of his pelvis as, body raised, his hands would support his weight. Our eyes lock in concentration, his seed speeds to spill, to trigger off the minefield of my bursting body. Pow! The fusion fix! I thought I would forget in time. How could I? I was lonely. I had no-one I could really open my heart to. Men made me feel less lonely when they held me. As a nun I couldn't do this anymore. So what would I do?

I'd take it with me to the next place. My time at St Francis was over. I realised things were not as simple as I'd expected. This was not going to be a piece of cake. I was still a human being. I still had desires and urges. If I could become more spiritual, if I could pray more or read more or work more, then maybe I would become holier. Then I'd be a saint. That's what I was hoping for after all. Recognition! But when would I begin to recognise myself?

I was asked to postpone my entrance to the novitiate for a year in order to teach at a mission station in one of the homelands — Bophuthatswana — at a girls' high school. I'd be on my own with no-one "in charge" of me. This was more like the real thing! What the "real thing" was I couldn't say. I wanted to be real — real close to God, real loving and really make a difference. The routine, the silence, the prayer, the focus, were all knitting me together. I had entered the convent as a mass of undirected energy with little self-awareness or self-knowledge. I arrived as a jig-saw puzzle clumsily interlocked into an unfocused, fuzzy picture. The years began to re-set the puzzle piece by piece, allowing a glimmer of the final photograph to emerge. St Paul's in Taung would take my ability to teach and strengthen it. It would take my thirst for contact with the Spirit and silence and plant it deeper within me. It would confront me with my motives for working in the missions and comfort me too. It would offer me another opportunity to look at my sexual urges. Slowly and irrevocably my desire to be whole was being met.

my life

Steps to heal the heart

Watching and saying nothing

At St Francis mission an opportunity presented itself for me to ask some questions of the sisters about having servants, or at the very least, to express how I felt. Were you ever in a similar situation where you felt uneasy, sensed things were "wrong" yet were unable or unwilling to say or do anything? Where were you? What was the situation? If you had spoken up what do you think would have happened? Why not write a script of the imagined conversation and outcome?

Sex across the colour-line

I was attracted to Themba. Have you ever been attracted to someone who was of a different race to you? Sometimes our conditioning is so strong that we never allow ourselves to go beyond it; we don't even think about the possibility. Think about it. What do you tell your children or what would you tell your children about a relationship with a person of another race that included sex? What were you told as a child?

The Shadow

I wanted to hide from my shadow side; from the parts of me I didn't think fitted in with being a nice nun: my judgement, my lust, my anger. When they flickered on the screen of my consciousness, I flicked them away like a windscreen-wiper flicks a raindrop. What about you? What aspects of yourself do you want to go away? What do you find hard to accept as part of you? If you have crayons or paint, get a large sheet of paper and paint those sides of yourself. Give them shapes and names and voices. What do the voices say? Do they talk to you? Do they talk to each other? If they had a perfume or a smell, what would they smell like? If you could touch them, what would they feel like? What do you think would happen if you let them out? If you acknowledged them, if you let them in, what then? Once you have drawn your picture, make a frame around it and colour that frame a different colour — one you like. Now look at your drawing. How does it feel with the frame? Turn your paper over and write a letter to the parts of yourself you have drawn. Talk to them, tell them how you feel. What's the difference now that you have completed this exercise?

Love at first sight

Ever had an experience something like the one I had with the children in the classroom next door? Where something bright and connecting just happens from nowhere. Write about it. Or make one up. One of those unforgettable beautiful moments.

Beating a naughty child

What was it like for you as a teenager at school? Were you ever beaten? Did you see a young woman beaten? A young man? Should boys be beaten but not girls? Who beats pupils more — male or female teachers? Is violence the way to educate? What are your thoughts?

Chapter 3 *Change and Challenge*

Once again I was moving. I had hoped that I would stay in one place for a long, long time. On the one hand I was flexible, ready to go anywhere. On the other hand I was traumatised by constantly moving home. From a Johannesburg flat as a baby I was moved to a farm in Sandown; from there to Dudley, England. From Dudley I was moved to London and three apartments — Camden Town, Belsize Park Gardens, Golders Green. From London it was on to a hotel in Scotland and from there back to South Africa to a house in Saxonwold, Johannesburg. I was twelve. I stayed in that house for four years. For my final school year I stayed in Rosebank with the Harrisons then briefly in a Hillbrow hotel, followed by a college residence for two years. While I was an actor I stayed in a Pretoria flat (when I wasn't touring) then left for London and two more apartments. On my return to Johannesburg I lived in two different flats before I entered the convent at twenty-four. In the first year I was moved from Aliwal North to St Francis mission and now I was going to St Paul's in Taung. Whew! How many other moves lay ahead?

Taung was in the heart of a black "homeland" — an area set aside for a particular group, in this case, the Batswana. By redrawing the South African map, government officials would declare a particular territory Bophuthatswana. All Batswana people who did not fulfil certain often complicated conditions of either employment and/or residence would have to "return" to a homeland they had never seen. These homelands were largely rural and the population returning would have lived their lives in the city. The government tried to entice businesses to build factories on the edges of the homelands to provide the "home boys" with work. There were not many takers.

Set miles from Bophuthatswana's capital Mafikeng, Taung hid in the back of beyond. Spread over two areas, a hospital and a school, the mission housed hundreds of nurses, student nurses and high school students. Central to the complex was the church. To the right of the church was the home of the Oblates of Mary Immaculate (OMI). Below stood the school with its upstairs dormitories. Most of the girls boarded. Our convent, home to eight sisters, was a short stroll away. To the left of the church, across the scrub, lay the huge hospital, constantly crowded. A dormitory for nurses separated the hospital from the nursing nuns who lived in a low rectangular building. Sometimes the teaching and nursing Sisters met.

Father Berndt, in his early twenties, was asked to be responsible for my spiritual development. Direct from Germany, Berndt was over six foot, his straight black hair combed back from his large forehead. Behind glasses his blue eyes blinked shyly at me. He felt awkward about his new position.

"What shall we talk about?" he asked in his German accent, laughing nervously. "Do you know music?" So we talked about music. He was an accomplished violinist. What he found hard to say in words he expressed in sound. So passionate was he about the violin that he lost all track of time when he played. So he stopped — I found that hard to understand. "It takes me away from God and my duties," he explained. How could it, I wondered? If he lost himself in playing, if the hours sped by, he must be doing what he loved. If he were doing what he loved, wouldn't love itself come through? Instead he chose to play the piano.

"What about you? Can you play the piano?"

"Not much," I replied, "I learned as a child but didn't continue."

"What about the guitar? It's easy. I can teach you and you can play with the girls."

I liked that. I'd been writing to my father. In the next letter I asked for a guitar. One arrived shortly afterwards. Brand new and waiting to be made mine. Berndt and I leapt into lessons and in so doing we became friends.

It seemed there were two classes of men in my life: men I was physically attracted to and who rarely became my friends, and men I was not physically attracted to who became friends only. My sexual feelings were so tied up with an abusive situation I still knew nothing about that for me to love someone who was a friend was completely foreign. I was safe with Berndt. He was much younger than I in male-female relationship experience; certainly he was uneasy around the sexual tension between us.

He was also lonely. I too, bore that burden of loneliness and I too, was unaware of it, had not voiced it yet. Behind the smoke-screen of our guitar lessons, Berndt bared places in his soul. I heard his words and felt his pain. I absorbed it like cotton-wool in milk, hardly conscious that I was taking it all in, harbouring.

One evening around six, when everyone was in church and stillness settled like a cat curled in my lap, I sat outside on a bench facing the emptiness of scrub and soil. I was full of his feelings. He had talked about his childhood — not a traumatic one, just sad. He triggered off my own still-sleeping sadness. As the sun stained purple-pink traces of itself in the sky, I began to cry. I sat there till the darkness covered me, finding a peace.

Berndt and I were aware that our meetings and friendship might be misinterpreted. We were careful never to stand too close. Africa is a sexy place; bodies, heat and energy sizzle. The students fried in it. Warm and demonstrative, they'd hold hands or link arms, finding it easy to sit close together. Often I was included in this. It was as if we were all just extensions of one another. One of the young women attracted me — tomboyish, androgynous Edith Malinga. Why? I didn't ask myself. I could talk to her; she listened. I didn't talk all that much to Berndt about myself, my heart. He was afraid of his sex and my sexiness.

I couldn't talk to any of the sisters. They were friendly; they'd help me if I needed help with school work and they may well have been there for me emotionally, but I wasn't drawn to any of them. Sometimes whiffs of my buried, repressed, denied, distorted fumes of feelings whispered to me. How could I recognise them? The mirror was up and I refused to look into it.

Edith and I could talk to each other. Yes, there was something sexual about it, something stifled, something unsaid. What did I want to say to her?

"Edith I like being with you. I like your gentleness and your presence. I feel attracted to you and I am afraid of that. I'm interested in your life and in you. I want you to like me. I'm lonely. I'm putting you in a bit of a spot. You're one of the students and I'm a teacher. How can we get the best out of this?"

I knew little about love. Later in the year when one of the other trainee-sisters arrived she struck up a similar relationship with one of the female students. I recognised that both of us longed for an intimate relationship; neither of us had yet given up the hope of someone special in our lives. Did we move towards women because men were forbidden? Maybe we're capable of a range of loving and we believe society forces us to make a choice, so we do.

"Sister Michelle, the girls just love you, you have a wonderful gift! You give them so much love!" That came from Sister Anne who was born in Taung and grew up there. I glowed with pleasure. It wasn't the full picture, but it was part of it. There was a natural ability in me to teach, an enthusiasm, a sincere compassion and caring. I liked being there, liked the students. My heart was open, big, warm. But there were aspects of myself I was not in touch with.

Circumstances arrive, usually uninvited, to offer us the chance for these hidden, harboured aspects of ourselves to peek out. Such was the arrival of Jacob Mogawa at St Paul's. When he called from Mafikeng to tell me he was not too far from Taung with his wife and some friends and they were coming to see me, I was thrown into a slight tizz. Jacob was the carpenter and handyman at the school where I had taught at Marist Brothers, Johannesburg.

"Oh, my God, am I allowed to have visitors? Who can I ask or shall I just go ahead and act like I can, because it's too late now and Jacob's on his way and I don't want him to think I'm an idiot, especially in front of his friends. After all, they've taken the time and trouble to come out here and I must look as though I want to see them."

I was uneasy about this sudden arrival. It was like you meet strangers on a trip in Spain and you laughingly say, "Oh, if you're ever in Johannesburg, do come over, we'd love to see you." You don't mean a word of it really, it just sounds nice at the time when you feel so magnanimous. Here I was, the great liberal, hard at practice for a gold medal, radically unsure of the procedure from this point.

"It's a man. Is it okay for me to have male visitors? Who do I ask? Never mind, Jacob's with his wife. Of course it's all right." Then, twenty seconds later, "Oh my God, he's black. Do you think that makes a difference? How will the Sisters react? Is this okay? Where do I take them? Is there anywhere I can't take them? Where do we eat? Do I introduce them to everyone? Help!" I announced I was having visitors and no one batted an eyelid. Good. I was nervous and fidgety waiting for them.

Jacob beamed as he closed the car door. Pleased now, I remembered how we chatted in his workshop. After a tour of the mission — which went off easily — I suggested we return to the convent to eat. I thought: "Oh my God, is it okay for me to go through the kitchen door? Will Jacob think I am taking him in the back way? But we all come into the convent through the back door." I had to be so careful! I was trying so hard. As we all trooped through the kitchen, I glimpsed the expression on the face of Sister Mechtild. Momentarily she lost the ability to hold her jaw closed. It gaped in a rather unwieldy manner. What could she have been thinking? "Oh no, Michelle has visitors and I'm not ready yet?" or "Michelle has black visitors?" Her eyes were jiggling right and left, her mouth apparently paralysed in its open position. The servants were equally surprised and appeared slightly embarrassed. They didn't quite know how to take it. What were their thoughts as they stared at the guests?

In the parlour-cum-dining-room, my guests were seated at the table set for four. Instead of fetching another seat and joining the party, I stood hopping round the table keeping everyone happy. I was a nun now. I had to serve everyone. I couldn't be a human being. I wasn't a teacher relating to pupils, nor a teacher relating to a carpenter. We were just people, but I didn't know that. I was awkward and jittery, struggling to keep my halo from slipping off.

The main dish was served. Immediately I sensed something was wrong. Jacob passed a few words to his friends in Setswana. He lifted his fork and pressed the meat with his fingers. I got it. They had been served "boys' meat". In South Africa, servants were not fed the same meat as their "masters". God forbid. It was tough and had a peculiar, rancid smell. The smell was now in the room.

I died. "Oh my God, its boys' meat! What do I do?"

Jacob said nothing. I looked at his friends. They were eating it. I needed to say: "Excuse me, there's been a mistake. May I have your plates please?" and return them to the kitchen. And to Sister Mechtild: "What do you think you're doing, serving this to my guests? Do you realise how you are insulting them? Why should they be given inferior quality meat? Do you think they are dogs and not people? Would you serve this to your family? Why give it to my friends?" I said nothing. I pretended nothing was wrong and continued to hop about. Why hadn't I thought of this possibility beforehand? Because I was out of touch with the reality of myself and the reality of the situation.

My friendship with Jacob rested on our few talks, not much more. Why didn't he say: "Michelle, this is boys' meat. Neither myself, my wife, nor my friends are prepared to eat it." Why didn't he seize the plates and fling them against the walls? Maybe he was afraid? Maybe he was too polite? Maybe he was holding back his anger? Did he not want to embarrass me? Was he too shocked at my acceptance of this? I don't know. And I didn't ask. Nobody said anything. I didn't apologise to Jacob. He said nothing to me. I said nothing to Sister Mechtild. We were all one big happy family. Five Hail Marys and three Our Fathers later and nothing had changed. All the unsaid words hung heavy in the air. I wasn't as perfect as I thought.

During that year I had another visitor — my father. Since December of the previous year when I had entered the convent I had been writing to him, slowly coaxing him into an acceptance of my decision. I was surprised when he wrote of his intended visit. Dad was relaxed with nuns. After all, he had first sent both his daughters to convent schools. A showman at heart, he loved showing his two daughters off to the Holy Family sisters. I wondered what it would be like having him on the mission.

It was easier than I anticipated. The sisters rallied round, welcoming him. He loved it. He had never remarried. I remember only once his expressing interest in a woman he knew. It must have been very lonely for him. Now he flirted and giggled with the sisters as far as he could. They tolerated him kindly, enjoying his humour, feeding him well. They fussed about him and he bore it all gracefully. The drive to Taung from Johannesburg took six hours. It was brave of him to come. We did no heart-to-heart talking. He saw I worked well, had plenty to eat and that I was happy teaching. He had an ability to accept what was.

What had I gained from this year? Time on my own to read in the secluded hospital garden. I could walk for hours across the scrub. At twilight I meditated, drinking in the purple-ochre sky as the sun sipped the last few day-drops. I had space to begin to gather myself together. And what else?

Intimations that all was not well within me; realisations that I had a long way to go before I was comfortable with whiteness; awareness that I was incapable of confrontation; confusions about the way I related so well to the students in class, then tottered precariously on the edges of roles.

Staying within appropriate boundaries with Berndt was easier. Had he been less apprehensive, it might have been difficult. Other priests lived at or stopped by the mission. A couple were attractive to me and I became something short of an idiot around them. I didn't know how to behave. I had to remember that the priests were not prey, nor were they after me. They were people who also happened to be male.

News came from Aliwal that I had been selected to form part of an inter-denominational start-up team for a new Catholic movement called Christian Life Groups. Its founder, Father John Golder, had met me on a trip to Aliwal and had asked our Superior for me to be trained for four months as a Christian Life Group leader. I'd be travelling around the country, meeting teenagers, visiting schools, setting up conferences, learning.

I was excited about the social aspect of this and the possibilities of developing new skills. Life on the mission could become boring and repetitive. I had no authority to make changes. Yes, my time at Taung was up. Little did I know that I would return in another capacity. Ahead lay adventure, stimulus and challenges on quite another level.

my life

steps to heal the heart

Home

For how long have you lived at your present address? What has become important to you about your home now? If you had to imagine, draw or sculpt an image that reflected your relationship with the place where you live, what would it be? Do this and share it with someone you trust.

Moving home

I moved approximately twice a year for most of my life. What about you? What has your experience of moving home been? Can you describe the move you most hated? The place you didn't want to leave? I felt a lot of grief and loss around moving. And you? Have you allowed yourself to mourn the loss of a home, or many homes? Do you remember all the packing and unpacking, sorting out your belongings? What about writing a letter to yourself and talking about what moving means to you.

Unspoken conversations

I didn't tell Father Berndt how I felt. Neither did he tell me his feelings.

Is there someone you know or have known who meant more to you than you ever told her or him? Imagine that person is present and you have the opportunity to say what you never said. Write to her or him now.

Secret sadness

Not all of us have had an opportunity to release sadness and sometimes we're not even clear why we're sad: the sadness is just there, like an itch that's hard to reach. I remember weeping at the film *Kramer vs Kramer* about a couple who divorced. Afterwards I realised I was crying for the tears I never shed when my family dissolved. Is there a poem or a piece of music that captures your vague feelings of loss, loneliness or longing? Sit with it for a while and let it seep into you. Be very gentle with yourself and take care of yourself. Make yourself a hearty soup or have a slow hot bath or nurture yourself in a way that is respectful and loving. In spending quality time with yourself, you remember how precious you are. Any sadness you may have will come quietly out and present itself to you.

Hidden aspects of ourselves

"Circumstances arise, usually uninvited, to offer us the chance for hidden harboured aspects of ourselves to peep out." This was the case with Jacob's arrival. I was unaware of my pseudo non-racism. What about you? Has there been a situation where you acted in a way that was a surprise to you, and later you realised things about yourself that you were not aware of? Was the situation amusing? Appalling? Disastrous? Is thinking about it enough or would you prefer to turn it into a script or a poem or a story?

Taking it out on others

As well as reminding me of my attitude, the visit of Jacob and his friends to Taung highlighted racist attitudes in the convent. Were you ever in a specifically racist situation? Where you saw someone humiliated because that person was a different race?

my life

Describe the situation and what you thought, felt and did or didn't do. Maybe you were humiliated? Go back there and write every detail of what happened to you, how you felt. Write the conversation you might like to have had with the person who humiliated you. See what happens.

Maybe you humiliated someone else? Think back. What prompted you to do this? How did you act in the situation? What were your feelings afterwards? Write a letter of apology to the person you humiliated. Let them reply to you.

If you were an observer of such an incident, were you able to speak up? What do you think makes us ready to act on behalf of someone who is humiliated? How did you handle the situation? Did you reward yourself for your positive action? Do so now.

Racist attitudes

What does it take to be clear of racism in oneself? What has your journey been like? Were there stages where you recognised shades of racism blunting your interaction? What quality does it take to be able to recognise this? Write or draw your history of healing as regards racism against another or against yourself.

Reconciliation

The arrival of my father was evidence of his change of heart. It was particularly difficult for him to accept my decision to become a nun because he was Jewish. The suffering of the Jewish people is connected to a large extent to the misinterpretation by some Christians of the message of Jesus and to their readiness to provide a scapegoat in the form of the Jewish people. As a father he had to deal with the loss of a son-in law and grandchildren. It took courage and love for him to visit me. Write, relate, dance or create the story of a person you know or have heard about, who overcame her/his resistance to a difficult change in life or to a loss. Perhaps you know someone who took steps to reconcile her/himself to a relationship like the one I had with my father. Maybe it was you?

Choice and sexual orientation

"Did we move towards women because men were forbidden? Or maybe we are capable of a range of loving and society forces us to make a choice." Are we "forced to make a choice"? How do you think sexual orientation is formed? Do you think you could be gay but unaware of it? Do you think you are bisexual? Because nuns are not allowed to date men does their suppressed sexuality turn to women? Do you think men become gay because they are priests? Or because they are gay they become priests?

Patterns in relationships

Do you notice a pattern in my relating? Do you notice a pattern in your own? Do you repeat certain kinds of relationships? What do you think your pattern is telling you about yourself?

Chapter 4 *Building and Blocking*

The brain behind Christian Life Groups (CLG) was a Jesuit, Father John Golder. Short, plump and balding, he spoke with a quiet certainty, dreamed the impossible and made it happen. Believing the best of people, his insight enabled him to gauge a person's potential, envision what the person could become and so often that's what happened — the person blossomed. His patience exasperated me. I was always in a hurry, with myself and with others. Not Father Golder. Had he been a camel, his hump would have been filled with compassion. He moved as fast as the slowest person in the group.

The concept of community was central to CLG. I accepted that community was just people living together and sharing the same ideals. It was a "doing" thing, I assumed. For Father Golder it was a "being and then a doing" thing. It wasn't enough to be bodies brushing past each other as we whisked about our everyday duties; bodies that occupied the same living space, ate the same food, prayed the same prayers, followed the same rule. It had to be something that happened inside us and between us. In order to establish this, Father Golder set up his CLG team of ten nuns and one brother for an encounter group with two Jesuit psychologists.

The technique of sitting in a circle for five days confronting each other was aimed at removing layers of protective barriers hoisted over years. It was slow going. The barricades were strong; bruises were buried and memorials laid. Several skins of resistance stretched, mask-like, over faces and as the days wore on mercilessly, the layers peeled off one by one, revealing the person underneath. The metamorphosis was like watching a birth. One sister refused to participate. She sat outside the group in stone.

Riveted, I watched the transformations, often anticipating who would "come through" or reveal herself next. I didn't have that much to break through (or so I thought) as I hadn't the backlog of years of religious life to produce that hard layer of skin. This protective sheaf is not limited to religious life. Wherever people form a community (and marriage is certainly one) there is the likelihood of conflicts unresolved, pain suppressed, wounds festered, intimacy avoided. Even telling others how much we love and respect them can be as difficult as expressing our dislike at what they do or don't do.

I leapt into the interaction, thriving on it like air to an asthma patient. As yet I had few defences to drop. I was open and absorbing, moving further and further with the intensity until I reached a point of fragility. Like a penis head pushes against the vagina, pressurising the thin membrane to give, to give in, to divulge its secret, so was something lurking under my surface threatening me. What was I hiding?

Because of the warmth of the group, the level of intimacy, the necessity to contribute, the ceaseless interaction, I was worn away to a point that scared me. Intuitively I shrank back, afraid that if the shell cracked there would be no nut in the centre. On the surface I seemed concerned about my lost virginity and being unable to be a sister because of this, but that was only a smoke-screen for the sexual secret my subconscious was guarding, like a hand holding a head underwater not allowing it to breathe. Do I shake off that hand, rear my head and face my assailant? No. In the process of finding myself and that self still flimsy, I chose to protect myself from confronting the lurking darkness.

I could not have integrated the knowledge that I had been sexually abused as a child.

This was the monster moaning in the depths, the penis pushing its entry. Had I allowed myself to go deeper into the feelings and explored them I might well have found this secret. But it would have shattered me. I had nothing to hold it with, nowhere to place it. I would have disappeared into the nothingness that lay beyond; into the awful emptiness.

The hiding of the truth was a protection. Memories of my experiences had sunk so far into my subconscious that they'd swim around for the next twenty years until I was ready to receive the knowledge, integrate it, and begin to heal. My intuitive refusal to confront this prematurely was a safeguard. I trusted my instincts. Did I take a risk and grow or jump in too soon and damage myself? I held back, held on and was glad when the interaction was over. We had grown close; we loved and appreciated each other.

It was as this team of individuals that we met hundreds of teenagers and young adults over the next four months. Fr Golder developed a weekend workshop called a Koinonumen which was similar to an encounter group without the encounter! Using a religious theme as a backdrop, groups would share how they felt about the subject and about themselves. This would bind the group and defuse conflict. We learnt how to facilitate the groups. It was Rogerian group-therapy. People formed close bonds and felt understood. For teenagers this was a miracle. Their enthusiasm was then channelled into action in the schools and community through CLG.

By the end of the four months I had learned that I could be comfortable with both black and white students in this setting. I could establish a trusting environment for individuals and groups. I had insights and valuable contributions to make to the programme. I preferred this kind of work to teaching. I wasn't lonely when I could be open with others and I learned I could love a man who was shorter than me!

We all loved Father Golder. How could we not love a man who listened to every word as if it were our last? Who was so patient it was annoying? Who challenged us to be all we could be, so we were that? Who had a vision of a community we all wanted to live? Fr Golder kept his guard up though. Throughout the encounter group he refused to be baited. He held out; he didn't reveal himself. I thought he might find it necessary to do so as he was "our leader". In my eyes he could do no wrong.

Out of this womb of women and warmth, of fun, music and laugher I burst, alive with a new energy, eager to be let loose, a filly primed for the race, whinnying in the stall, skittish at the gate, held short by the jockey. When would I hear "And they're off?" Before me loomed the Novitiate in Aliwal North, two years of separation from the flow in which I had just begun to flourish. A far cry from the open track for which I pranced and snorted.

It was easy to be open and take risks when a leader was there to make it happen. It was easy to experience conflict when you knew there was a safe and sure way of releasing it to everyone's benefit. It was easy to be my own person when everyone around me was telling me how wonderful I was and encouraging me. It was easy to be loving towards the team when I liked everyone anyhow. None of this was "forever".

I knew it was only for four months. It was a breathing space, a pat on the back for my efforts, a bit of cement in the cracks. A little love goes a long way.

In the two years ahead I'd be confronted with a blurring of boundaries as I'd struggle to maintain my identity and fail. Challenged to confront, I'd shy away, unable to hold my ground. I'd become a child again — dependent, relinquishing power, desperate for approval. The price I'd pay for peace would be exorbitant.

my life

steps to heal the heart

The past in hiding

A past that is not ready to reveal itself stays in hiding. It emerges only when we have enough strength to face the news and integrate its effect into our lives. Often bits of it flicker across our minds, like a glance of a person in a train going the other way. Sometimes a memory arrives unannounced and you don't know where to put it — rather like an uninvited guest when you have no spare room. Never push the past onto someone who is not ready for it. When it chooses to arrive in your life, treat it with great care and realise this is your opportunity to heal yourself. It hasn't come too late or too early; it is right on schedule.

Communication in the family or with the persons most close to you

Often in living with others we might live in the same house or apartment but we live separately. Over time we drift further apart. One can be lonely even as a wife, a husband or a committed partner. How can you protect the inner life of the people you love and live with? How can you ensure real communion?

Someone who believes in you

Who in your life saw you as you really are? Who encouraged and supported you? Write the story of your relationship. How you were when you first met; how the person influenced you and how you are now. Did that person ever know how important s/he was to you?

Perhaps you wittingly or unwittingly encouraged someone to be their beautiful self. Write about the person and what happened. What is it about you that made this possible?

Perhaps there wasn't a person who stood by you. Perhaps the young person who needed that encouragement is still waiting for it. Write to your inner teenager or inner young adult or inner child. Tell her or him how wonderful s/he is. Say all the words you needed to hear at that stage. Then write your own reply to yourself. Let it just happen.

Family

Write about your family — the one you are part of now. What aspect of it do you especially appreciate and value? If there was one aspect you could change, what would that be? What is it about each member of your family that endears them to you? What is your wish for each of them? If it is difficult for you in your family now, what would make it easier for you? What would you need to say to each person?

Chapter 5 *Special and Separate*

What is the objective of the novitiate? It is a time set aside to ground the sister in her personal relationship with God, and give her an in-depth understanding of the three vows upon which her life is based. It's a honeymoon period where two lovers, committed to one another, gaze deeply into each other's eyes. They spend quality time together to form an impenetrable bond which will withstand the inevitable rigours of the future.

The emphasis was on our being separated from "ordinary people" and even from most of the sisters. We were to be exposed only to the best of the bunch in case we got the wrong idea of religious life. Like budding exotic plants, we were to be hot-housed, kept at room temperature, not allowed out and about, watched solicitously so that we would grow straight and healthy. Set apart, we would not be distracted from the inner life we had to cultivate. Contact with the children I had taught was prohibited. They were bewildered. "You may not speak to Sister Michelle," they were told, "she's in the novitiate now and can't be distracted. It was hard for me, unnatural.

Many of the sisters who lived and worked in Aliwal North were from the "old school". They wanted religious life to stay the same. No change, no new clothing attire, no new work, no new! A novitiate in this atmosphere was going to be a challenge, especially for the novice-mistress. For this exalted and powerful position of caretaker-guide a Sister was chosen who was regarded as an exemplary model of the religious life; one whose depth of spirituality and insight would be an inspiration to the budding nuns placed in her hands.

Would she be a German sister, South African, Swiss or Irish? She was chosen by the Council of Sisters elected to lead the congregation together with the Mother Provincial and her assistant. Their decision would have political overtones and implications. The congregation was top heavy, in that most of the Sisters fell into the fifty-plus age bracket. They tended to want to retain the status quo. Few women were entering the convent in 1971 and, if they did, they could look forward to change only if the younger sisters and some of the forty- to fifty-year-olds pushed constantly for it. The allocation of votes limited the power of the pushers. The system wasn't easy to sabotage.

Sister Stephanie was Irish. She'd worked with the formation of sisters before, had been through a personal renewal course, was experienced as a teacher and had taught in coloured areas. (In South Africa people were divided according to colour. You were black, Indian, coloured or white). We assumed she had all the qualifications, seen and unseen. Sister Stephanie had "modern" ideas. She didn't think Aliwal North was a suitable place for a formative programme. Where was the interaction with novices from other orders? Scintillating teachers to draw on for information and inspiration? Who would she confer with? In the words of Willy Loman in *Death of a Salesman,* she was not "well liked". Perhaps it was her demeanour, perhaps it was that the other sisters resented her "not-good-enough" attitude. "It was good enough for us, why isn't it good enough for you?"

She found she was alone and responsible for two budding beauties — Liesl and myself. Liesl, from a small town in Germany, was new to South Africa, a nurse, twenty-nine. She was there for me. I took her so much for granted that I tended to overlook her, if anything. She could be relied upon totally. She never pushed herself forward as I was inclined to do in my constant need for attention. We never fought or quarrelled.

Leisl was guileless. She said what she thought, chose her words carefully, sometimes struggling with a foreign language. She was the epitome of someone happy in service to others. If she was hurt or in pain she'd keep it inside. I could see it on her face and would pry it out of her. She'd grown up in a basic, strong, supportive large family and this grounding saw her through. She appeared quite fragile in her thinness, but she was physically very strong. Her spirit was a straight arrow, totally committed to the life of a nun. She loved God and that always came first. She indeed was a sister to me.

The word "special" set us apart even more. When I first thought of becoming a nun, I bought a book entitled *Chosen by God*. Sisters felt they were specially chosen by God for this unique relationship and I think it is a choice. They chose to respond to God's invitation in this way. But choice doesn't mean "better than". It was inferred that nuns were better than lay people because we had this core relationship as a bride of Christ. The laity may have been sisters or brothers of Christ, but they were not brides. What the priests were, I don't know.

The idea of being special is particularly dangerous, especially for anyone who comes from a dysfunctional family. It wasn't helpful for me. As a child performer I liked the notion of being special — apart from everyone else. As my mother's favourite I was special. As a singer up there on a stage I was different and, of course, special. Now as a nun I was extra special. An insidious "better than" attitude was ingraining itself into my psyche. I latched onto this idea and attitude because, at rock bottom, I felt unworthy, not good enough. Cover this up with a "special" label and you have a person with a whip in her one hand ceaselessly beating herself for not being good enough, and a sceptre in the other as she graciously rewards her subjects. "You're nobody till somebody loves you", goes the song. They forget to mention that the "somebody" who needs to love you is yourself. As yet, I could not love myself. I needed approval from others. I felt I had to entertain to win attention and I'd vie with others to get more than my share, for my share could never be enough. Any compliments I'd receive, I'd brush aside unbelievingly. I was a shadow looking for substance outside of myself. Who could give me myself?

In my need (now that there was nothing to divert me) to be loved and accepted, to be mothered and nurtured, to experience the harmony of a love tryst, of intimacy, I gave myself, my power, my will to Sister Stephanie. I quickly sized up the situation. There were only the three of us in the novitiate. It was going to be a long two years. There was much about Sister Stephanie I respected and liked. She was intelligent, sensitive, future-oriented in terms of religious life, well-read and she enjoyed the company of men — though she only allowed this to leak out occasionally. On the other hand, she was punctilious, somewhat of a prude and inconsistent in her behaviour towards us — open and warm at one encounter, closed and cold at another. It was as if she didn't quite know how to be a "good" novice mistress, as if she didn't trust herself.

I sensed her acute loneliness. Because of it, I wanted to be there for her. Add to this the nature of the novitiate where the novice believes that the novice mistress is God-incarnate, a guru one has to listen to, the person who holds one's life in her hands. One word from Stephanie and we were out. This sword over my head I had either to fight or surrender to. I didn't realise I could do both. So terrified was I of confrontation and conflict, so eager for peace at any price that I became what I thought she wanted me to be. I said what I thought she wanted to hear. I gave up the little I knew of myself to become a reflection of her. If she was happy, I was happy. If she was upset with me, I was dead. My moods hinged on hers. And I had no idea I was doing this to myself. It just happened over time, imperceptibly, like the gentle ticking of a clock that nobody notices. The line at which I stopped and she began was gone.

Now that I was in a situation that I perceived as threatening I gave up. Without a fight. Because of the abuse I had experienced as a small child where my boundaries had been invaded, I was unable to defend myself. I let my borders blur but only when I was "the child". When Stephanie was sad or down, I became "the mother" and I'd listen to her and be there for her. Then I'd switch back to "the child" and be helpless and a victim again. It was a familiar feeling. Perhaps I'd been called upon as a child to mother my mother, to be her confidante and assume a role I wasn't ready for. But I was a child then and I needed her to be a mother. I was repeating a pattern. I was co-dependent for sure. Stephanie had no way of knowing that subconsciously I was betraying myself — being there for her instead of being myself.

"A deep loneliness wells up inside me. On the outside it all seems perfect. I have a bed, clothes, a regime, a routine, am surrounded by people who hold the same ideals and yet, and yet ... why am I so alone? Why do I feel so empty? When I am alone, sitting in the orchard, walking, I get in touch with a presence deep inside of me, a presence I can spend time with. In a retreat and in the hard times of silence when I feel like screaming, I pass a point where the peace pushes away the scream and there is this stillness of being, of being filled. I run to this place."

What I did now was to replace that still spot in my heart with a person. I put Stephanie in the secret garden of my heart. The trouble with that was she couldn't stay constant. She had her own problems. Also, she was a person, not the almighty presence I was used to tapping into. I chose to sacrifice myself, my personality, to give it away, because on the human level I was so lonely. I wanted to plunge all of myself into her so that I no longer had to take any responsibility for my life. I shrank myself to fit who I thought she was. If I wanted to be myself, I'd have to fight for that. And loneliness was stronger than courage at that stage.

I could only love someone when I was a person myself. Here I was denouncing myself, renouncing myself as a trade-off for acceptance. But the person Stephanie was accepting wasn't me, so how could that do me any good? Better to wait until I met someone who could accept the real Michelle and then open up. Better still to begin to accept myself and then I would only be giving from a secure place, in tune with the inner self, the all-powerful presence within. There is no substitute for the unique feeling of being in touch with your own self.

So, on the one hand I had slipped into a co-dependency relationship and on the other I was in a very safe place for at least a year in that I had plenty of time to just be. We'd study in the mornings, do a spot of cleaning, take long walks in the afternoons, live life at a leisurely pace. I had space.

The year followed a cycle of religious events from Easter to Christmas. In between this there were personal feast days where Liesl and I would create a mini-concert to entertain the sisters. It seems we had the time. When we needed a gift for a feast day or celebration, we'd make it — a card, a drawing, something small but personal. We had no money to buy a gift and this form of giving I found enjoyable. Sometimes we had "recreation" with the community. Here we'd play games and generally fool around. I found this ridiculous at first. Perhaps because I'd never been part of a family where games were played. My father played cards with his friends. The only game I remembered was "spin the bottle" at the age of twelve or thirteen. The thought of grown women giggling like kids, playing charades or some other evilly concocted torture sent me scuttling to chapel or to my room. In spite of my cynical attitude, I had to admit that sometimes I actually enjoyed being silly. "Fun" did not have to involve men, it seemed.

It also gave me an opportunity to let off steam. But not enough.

My body chose to let off inner steam and frustration it was accumulating by repeated migraine attacks. As a ten-year-old waiting to run in a race, the first migraine attacked. My eyesight blurred, my hands numbed, my lips got thick and puffy and I was left with a searing pain inside my head. Terrified, I grew to fear an attack. What brought them on? I kept a couple of strong pills with me to knock me out at the first sign.

One of Stephanie's better ideas was to move the novitiate to an area called the East Rand for a short period. In a town called Boksburg we were under the guidance of two Dominican priests. In this environment I began to write haiku poetry.

An idea that was basically sound but poorly implemented was to send the novices to a mission station to integrate the theory with practice. We were both sent back to Taung but this time to the hospital. Liesl was a nurse so that made sense. But what did I know about injections, bedpans and treating burns? I was not to contact my old friends on the school-side at St Paul's, nor was I permitted to learn Setswana. No, rule 135b states that "in the novitiate, the novice does not study secular subjects". Black is black and white is white. An *i* is dotted, a *t* is crossed. Flick water off hands, dry thoroughly on paper towel ripped perfectly at perforated line, discard same in bin, straighten veil, flush toilet, check to see all excrement has vanished and no tell-tale spots remain in bowl or on rim, sniff, grab hold of door handle with vigour, emerge resolutely. If one was to be human, let's get it over with as quickly and as efficiently as possible! Heil Hitler!

The only way out of the situation was to contract a tropical disease. There were plenty to choose from. A lay missionary who escaped from the Congo stopped at Taung and passed on to me what she had escaped with — hepatitis! Gotcha! That meant weeks alone in a darkened room suffused in a yellow glow. Not very pretty, but useful. Now can I get on with my life?

The novitiate was drawing to a close. Where would Liesl and I be sent and what would we do? I was adamant that after my CLG experience I no longer wanted to teach. Sister Liesl was sent back to Taung to the hospital. Sister Michelle was to go to Maitland in Cape Town to teach white children.

I was stunned, disappointed and angry. But far worse than this, I had lost my centre. I left the novitiate, after taking the first set of vows for two years. I sat on the train for Cape Town unaware that I had separated myself from myself. I still did not know how much I had identified with Stephanie and how critically this would affect me in Maitland.

"MISSING. MICHELLE. LAST SEEN TWO YEARS AGO. COME HOME DARLING. WE LOVE YOU." The year ahead would be one of continual crisis as I struggled to find myself again.

my life

steps to heal the heart

Women who become nuns

What is your opinion of women who become nuns? Do you think it's unnatural? When I entered the convent many people thought I was running away. In a way I was; running to find peace and stability. What has your experience of nuns been? Were you at a convent school? Was that a positive or negative experience for you? Describe it. Sometimes all it takes is one person to make a difference in your life especially at school. If there is any unfinished business between yourself and a nun or a brother or a priest, write to that person now and express what has, as yet, not been said.

Co-dependence

A co-dependent relationship is where you want to please the other person so much you lose yourself. The other person's feelings, thoughts, actions become more important than your own. You act from outside yourself and make yourself into that which you think the other person wants you to be. So you lose yourself. In a way it's a kind of addiction. You are addicted to someone else's approval. Have you experienced this in any way? Can you describe what this was (or is) like for you? What advice would you give someone who is in a co-dependent relationship? (See Part 3 Chapter 4 also)

Loneliness

What's your relationship with loneliness? When you feel lonely what do you do? Do you run from it or do you befriend it? Can you sit with yourself and feel it fully? Often it is your inner child who is sad. Write to your inner child, console her. Tell her what you know she needs to hear. Be kind to yourself.

Chapter 6 *Hurting and Healing*

Set in a poor area, Maitland convent's grey walls reminded me of East Ham in London. Maitland was said to be a dynamic community of twenty five sisters. I'd be able to take part in all the activities offered in the Cape. Sister Stephanie thought she was choosing the best place for me. But Michelle wasn't there. The eyes that looked out at it all were empty. It was as if I saw everything from behind an impenetrable screen of opaqueness. The school principal seemed very friendly and confident of my ability. If only she knew.

"You'll teach commerce and biology, Sister Michelle," she told me blithely. "I'll help you; it's really very easy."

"But I can't," I protested, "I haven't a clue about them."

"You have time," Sister Thomas insisted, "you only need be one chapter ahead."

What would I do? I didn't want to teach anyway and I didn't want to learn commerce and biology. I was a reluctant dog on a leash, pulling back, sitting stubbornly, refusing to budge. Teaching became a nightmare. Had I been myself I'd have struck up immediate rapport with the teenage girls, been available to them, listened to them, got involved with improving the quality of their classroom time, made friends, contributed. Had I been myself, I'd have refused to teach what I wasn't trained for. But I wasn't there. I stood in front of the class feeling like a refrigerator with no food in it. I made the motions of teaching, never sure if what I was telling them was accurate. The drawings of plants and animals were not so bad. I'd put them on the board for the girls to copy. But the details of the species, their habits or anything vaguely resembling facts swam in a faraway sea, the waves of which never tickled my toes. I refused to knuckle down and study. Instead I'd spend hours creating biology games for the students to play. I didn't want to teach and I wouldn't do it. After all, I was a Taurus.

I was trapped in a gigantic spider web. Whichever way I moved, I was cloyed in strands of stickiness pricking my skin. I'd talk endlessly to Sister Ignatia who slept in the same building as I. Iggy was Irish, a bit of a psychic, a little fey. It did no good. I'd go over and over how miserable I was like an endless vomit. I'd write long letters to Stephanie late at night, pouring out my misery. She'd write back and I'd feel no better. I'd speak to the Superior, Sister Mary, but the next morning I'd be in the classroom again. Like Marcel Marceau in his glass cell, I could only palm the clear sheets, feeling their cold surface, seeing the faces and figures on the other side. I was a silent scream sealed.

Who could put the pieces back in place, I wondered, as I continued to muddle through the days, half-there, half-nowhere. Maitland had its problems too. It was a time of transition for the Holy Cross. We were reassessing our effectiveness and Maitland was on the hit list as being past its prime. The majority of sisters dug in their heels snorting: "We will not be moved." There were many apparently valid reasons for staying, but some of the unspoken ones were the spiritual and psychological iron bars of a mental maximum security prison gradually erected over the years.

As religious people we renounced ownership of anything, except what we wrote or created. Poverty called for an openness of spirit, a constant letting go the inclination to have, to hold onto. That included people and things, places where we worked, or whatever came into our lives that we might become attached to. The vows, taken once in a ceremony, required a daily commitment. After all, we're only human. Imperceptibly things and places inch their way into our hearts, creeping in when we're not looking.

Then suddenly we hear ourselves insisting that "This is the only classroom I want to teach in!" or "This is the only kind of clothing I'll consider wearing" or "This place must be kept up! I cannot live without this place!" Our anchor, our security has shifted. It was God, once; now it's my work, my space, my place, even my opinion. The community fought for Maitland to remain open. I ran from the fray; there was enough war within myself. I wasn't keen on Maitland surviving, but I wasn't there anyway so why get involved?

I couldn't continue to live on the brink of myself. At bursting point, I phoned Bishop Stephen Naidoo. I'd attended many of his talks and respected him. In answer to that frantic phone call, I met him at his mother's home one Sunday afternoon and it all came pouring out. Stephen took it all in astutely and quickly. He was a gifted counsellor and spiritual director.

"You have to get out of Maitland. Maybe you need someone to take care of you?"

"Like who?"

"Like a man."

What was he suggesting? That I shouldn't be in the convent? A man? I can't take care of myself?

"No, I don't want that," I assured him, having no idea what I did want. I just wanted to get myself back again.

He said he'd call our Mother Provincial.

"You need to be in Johannesburg. I can see you there."

With a sense of relief I returned to the convent and waited. Sure enough, within a few weeks, word came through. "Sister Michelle is to be transferred to the Mondeor community in Johannesburg. She'll be teaching in Soweto. Sister Stephanie is part of that staff now. Maybe it'll be good for Michelle." I felt almost guilty leaving Maitland, like the elephant held by a slim string, conditioned to confinement. On some level I blamed myself for not being happy and successful. I should have pulled myself together and got on with it, whatever that meant. How to do it was the hurdle. Now, with the string sliced, I could move away, and I did so, gingerly, unaccustomed to freedom.

Being with Sister Stephanie again seemed okay to me, until I got to Mondeor. A sleepy suburb, tucked behind purple hills, it hid its ten Holy Cross sisters in a house like all others around it. Luckily ours was the last on the block. Leaning over us rose a hill, alongside us ran a small river and trees surrounded the double-storied house. We were almost in the country. I still had not understood why I had such a horrible year until I began to live with Stephainie again. Now I was just another sister, not a novice, not under her.

Once a week I'd visit Stephen Naidoo for a counselling session. Before I began I was sent to a psychiatrist, Dr Bernard Levinson. I told him I felt like a golf ball, poised on the edge of the hole, not yet where I should be. A poet, he understood. Stephen Naidoo explained how infinitely complex a human being is, like a Swiss watch. If one small part of the watch is not functioning, we have one stopped watch. The human being requires sensitive hands to heal the "broken" parts so the person can be whole again. Stephen wore kid-gloves and week by week the shadow of Michelle inched back to her feet. It was the first time I had been counselled. I was relieved that I could just talk to someone and not have anything at stake. As this retrieval took place, as I moved back to base inside myself, I moved farther away from Stephanie.

Anger burned within me, anger at her, anger at myself. I felt alive with an electricity that might leap out like lightning and strike. I avoided conversation with her, sat far away from her at meals and bottled up when I was beside her. Underneath the unexpressed anger was the fear that I might lose myself again if I got close to her. Half of me wanted that closeness but not at the price I had paid. "Go away," I wanted to say, "you frighten me. You tell me so much about yourself and I listen and then you expect me to tell you all my secrets and I do, in spite of myself I do and then I am caught. You have all of me and I have nothing. Please go away. I want to be my own person. I want to be with you like anyone else. I can go so far and no further. I can't be there for you only. I have to be here for myself. I can't continue to betray myself, to abandon myself. Find somebody else to be close to. Leave me alone." Regaining my power I was not prepared to give it away.

Stephanie was bewildered. What had happened to me? Did she consult with Father Naidoo about me? Did he explain to her? I never confronted her directly about it. I was too terrified. The community was alert to this energy between us. It couldn't have made her position there any easier. One of us had to move away so we could both lead normal lives. Father Naidoo knew how much I wanted to continue with CLG work. A few words from him and I was transferred to the CLG community.

"Koinonia", the name of the CLG centre, was located in Judith's Paarl — not a distinguished neighbourhood by any stretch of the imagination. An old house, long a Dominican retreat centre, it held rooms now turned into bedrooms for the groups. A new wing allowed for more single bedrooms with a spacious hall for conferences and get-togethers. The house, surrounded by gardens, extended on the other side to an office and living quarters for Fr Golder; a cosy, carpeted chapel, and additional meeting rooms. Koinonia meandered in an informal low-key way.

My being with Father Golder again and an experimental community of Sisters from various orders, plus other young adults, proved to be the antithesis of my Maitland experience. I was doing work that I loved and was living in an environment where we really spoke to one another. Under Father Golder's guidance we'd meet regularly and he introduced techniques which made it possible for us to speak our hearts and confront one another. We'd meet each other in pairs and tell each other what we liked, found easy to live with or respected about the other. We'd also share the problem areas. Perhaps there were misunderstandings or hurts we had not spoken about but had kept buried. This time together gave us an opportunity to release those and to search for solutions.

Acceptance was always the bottom line. Our goal was self-acceptance and acceptance of the other as s/he was. Not as how we wanted her to be; or how, by giving her feedback, we hoped she'd change. I was impatient with myself, impatient with others. I wanted people to be like me. That made it easier for me to like them. I didn't yet know all the tunnels and trails within myself. I did my best with the picture of myself as I saw it then. Only once I had learnt to have compassion for myself could I show compassion for others. Compassion comes through self-knowledge and that has a pace of its own. I was receiving parcels of myself, fragments of who I was, bit by bit, portion by portion. Again and again I was learning, in cycles, round and round, deeper and deeper. There is no rush, no quickie, no "one book does all, one teacher, one workshop, one experience". It is all of them put together over years, over lifetimes.

Father Golder's calm and consistent presence made our attempts at community possible and successful. But who said he was perfect? I used to wonder how he kept so distanced from it all, so detached, so all-knowing. It seemed impossible to prick his surface of serenity. Once I saw it shatter. Jennifer's brother was seriously ill. She had to rush out and fetch him. I caught the look on his face. It was alive with concern. The mask had dropped. Alongside the concern was something else, himself. "What's going on?" I thought, "Where have I seen this expression before? Yes! Of course! I've seen it on the face of a person who loves someone else, not in a brotherly way, but as a man!" Soon after I left Koinonia Father Golder left the Jesuits and married Jennifer. He was fully alive!

I was also regaining some aliveness. For close on a year in Koinonia I helped organise and run multiracial conferences, introduced and edited a CLG newsletter, designed and created new and exciting themes for Koinonumens and continued to learn counselling, community-building techniques and spiritual direction. But best of all, I danced again! Flashback:

It is the farewell dance for the graduating class at Maitland. The girls look gorgeous, their partners prickle with excitement, the band blasts into action and I sit. I sit in my habit, my black-shoed feet tap the floor in perfect rhythm, perfect. My body bounces off the edge of the chair as my shoulders march, left, right, left, right, to the beat of the drums. My fingers click to accompany my swaying shoulders. I am alive, of that there is no doubt. Scanning the male faces about me, I search for someone I could approach who is partnerless and equally revved up. Breathlessly I wait to hear the magic words: "Would you like to dance?" I wait. Is there anybody out there? Yoo-hoo?

I watch and wait until the penny drops. My fingers fall silent into my lap; my shoulders slump as though a weight has just been dropped on them; my fretting feet find a place on the floor and hold it as my body returns to normal, inert. "You are now a nun, Michelle, and N-U-Ns don't dance. Well, at least not in public and certainly not with members of the opposite sex!" Disappointment digs into my palms as I close my hands in on themselves, cross my legs in resignation and leave as soon as I can, walking away from the call of the music.

But now at Koinonia, at conferences and parties and sometimes just for the heaven of it, we danced! All of us! We weren't "nuns", we were people. At last! And we danced with "them". Yes! Males. (May the protection of all the saints ...) And no-one fell pregnant. We came away happy, healthy and unscathed. We might have lost our veils in the process, but that's a small price to pay. It's better than losing our you-know-what that also starts with a V and gives us all one helluva lot of trouble.

I may add, while I'm on this roll, that there were times, oh beloved ones, when the huge, carpeted, multi-faceted hall was empty and into this temple of delight I would dive with my bare feet (I cannot but weep) and bare head (oh vile she-devil) and placing a tape (how cam'st thou by that wicked piece of futility?) in a tape recorder (such torments do now assail me), I would swirl and prance and pirouette and prostrate myself in a multitude of poses and movements that your heart would burst with joy to behold! (Now splits my soul from my body, and all heaven dost my passing mourn!) So be it. I prefer to dance.

I had two very close friends: Sister Patricia (Trish) from Germany, and Brother Christopher from South West Africa. Trish was like a sister to me, and Christopher, an OMI brother, took me a step further into the black-white world we lived in. He called me Ish and I called him Tophs. He once told me how he had come to discover he had a mission. As a small Ovambo boy in the bush of South West Africa, he herded the cattle for his father. One evening, around sunset, the barking of dogs alerted Tophs to the presence of danger in the kraal. Sure enough, a lion bounded out of the bush straight for him. He fled into his hut, the dogs hot on his heels. Throwing himself into the corner against the wall on his knees, he covered his head under his arms. The dogs leapt on top of him. The lion grabbed the dogs and left Tophs alive.

We'd drive together into Soweto — the Johannesburg black ghetto — for functions at the OMI church in Moroko but we had to be very circumspect. I was white. Tophs was black. This alone would draw attention to us. The Immorality Act forbade sex across the colour line. Mixed couples travelling together were immediately targets for police surveillance and questioning. Often the couples would swap: the white couple would sit together and the black couple likewise, till they got to their destination.

The fact that I was a nun in a habit and Tophs in a priest's collar helped defuse the suspicion slightly, but on another level, a black priest or religious man may have been viewed with contempt by white policemen suspicious of the possibility that any black man (or Kaffir or Bantu) "had it in him" to become an ordained minister. "Who does he think he is? A white man?" At the same time Tophs might have met with disapproval from some of his people for "going over the other side" separating himself twice — once as a celibate unable to have children (a concept foreign to his culture), and twice as crossing the border into a white world. "Going as white." As a sister I was probably viewed with less hostility by the Sowetans than had I been a white woman, only. On the other hand, many black people were outraged at the missionary zeal and what religion had contributed to "keeping the black man in his place" so the habit would not have saved me.

Tophs stayed at Koinonia for a brief period. After he left, we wrote often. Our relationship was healing for us both. He was as black as deep chocolate, with a smile as brilliant as a comet. High cheekbones and clearly mischievous eyes, he was impossible to overlook. Yes, we were attracted to each other physically, but the possibility of a life together didn't exist. Each of us was committed to a celibate religious life in our own countries. We touched and held each other, but gently, knowing that we were playing with a fire that could burn for only a few months, if that. Tophs later left the brotherhood, married and disappeared from my life. His imprint remains. He had an earthiness, a way of being with me that was uncomplicated and nourishing.

I knew my stay at Koinonia was temporary. I had entered the Holy Cross, a teaching and nursing order. That's where my permanent place had to be. In order to see if I could lead the regular life of a sister-in-vows it was necessary for me to return to a Holy Cross convent. One of my reasons for entering had been to be closely involved with the black community and there was no better opportunity than Soweto where our sisters had a school. Mother Provincial asked me to return to Mondeor and take up a teaching position at Immaculata High in Diepkloof, one of the areas within Soweto — South Western Townships. I had to take with me what I had learned from Koinonia.

In Koinonia I had learned to live the religious life of the future. Not only the religious life, but perhaps life for any people living together. It was based on openness and honesty and not trying to hide who we were. The basis of our lives was vulnerability and trust. We trusted that as we revealed who we were, we would be respected, accepted for that and never betrayed. In this climate of listening, I began to accept my strength and I could see how I contributed to the success of both the community and the groups.

Our life wasn't tightly structured. There was a flow to it, an unexpectedness, a creativity. Could I gather this together and take it with me, like a traveller with a knapsack, into Mondeor, back into a world where people passed one another without looking inside; where the doors to closeness and intimacy rarely opened? Had I enough faith and dedication to live without that openness, to trust and accept without revelation? Could I return to a nine-to-five routine, teaching a class within the confines of a community of ten sisters? This was bread and butter; I had been living on a diet more like sole, champagne and strawberries.

I had come a long way in terms of intimacy. Trish and I were close confidantes, but we were equals. We gained by our friendship; we gave away nothing of our individual power. Quite the opposite, we reinforced each other. I'd miss her, but she wouldn't be far away. I'd made other friends, students from the groups, part-time CLG workers. There was always the tendency to move beyond a boundary with some people and I'd recognise this and move back. My needs were largely met.

My stay at Koinonia had been a time of healing for me. There can be waves of growth, waves of healing, waves of integration. In the novitiate I had gone too far out of myself. In Maitland I was a fish out of water, floundering as a result of my relationship with Stephanie and my conviction that I no longer wanted to teach. Stephen Naidoo, John Golder and the community at Koinonia had eased me back to a place of comfort and integration. Now I would return to the so-called "real" world.

In terms of my spiritual development, Koinonia had introduced me to an expression of Catholicism that included intimacy, music and spontaneity. We'd sit in a circle for the Mass and remain seated, allowing ourselves to become absorbed more easily. We'd be able to participate more by sharing our thoughts on the reading for the day, or spontaneous praying at a time for opening our hearts to God in the presence of others. We'd choose hymns that reflected how we felt, hymns that more realistically expressed ourselves in contact with God. We had more power.

Our living together reinforced our understanding that the closer we drew to one another, the more we could give of who we really were and therefore the more we could see and feel God in ourselves and in the other. God is not some isolated being sitting away from us, like a potentate. So often in a church the experience is all focused forward towards an altar. The routine is repeated each time and the Mass can become another dead ritual. You come in, say the prayers, stand, sit, kneel, go through the motions, have communion and leave without saying anything to anybody. Was this an experience of God? It's like having sex without loving your partner. You just do it. There are, of course, times when the need for worship and thanksgiving pours out of one's heart and is directed through the priest to God. Yes, but our relationship to God is nourished by our relationship to one another and vice-versa. The novitiate certainly gave me that one-on-one certainty. Koinonia expanded this to include people.

So here I was in my late twenties, wiser, still convinced that this was the life for me and heading towards another adventure. I agreed to return to Mondeor as a teacher. Little did I know that in June of 1976 I would be caught up in one of the most violent outbursts for freedom South Africa had yet known — the Soweto Uprising.

my life

steps to heal the heart

Talking it out

I held a lot inside me in Maitland; I didn't know who to talk to. Have you thought of talking to a trained listener who knows about people? Like a counsellor? Talking to a friend helps of course, but talking to someone you don't know is sometimes easier. If you prefer to write it down that's also effective. Often in the writing or the talking the truth of the situation comes out and you see what it is you need to do, or you gain insight.

Relationships on the rocks

You had a break-up or a misunderstanding with a friend. What happened? Can you talk to this person now and say what you never could? If not, why not act out the situation and take both her/his role and yours. You might discover something unexpected.

Compassion

"Only once we learn to have compassion for ourselves can we show compassion for others." Do you like yourself? When you look in a mirror, is there acceptance in your eyes? A tenderness perhaps? Or are there voices in your head that condemn or judge you? Do you find it possible to forgive yourself? Is it easy or difficult for you? Do something loving for yourself today. How does that feel?

Catholic Sisters and Brothers misbehaving

Did my relationship with Brother Christopher (Tophs) shock you? What do you think happens when people promise to be celibate and then break their promise? Has that ever happened to you where you promised to be faithful to one person and then you landed up having sex with someone else? Write a True Confession.

An either-or relationship

Do you think that a relationship must be either a love relationship or nothing; a friend but never a lover? I wonder how many of us put the sex we are attracted to into a box and we limit the extent of our relationship. If you are a straight woman do you have close straight male friends, people you do not have sex with? If you are a gay woman do you have a close female straight friend? If you are a gay man do you have a close straight male friend? If you are a straight man do you have a close gay friend? Describe one of these relationships in your life.

Sex and religious ritual

If you belong to a religious group what kind of worship do you find most comforting? Do you prefer formal or informal worship? Do you agree that going through the motions of a ritual is "like having sex without loving your partner"? In which other ways is worship like making love?

Chapter 7 *Revolution and Resolution*

As the first slats of light seared the sleeping sky, we'd back out of our cosy Mondeor convent till amber slithers of sun cracked the black mirror of a Johannesburg morning. Welcome to Igoli, city of gold. A fifteen-minute drive took us into Soweto, South Western Townships, the sprawling ghetto that sardined well over a million inhabitants. For blacks only.

Soweto — almost a secret dirty word among whites, few of whom had ever seen it, let alone been inside. "Unarmed? Unescorted? Never!" The gargantuan subconscious of the white world, Soweto was pushed back into the darkest recesses of our brain like a brooding cancer, while we ate our steaks, dressed in silk, drove BMWs to work, drank cocktails at clubs and kept our nails clean. We attempted to flick this troublesome spot out of our consciousness, like a stray crumb on a trouser leg. But it was there, and we were driving into it.

In these earliest hours, mists of smoke hung heavy over the slumbering city; dense smog curtains rose from countless chimneys loosely attached to rows of leaning matchbox houses crouched together for comfort. Hints of light in sanded pathway streets hid behind the grey morning cloak. Like a huge quilt, the hazy morning fabric hovered. Soweto, violent, mysterious, troubled, sprawled for miles like an oil slick, coating its inhabitants with a "second-hand-not-good-enough-skin" which would not wash off easily.

Into this barest glimmer of day we'd slink between the brooding blocks passing shadows bent towards the bus ranks, park our two cars in the makeshift garage and in silence we'd set the table in the sisters' staff room for breakfast. Down the long, cement, open corridors we'd patter to the hall where Father McNaughton would say the Mass. Immediately after we'd retrace our steps, eat a hurried meal and move into the classrooms. So begins another day, and another and another.

Black education was under a separate government department: the Bantu Education Department. From school entry until the beginning of high school (Standard Six), children were taught in their mother tongue, which could be either Zulu, Southern Sotho, Northern Sotho, Setswana, Venda, Xhosa, Pedi or Tshangaan. Once in Standard Six, children were taught in English.

The young black student of 1976 was a far cry from his parents who, by and large, still carried a "yes, baas" mentality. Their attitude was: "You can't change it, so accept it." Poorly educated and often deeply religious, they believed that the "will of God" put it all into perspective. Often the student's mother was a domestic servant who'd be up at four at the latest to get to her madam's house by seven to make coffee for the master before he left for work. She'd nurse her madam's children all day while her own came home from school to an empty house. After housecleaning all day, she'd return by bus and then by train to begin again at seven with supper for her own husband and family. He would probably be a blue-collar worker, or, at best, a clerk, maybe a petrol attendant and their combined wages would be unlikely to make ends meet.

Often the oldest child would have to leave school without completing, to find work and help the rest of the family, who extended to cousins and nephews, aunts and uncles. If the oldest child was a girl, her chances of finishing high school were considerably less. The oldest boy, however, would get as much support and encouragement from his parents as their meagre earnings could muster. With much hardship and going without, they would endeavour to send him to a black university (such as they were). At least one of their children would have the opportunity of a future. He, in turn, would be responsible for supporting his parents and other siblings and relatives once he had made his fortune. The price he paid was a high one.

The family of at least six generally lived in a two-roomed house. Privacy was not an option. Few homes had electricity, although this was gradually being introduced. Television was a luxury, besides, where would you put it and who could afford it? Clothes lay neatly ironed and folded in trunks under the bed. Children studied by candlelight between the hours of midnight and 4am, accompanied by the troubled township noises. A black middle-class was emerging, but in 1976 there were few who fitted into this bracket.

The young black student was sometimes ashamed of the illiteracy of his parents and communication would break down between them. The parents appealed to the teachers to "speak to our children!" but the teachers knew how angry the students were and how inadequate the system of education was. Aspiring young teachers were often pushed into the classroom with insufficient training and education. Many just gave up and sat at the desk reading a newspaper, ignoring the students. The colleges for training black teachers were few and of mediocre quality. Why should the government care? The less educated a black person was, the better. Whites would not lose their jobs and blacks would remain "in their places".

But the students acknowledged education as "the key to success" in that a degree meant a better position, money and power. The sad part was that the type of education offered was hardly a key to anything but disillusionment. The corporate world was sophisticated on a level few black graduates had encountered. The end of one mountainous climb — a school-leaving certificate — meant the beginning of a so-called university climb, which ended in the devastation of entering a corporate world which was, by and large, a foreign country where many entrants spoke little of the business language. Checkmate.

In high school, Afrikaans was studied as one of the official languages; English was the other. The majority of the population fell into neither of these two categories but they were ignored. Then in 1976 the government wanted to enforce Afrikaans and not English as the medium of instruction. This tipped the scales. Afrikaans was equated with the oppressor — just as English had been to the early Dutch settlers as they strove to break away from the grip of the British — and the students resisted learning it anyway. In the English-speaking schools, white children objected to learning Afrikaans because they thought it "below" them, and a bastard language. However, they were not obliged to study other subjects in Afrikaans.

For a black student to have to learn Afrikaans was irritating enough, but to then insist that every other subject be instructed through the medium of Afrikaans was extraordinarily insensitive. The oppressor would then infiltrate his mind like a subtle poison insidiously seeping into his veins, drumming in his heart. This was intrusive, abusive. Acceptance would mean annihilation of any vestige of self-esteem.

June 16, 1976 began, for us, as any other day. Up early, out to Immaculata High, Mass, breakfast and into the classroom. The day passed as did most, with one exception: we heard that the daughter of Mrs Ndlovu, one of our teachers, had been shot. (Shot? Where? By whom?) Regular school ended at two and adult education classes began later, from four to six, late afternoon. Sister Michael, the principal, and Sister Aquina the Superior, had left and I was to see to the afternoon school. No big deal. There were three other Sisters with me.

But something was wrong. There was a restlessness in the air. An intangibility hovered around us, like a spider web you can't see, but which keeps tickling your face. No adults arrived for class. The school seemed suddenly deserted. Something was wrong. We were not being included in the secret. What was it?

"The children are marching!" came the whisper.

"Marching? What do you mean, marching?" we echoed, lost.

"Someone has been shot, a boy called Hector Peterson."

"Who is Hector? Who shot him?"

"The police are in the townships!"

"What for?"

"A white man has been murdered!"

"Murdered? A white man? Never!"

"Emdeni. It started in Emdeni."

"But that's on the other side of Soweto! It's miles away from here!"

Rumour by rumour, the news began to steal in.

Like a wave starting on the far side of Soweto the marching students had spread. Gathering momentum they crossed to Diepkloof. It was a peaceful march to begin with. Wave upon wave of uniformed school children carrying signs protesting against the introduction of Afrikaans and singing songs, broke on zone after zone. As the roar of their indignation filled the skies, the spray of their demands for justice splattered on the nervously watching and waiting policemen, itchy-fingered. Student rage formed a wall of water poised before barrels of guns.

"Stop, or we'll shoot!" Someone threw a stone, a pebble. That was all. That was it. Piet Smoller, or a man with a similar name, moved a finger and the furious wave, its head held high, gave a mighty heave and crashed, splintered, splayed, split, smithereened onto the dry, dust-filled streets of Soweto. Bullets bore into legs, breasts, backs, bellies and bottoms. Bodies, baked in blood, quickly carpeted the sand. Winds of wails hid behind the roar of rifles. *Amandla? Awethu?*

Meanwhile, back at the school, we waited unaware of the rushing, rampaging torrent close by. As the rumours trickled in, we stood back, hesitant. I walked to the garage. Simon Nakene, one of my students, leaned casually against one of the poles, as if it were just another day, as if he had with nothing to do and nowhere to go.

"Simon," I said quietly, almost offhand, "What do you think?"

Not moving a muscle, not even with a shrug of the shoulders, glancing at me from the corner of his eyes he matter-of-factly answered.

"Go, Sister."

I stood.

"Go!"

"Out! We're out of here!" I yelled and, grabbing keys, fled from classroom to classroom locking the doors as if that was going to protect the school or us. Now I was shake, rattle and rolling much better. The huge assortment of keys kept falling from my hands as I fumbled to find the right one, dammit! Sister Regina Maria joined me in the locking mania. Shouts from the streets, the crackling of gunfire. Move it! Move it! Forget it! Into the car! We were running, at last.

The school was deserted as I leapt into the station wagon and lurched out with the brake on into the dusking streets. Whroooom! (Our Father who art in heaven — get the beads out girls, this is prayer time!) From the school to the main road was a matter of minutes. (Please God, let us get out alive!) Turn left out the school, drive fifty yards, then left again (mind that child!) until the end of the road (duck, duck, keep your heads down just in case). Stop. Not too long, idiot. Turn right (Oh, my Jesus, forgive us our sins, save us from the fires of hell) and keep going till you get to Baragwanath Hospital.

Whatever happens, don't stop. Just keep going.

A grim silence shared our space as we held our breath along that stretch, not daring to look around us. Baragwanath, the largest black hospital in the Southern Hemisphere sat ahead of us, stolidly waiting for the hundreds and thousands of victims who would be carried into its patient arms in the next few days, week, months. Wait at the traffic light. (Change, oh please change!) Then left along the main road and out of Soweto.

"Look back. What do you see?" But the evening smog was descending on the seething cauldron; nothing was clear. Ahead of us were the roadblocks. We were waved through. Incoming cars were stopped and searched. The line backed up all the way to Uncle Charlies — a roadhouse at the turnoff to Soweto. We began to breathe again.

Safe in the convent, we sat glued to the TV watching as the accounts of the day were relived again and again. Yes, a white doctor had been dragged out of his clinic and battered to death; yes, schools were burning; children were being shot at — with rubber bullets only, of course. Shops in the township had been looted, beer halls were ablaze, cars had been overturned and torched. Blacks were on the rampage. What can you expect, insinuated the report.

I held the secret hope that this was the start of the revolution. Not that I welcomed violence but I was exasperated with the situation and change would never come if it were left to the half-inch seam of generosity of us whites. Rights had to be taken, not waited for. Apartheid, a meticulously planned violence, kept people poor, insufficiently educated, and unable to compete in the economy. The Nationalist government and its many supporters — both English- and Afrikaans-speaking, both Christian and Jew — had helped to attempt to brand their black brothers and sisters with the mark of inferiority. The flip side was showing now.

Through the Soweto revolt I glimpsed hints of my own freedom. All the restrained anger buried within me wanted to rise. "Get off my back! I want to be free of not being myself! Free of my fear, free of having somebody else control what I can and cannot do. I want to be able to love who I want, work at what I want, live where I want and with whom I want! Give me space!" I needed to realise that the only person who prevented me from experiencing freedom was myself. The struggle around me reflected the struggle within me. My soul stirred to the action I saw. It pointed to a future where we could all be free, personally and politically.

Over the next weeks our only contact with Soweto was via our teachers who phoned when their lines weren't down. The city was in an uproar, food was scarce, children were terrified — afraid to be in their homes; afraid to leave. "Black Power" was becoming a feared term. Genuine protesters were joined by gangs and tsotsis who jumped on the wagon of chaos, taking advantage — burning, looting, raping, killing. Police with teargas and guns were having a field day. No questions asked. Shoot, kick open the front door, release gas, fire at any figure. Next house. Shoot, kick open the front door, release gas, fire. Mrs Zwane opened our school and the classrooms were used for shelter from the police, the tsotsis and some Black Power students who petrified the children.

Soweto was a fuse igniting South African townships. Among the white population the reaction was mixed. A typical one was: "Look. We gave them schools, we pay for their education with our taxes, and what do they do? Are they grateful? No! They burn them!" Amongst the sisters I heard this argument. Let us all bow to "The Great White Handout of Second Class Education" where money spent on a black child was not half that spent on a white child; where syllabuses for black children were nowhere near the standard of those used in white schools. Our black children paid fees and had to buy their books. Classrooms were overcrowded. In government schools for black students, there was no science equipment, no library, no gymnasium, no sports fields, no swimming pool, no grounds to play on. "But we whites expect to be thanked for all we do for you!"

The white voter (the only voter) also forgot to think about the social conditions under which most black South Africans lived. The average white English-speaking child grew up with parents who read *The Rand Daily Mail* newspaper each morning. They sat at a food-filled breakfast table in comfortably furnished surroundings and scanned *The Star* in the evening after a lucrative day's work. They listened to conversations about the economy and world events; their parents surrounded them with books, toys, gadgets. Hooked on TV as soon as their eyes could focus, they were using the telephone by six, playing with dad's video camera at ten, and restlessly awaiting their first computer for their thirteenth birthday. The black child had none of this. Most whites had not yet made one relatively important connection — black South Africans were human.

Why the beer halls were burnt also remained a mystery to most whites.

"I mean, we would never dream of destroying our bars, would we now?"

They were not aware that the government had carefully built beer halls at every block as an inducement to the people to spend their money, drown their sorrows and by so doing achieve two objectives. Resistance to the "system" would be lowered and the prevalent belief among whites that black employees were loafers who drank their wages away would be reinforced.

At the end of July we re-entered Soweto. Our school had not been set on fire. We waited. News of deaths poured in as, one by one, like stray birds, the students dropped in. But not in uniform. The newly formed Soweto Students Representative Council (SSRC) had ordered a boycott of schools until their demands were met so our students dared not look as though they were coming to learn. They told me about their experiences — running from home, not knowing who to trust, sleeping in ditches, dodging bullets. Our students wanted an education; but they had better listen to the black consciousness students and stay out of school or they'd be beaten. At the same time they wanted apartheid to end.

I was particularly concerned about Moses (or Moss as his friends called him) Maswanganyi. He'd come to Diepkloof from a Seminary in Hammanskraal just outside Pretoria. Shy and awkward at his first co-ed school, Moss was politically active. We became friends. I was lonely, too. He was on the SSRC and it was due to his influence that our school stayed in one piece. He was in constant danger. Student leaders were disappearing fast — they were either imprisoned, shot, or they fled to Swaziland and from there to other parts of Africa, to Europe or America. A dense network of black informers made it imperative for messages to be relayed to members of the SSRC in complicated secret ways. Sometimes a leader would come into the school, whisper a few words to Moss and ask to address the students. Asking no questions we'd leave the room to hover outside, wondering if the police were hot on their heels. When the police arrived, the students, tipped off, would begin singing. "Hymn practice," we'd say with a smile.

Gradually the children mustered the courage to come to class and the semblance of a regular day began to flit on our reality screens. But it was a fairly loose connection. The scene: a crowded classroom. Time: 11.30am. We're studying a Shakespearean play, *Macbeth*. Slightly tense, we're alert, and not because Lady Macbeth's walking in her sleep. Maybe this will be a quiet day? We begin to relax. Something on the other side of the school in the lower quadrangle attracts Lindiwe's attention. Raising her arm, she points through the window, then makes a fist: "*Amandla!*" The trigger words raise the forty students as one. Squealing with fear they surge towards the small door squashing each other through in panic. Within seconds the room is cleared. Flattened against the wall I begin to breathe again as I stagger out. In every classroom the scene repeats itself. Small dots dancing in the distance are all that's left of the disappearing figures.

Heading for the staffroom I spy Sister Aquina standing at the entrance to the school. Her arms hang loosely at her sides as she watches the students fleeing in all directions. "Are you aware of what's going on?" my look says. Reading my surprise at her reluctance to run screaming with the rest of the pack, she answers quietly:

"Michelle, if God is in Mondeor where it's calm, then he must also be here. Not so?"

"It's possible," I respond, jumping from one foot to the other. "but can we continue this conversation in the car?" And I drag her away.

News came that Dennis Mlambo had been arrested in a march through the streets of Johannesburg. Where was he? We began to phone all the prisons. Sister Aquina had connections with government departments; she succeeded in tracing Dennis to Modderbee Prison on the East Rand. We decided to accompany his mother, taking food and clothes.

Dennis was quiet, moderate and mildly active. We spoke to him through wire mesh. "How are you?"

"I'm okay." He smiled. He was without his glasses.

"Where are they?"

"They were broken. I've been beaten. A hood was placed over my head and my body was pricked with electric shocks. They pushed my face down the toilet and flushed it many times."

"What did they want?"

"Names. Names of students. I don't know who they want. I had to keep saying: 'I am a stupid kaffir'." He fell silent.

"Can you breathe?" his mother asked, concerned about his asthma.

"Sometimes," he muttered. "I feel sorry for them." He shook his head. "They're ignorant, they know nothing."

We leave, humbled by Dennis' courage, awed by his spirit. A few weeks later he was released. How long his recovery took is not so clear. He's one of the few who didn't die, who didn't have to live in exile, who wasn't maimed or lost without trace. Parents went from police station to mortuary to hospital to prison searching for their children. A student picked up by the police had no rights, no defence, no lawyer. He was not permitted to contact his family; he was rarely identified. If a body was brought in — tough shit. The officials were providing no information. Numbers were kept low, officially.

The 1976 uprisings were a watershed that changed South Africa. An irrevocable step had been taken. Afrikaans would not be afflicted on students. Radical improvements would be introduced into the school system which, like a giant cement eggshell, was cracking. Within it surged the life force of a people committed to justice and freedom and prepared to die for it. "We have nothing to lose" was the general feeling. Children had taken the responsibility for a new order. Adrenaline pumped through the veins of black South Africans. A livewire tension crackled and hissed. Townships were bombs, tick-ticking away. The movement to dismantle apartheid was a dawn bringing day and only the slowing of the earth around the sun could stop it now. *Amandla! Awethu!*

95

Just as the inevitability of change within the fabric of South African society was a reality impossible to dismiss, so did I have to face the reality of my situation in Mondeor. I did the best I knew how. I would be up early, go out to school, teach all day, come home late in the afternoon, have a bit of a rest, a bit of a walk, and plan the evening ahead. Maybe we'd sit and read, maybe play a game of cards. We were all exhausted and ready for bed by 8.30pm. Day after day after day. It was tight and fixed and I felt as if I was in a prison, an emotional prison.

I didn't know what I was feeling. Like a robot, I carried on. If I had known, I would have cried: "I'm lonely! I want someone to talk to, someone to pour my heart out to. Someone's shoulder to lay my head on. There are walls around me; it's hard, all hard. There's no softness, there's no bosom. I'm a marathon runner. Must I go on and on and on?"

I'd sit in the car to and from Soweto feeling pinched into a space too small for me, not wanting to say the words of the Rosary over and over. "Shut up! I want to be still." In the breaks I didn't want to sit in the Sisters' staffroom; I wanted to be in the general staffroom. "I can do that. Why don't I do that more?" I'd ask myself. As we rode home I'd feel tight again. Looking out of the car like a prisoner in a police van I'd wonder: "What's the matter with me? I can't breathe. Who can I talk to? What will I say?"

Father McNaughton belonged to the community. He'd say Mass in Diepkloof for us every day and on some nights he'd eat supper with us, play cards and sleep in the guest room at the back of the house. One morning after he left I had to go into his room to collect the sheets. In the doorway I stopped, struck by the smell of a man. I slumped into a chair. All the memories of making love, of being held, of the reek of sex, the shift of semen and the salt of sweating flesh, bombarded me. My mask of control that pretended everything was alright slipped and for an instant I was aware of the gap within me. What is it? It was as if my body sprang open; a giant gate clanged back and emptiness yawned. For an instant I tasted the hunger, the need, the falling through space. Zap! Swiftly I shut the iron gate. Terror barricaded the feeling as a small voice whispered: "Isn't this what you want Michelle, a male lover?"

Was there satisfaction in teaching? Yes. The uprisings drew the students and me closer than our combined attempt to go beyond the education system by passing the exams. We knew that the piece of paper qualifying entrance to a university was still "not good enough". The system itself would have to go. Hunched around the desks we'd talk about being black and being white.

"White kids have such a good life," Solomon Mooke complained, "they're never unhappy, never sick."

"Do you really believe that?"

"Yes!" A chorus of voices.

"White kids are unhappy. They've problems with their parents, they feel misunderstood, they suffer from complexes ... "

".... but they're not hungry, and they're not poor, and they aren't second-class citizens."

I fell silent. In the light of what the faces turned towards me were going through, white children had no problems. Yes, being with the students soothed me. "You don't have to wear a habit to be involved in justice, Michelle," urged the small voice inside me.

The daily grind of crowded classes, slow learning, limited resources and harsh architecture was gruelling. Undoubtedly the prettiest in Soweto, Immaculata High School consisted of long red-brick buildings with small efforts at grass patches and sometimes a spray of flowers. As far as the eye could see it was dusty and bare. No trees, no colour, no moisture, no rest for the eyes. My soul grew weary of the aridity, of row upon row of sameness and smallness and misery. It would take hours for me to revive. Yes, Diepkloof drained me. "Is this what you want for the rest of your life, Michelle?" That voice again.

In spite of the murmurs hissing for my attention I consistently denied that anything was wrong. I continued to believe that all I felt and lived was par for the course. I was meant to be a nun and meant to teach in Soweto. So when Moss called me aside one afternoon and told me he was considering becoming a priest, I readily agreed to contact the man whose name and number he gave me, Father Riordan Kavanagh.

I had been living for seven years with structure, discipline, boundaries. This balanced my previously chaotic life. With little sense of belonging, I had started out. Now I was closer to my family of origin and felt strongly part of Holy Cross. I had entered not knowing who I was. I was Sister Michelle now. My understanding of sexuality, of sex and of loving was clearer but the clarity resided mainly in my head as my body bounced to its own rhythm. With a limited understanding of my gifts as a teacher in 1969, I had offered myself to the order. In 1976, after considerable experience, I knew I was a talented teacher. The lengthy periods of silence and solitude had tightened the bond with my inner source of strength. The exposure to spiritual teachers, writers, speakers, thinkers had fed and formed me. So everything was okay, wasn't it?

The little voice continued: Could it be possible that what I construed as an end was a means? Who would leave a delicate plant to run wild — untended, unguarded? No-one. You would harbour it until it was able to withstand the elements. Was there any likelihood that like the growth of liberation, I would grow and then outgrow? "Until death do us part," I had sworn in my heart. What did that mean now? Had I become so alive that my continued growth depended on new soil?

As I dialled the number for Father Kavanagh I couldn't know that as resistance to Afrikaans was the spark that set off the uprisings that began real change in South Africa, so would our meeting be the flame lighting the fuse that would fire the missile into a wider, unknown space.

my life

steps to heal the heart

June 16, 1976

If you were alive on this day, where were you? Describe in as much detail as you can what that day was like for you and how or if it affected your life.

The Student Revolution

Do you remember this event? What were your thoughts on it? Did it affect you or your family in any way? What significance does it have for you today?

Racism

South Africans find it difficult to escape racism.

- Do you consider yourself a racist? Partly racist? A situational racist?
- Would you recognise a racist statement or a racist act? Examples?
- What do you consider to be the strengths of South Africa?
- What do you consider our weaknesses?
- How many official languages do you speak? Do you think it is important to speak a language other than your own in South Africa? Why? Why not? What is your experience when you can speak another person's language? What is your experience when you can't? Do you think one language is more important or better than another?
- Where do you see South Africa in ten years time? What will your contribution have been by then?
- How do you feel about being who you are in South Africa today?

Early messages

As a member of the black community what were the early messages — both positive and negative — you got about yourself when you were a small child? Write them all down.

Were they messages about you in particular or about black people in general? How many of these messages do you still hold today? How many have you changed? What happened when you decided to change some/all of the early messages you heard? Did you do this with the messages you got of the white community as well? Why? Why not? When you read "black" community who do you include? Who do you leave out? Why?

As a member of the white community what were the early messages — both positive and negative — you got about yourself when you were a small child? Write them all down. Were they messages about yourself in particular or about white people in general? How many of these messages do you still hold today? Have you changed any? Which ones?

What happened when you decided to change some of the early messages you heard? Did you do this with the messages you got of the black community as well? Why? Why not? When you read "black" community who do you include? Who do you leave out? Why?

An emotional prison

"Day after day it was tight and I felt as if I was in a prison, an emotional prison." Do these words ring true for you now or at another time in your life? Can you expand on them, explain what the circumstances were and how you coped or didn't cope with them?

my life

_____
_____
_____
_____
_____
_____
_____
_____
_____
_____
_____
_____
_____
_____
_____
_____
_____
_____
_____
_____
_____
_____
_____
_____
_____
_____
_____
_____
_____
_____
_____
_____

The smell of yesterday

Sometimes it takes only a smell, a scent, a sound or a touch to waken a memory. My memory in Father McNaughton's room caught me off-guard. I was busy pretending everything was okay. Has this happened to you? You thought you had it all under control and suddenly something slight happened and it all fell apart — you knew who you were pretending to be was not who you really were. What did you do?

Doubting a relationship

At that time I began to doubt whether I should be in the convent. Have you gone through a divorce or considered breaking up a long-term commitment of some kind? What were the early signs that all was not well? What made you realise that you were not imagining your feelings? What did you do? Did you tell anyone? How did you go about separating yourself from the person, the job or the situation? Are you glad you made the choice you did? Do you think it was the correct or best choice? What were the outcomes for you?

Using youth to win a war

Perhaps you fought as a child for a cause. Perhaps your child is fighting for a cause. What is your opinion of adults using children as soldiers in a war? It has happened in Africa and in the Middle East, for example. What is the result of this — for the children who remain alive and for their children? What do you think about adults who train children for war?

Seeing violence

Did you see any violence when you were young? Let's say, when you were under eighteen? What happened? What did you see? How did you feel? Can you talk about your experience? Can you write about it? Perhaps you'd prefer to paint it? Getting it out is important both for yourself and everyone else you know.

Being violent

Did you ever enjoy being violent or receiving violence? Can you remember what led up to it? What was your reaction to hurting somebody or to the feeling of enjoyment when you were hurt? How do you feel about this now? Write or talk about your experience.

Is God in violence?

Sister Aquina found God in the middle of a possibly violent situation. Where do you think God is when people are being chased, hurt, tortured or murdered? Where do you believe God is when there are massacres, when millions of people are systematically exterminated because they are a particular religion or race or because they weren't the right race or religion? Does the question of God's presence or absence in these times matter to you?

Can we all be cruel?

Sometimes torture is physical; sometimes it's emotional or psychological. Sometimes we can refuse to share what we earn with the people we love or we misuse the money other people have. This is financial abuse. We can all be cruel to varying degrees. I realised that particularly when I visited Auschwitz and saw the gas chambers. The "they"

my life

_____
_____
_____
_____
_____
_____
_____
_____
_____
_____
_____
_____
_____
_____
_____
_____
_____
_____
_____
_____
_____
_____
_____
_____
_____
_____
_____
_____
_____
_____
_____
_____
_____
_____
_____
_____
_____
_____

who do these things are not too far from the "we" who judge them. We share the same capacity. Under the same circumstances we do not know how differently we might act. Tell about a time when you were cruel to someone. It could be something slight, but the intention was to hurt or humiliate or disappoint. What do you think triggered your action? Write a letter to yourself. Ask for pardon. Reply to yourself and forgive yourself completely.

Forgiving a stranger

Let's imagine someone comes up to you and attacks you. He doesn't take anything from you. He just beats you up. Is it necessary to forgive him? What if he does it to someone you love? Your child? Your mother? Is it necessary to forgive him? What are your thoughts on this? Does it matter what you think? Why? Why not?

A place of bad memories

Have you ever returned to a place that held awful memories for you? Was it like reliving that incident or that time? What made you go back? What did your reaction to your return tell you about yourself? Would you advise anyone to go back to the place "where it happened". Why? Why not? If you went back did you devise a ritual to release all your associations with that place or person?

Responsibility

In the 1976 revolution, hundreds of young people took responsibility for changing the country. It might not have begun as a systematic attempt to overthrow the government but, once under way, it was the spear that broke the apartheid shield. Many young boys and girls died; many were maimed; many went into exile and were lonely. Many dropped out of school and were never able to return. Their lives were ruined because they had no education and therefore little access to work. Who is responsible for changing an unjust system, for ensuring that a country remains stable? What are you doing to ensure the stability of your country now?

Chapter 8 *Loving and Leaving*

*I*t was one of those speckled days where, in the morning, it appeared as if it could be a regular school day. The children jostled in through the small doorway and flooded the corridors and open assembly ground expectantly. No bell rang to start the day, as the less attention we drew to ourselves the better. The children responded to directions that passed from one student to another from the Soweto Students Representative Council (SSRC). It was either "Yes, school today" or "It's a stayaway". Some days began as a "Yes" but broke up into a "stayaway". Such was the day Father Riordan Kavanagh had agreed to meet Moss. There was no way I could know that Moss's urge to become a priest was the link drawing Riordan and myself into a relationship. What did I have to learn from him? Why did I come into his life?

In the library waiting for Moss we sat making small talk.

"Maybe he wasn't able to make it today," Riordan offered, raising an eyebrow questioningly as a shaft of light falling through one of the broken windows fell onto the side of his face.

"Yes, Moss is involved with the students' council and it might be dangerous for him to come," I agreed, finding it a bit unsettling to return his gaze. "The police are hot on the heels of students who assume responsibility."

"Why not bring him out to the house in Boksburg?" he suggested running his hand through his auburn hair which was just turning up on his collar. "We could have a bite to eat and show him around. Of course, we'd love you to come, Michelle." And his blue Irish eyes sparkled irrepressibly. He was a natural flirt.

The meeting in Boksburg was the first twist that began the unscrewing of the cap on my emotions. Riordan drew me on every level. Unlike most priests, he was relaxed and present. Women didn't derail him in the sense that he felt threatened by them. He responded openly and eagerly to us, was genuinely interested. He talked freely and easily about politics or the church, or anything. He wasn't hung up on race.

Riordan could see I was clenching my teeth emotionally. Perhaps he sensed how tense I was, how much I was hiding from myself. Used to working with Sisters and not afraid of intimacy, he'd follow his intuition as to where the person was holding in, holding back, unhappy. At first, this was what drew him to me. He sensed a pain and as a healer he wanted to ease it. He came to Mondeor to visit me.

In my usual manner of not allowing myself to see, to listen to myself, I resisted and refused to acknowledge my unhappiness in the convent and my attraction to him. Denial was a stronghold. My annual retreat was due. Each year a sister spent a week or ten days away from her work, away from her community, in a period of intense prayer and reflection. This was to recharge her spiritual batteries. Sometimes the retreat consisted of a priest delivering sermons, the sisters taking notes and praying on them. The week was spent in silence. Alone with God. Before I left, I spoke onto a tape and sent it to Riordan. "I'm nervous with you, I know you want me to talk about myself and I'm scared. I feel I'm walking on the edge of a swimming pool and you're inviting me to dive in. I want to and I'm reluctant to." What was I scared of? In the retreat I learned.

Closeness scared me. Riordan was warm, open, receptive. Able to grasp who I was, he could understand me. Because he was focused on God, I could trust him to respect that in me. He wasn't going to abuse me; he wasn't going to use me. He was just going to be my friend. It was like you find a stray dog cowering. "Here little one," you coax, "come, I won't hurt you." The dog shivers in fear; his eyes tremble with a mixture of belief and betrayal. Longing to be in your arms, he holds back, programmed by abuse. So every day you leave food out, speak tenderly to him until, beginning to trust, he moves towards you incrementally. Riordan was luring me into love. He didn't bargain for his foot to slip; he didn't think he'd move beyond his role of healer.

One afternoon we met and drove to a house in Orange Grove. Who did it belong to? I had no idea. I remember standing at the mirror and looking at Rio through it. We were tense. "Different," he murmured in a kind of wonder, "every time I see you, it's different."

That time had come, the time to touch. We were two boxers circling one another. I was in lay clothes. It would have been so easy. Rio excused himself and went upstairs to rest. Was that an invitation? Should I follow him? No, if he'd wanted me to, he'd have taken me with him. Or would he? Maybe he was scared? Maybe he didn't know how to make the first move? I stayed downstairs, taut. Waited. The frustration grew. I knew what I was missing. Did he? After an hour he came down. Thanks very much.

I didn't become him or lose my identity. My tautness melted. I relaxed, allowing myself to be. I breathed easy. He took away my loneliness; he curled into some space inside me that read "vacancy". He activated what was dormant inside me. I was learning how to love a man. By trusting him I was removing resistance, enabling that spring of love to bubble.

I was sent to study for a year at the Witwatersrand University. Mother Provincial was convinced I needed a professional qualification as a teacher. I lived in Victory Park, an affluent white suburb closer to the university. I was under a vow of obedience and that means saying yes to God. Her request was reasonable. One year away from Soweto would not mean I could never return.

My time was flexible now. Rio and I could meet often, could walk in the park at the Zoo Lake, could even go out to dinner. I introduced him to my mother. We'd meet at her apartment where I'd change out of my nun's uniform into a skirt and blouse and we'd go out in disguise. We knew we were in love. Should we express this? One afternoon before we went out to dinner we were sitting on the couch. I dropped my head onto his shoulder and turned my face to him. Our lips met. I sensed his hovering. Slowly he opened his mouth and we began a fragile exploration. Shaking, we separated. Rio stood up shyly. "I have to change my trousers," he smiled. Quickly he rinsed them and ironed them dry. Before my mother returned. We were teenagers again.

My background was rife with sex; Rio was a virgin. If we had to make love, would I be the teacher? What should we do? My attraction to him was not like the raw sexual urge I had felt before. Rio had a gentleness about him which made it slightly difficult for me to be aroused by him. Why? Because (and I did not know this) I had been abused as a child and I would only respond to men who could abuse me, who were emotionally distant. Rio could never fall into the category of abuser. He knew how to love, was emotionally accessible. No man had been there for me on this level before and I didn't know how to respond.

The fact that we were spending so much time together was already a blurring of our vow of celibacy. We pledged to love God first, ensuring that God be the pivot of all relationships. This shifted as our eyes and hearts held each other in a way that excluded other people. Being a nun or a priest is being for everyone, is loving people without favourites. No exclusivity. Once we included sex, we'd be on very shaky ground. Could we continue to be close and keep our loving "on the level"? Rio was committed to the priesthood. His was not a divided heart. How could he balance his love for his vocation with his delight in being with me?

What was happening in my heart? I still felt called to be a nun; I didn't seriously consider being anything else. But where were we headed? The more we were together the more difficult it was not to express our feelings sexually. It was a stop-start situation. I felt guilty in the face of God. I shouldn't be competing with God for Rio. The way the priesthood and the system was set up it was an either-or decision. It couldn't be both. Not for us anyway. I wanted him to be mine, yet I saw how effective he was in relating to others, how extensive his influence was and how happy it made him to be of service. Rio wasn't lonely. I was a powerful attraction but he could be who he was without me. I was lonely. He exploded and explored my loneliness, made me confront myself, express myself. I tended to want to hold on to him. Part of me also knew that I too, wanted a wider sphere of influence. I couldn't see myself as the parish priest's wife. I needed to develop and use my own power. Riordan's love softened and consoled me. I had to see that love as a gift, draw back and release him.

I ran back to God. I went to a retreat with the intention of drawing strength from God's presence and with that power, deciding to allow Rio to be his best self, as I saw it, and continue to give himself to everyone, not only to me. This time the experience of prayer and silence was more intense in that I had a personal director who, based on who I was and what I wanted from the week, would give me four passages from scripture to meditate on. I'd pray for an hour on each passage, then write my responses to them. That was four hours of prayer. We'd meet once a day and I'd tell my director, a woman, all the thoughts and feelings I'd experienced. From this she'd choose another four passages. So the retreat would take its own shape. The director, trained in both spirituality and psychology, kept open to inspiration and was sensitive to me.

It became a journey with myself and with Spirit. There is no escape in the silence. I had to face myself. In the facing of myself I experienced that inner eternal outpouring of warmth and fullness. I had nothing to be afraid of. I could never lose Rio. What he embodied was essentially God-in-form. This God-in-form could and would come to me in countless ways. God is not miserly. There is more than enough for all of us. Why do I think that only this person can love me? That only this person is my source of happiness? Why do I confine myself and then want to contain and keep the bearer of this love? Can I love only one person? Of course not! I was afraid that there would not be enough, that there would be no more. Once I touched that well of being within myself which is God and which is me, I knew that there would always be more than enough.

It was in this knowing that I came to accept that my partnership with God was ongoing; that I would be maintained and supported and that Rio's presence in my life was an enrichment I did not need to hang on to in fear and possessiveness. What drew me to him was his essence. I could release the form, allowing him to continue on his unique path. I called him and asked him to visit me. The Sisters were looking after the home of a parishioner who was on holiday. We could meet privately there.

When we looked at each other in the sitting room of this stranger's house, Rio saw in my eyes that I had drawn strength from the well. Had he been waiting for this? Did he know we had to redirect our energies? If he had "cut the cord" I would have been too weak to benefit from it. Now, at this moment, I was strong and firm. He met me in my moment of power and, with no remonstration, gracefully agreed I had come to the best decision. He took his leave gently.

He also knew that once the aura of the retreat had worn off, I'd be on the phone in tears. Which I was. I knew I had done the right thing, but my fear and need re-emerged screaming: "No, no, I was only joking! I need you, don't go away!"

Patiently he held me through this, over the phone, in letters.

"I know it's hard for you. I miss you too. Yes, speak to me, tell me how you feel; I'm here Michelle."

"But you're not, Rio; you're not here!"

We did not see each other, and little by little I let him go.

That a man of his calibre could love me was a major indication to me of my self-worth. That we could spend hours together talking in depth of matters of the spirit; that we could laugh so easily and be so comfortable with each other; that we could have the strength to honour our vows, finally, and choose what was best for both of us, meant we were gifted with a precious and unforgettable friendship. There was a promise, unseen until now, that a relationship based upon a spiritual connection was the only one for me. Sex was the outcome of a connection already there, not the attempt to make that connection. One day I would have the courage to be vulnerable to a full relationship where the man was available and love would be called for in all its dimensions. This was a hint of possibility, a whiff of perfume from a distant flower.

I wrote a letter to my love ... and never mailed it.

"Rio, my love, I thank you for being in my life, for the hours we spent together, for all I learnt from you and with you. I am sorry for the times I acted strangely without consideration for who you were or what you had chosen, for the bewilderment I might have caused you when you were only being there for me. I love you and I hold you in my heart which has softened now that so much fear has gone from it. Wherever you are, here or no longer in this world, I will remember you with thanksgiving and joy. I hope you remember me in the same way."

I wondered who he had talked to; who had been there to comfort him as he plunged into love and then gradually found his way to another place without me. Did my love change him as a priest? Did our love make him more of a man? More human? Did it need to? Did it change him for the better as a priest? And what did he take with him, what thoughts, what memories, what misgivings or regrets? Who comforted him? And did he ever fall in love again?

It seemed as if I was being pushed back into "the world". On an emotional level I was like arid ground softened by a long rain. At university my intellect and creativity were nourished. Surrounded once again by literature, poetry, plays, music; tutored by dynamic teachers who became my friends; stimulated by a plethora of ideas, issues, philosophies, my spirit sniffed then drank the fare in gulps of glee. "Is this an alternative I see before me?"

The situation raised problems. I didn't want to go to classes in a habit. I felt awfully conspicuous, as if I were in a fancy-dress costume. Wits campus was my old haunt! I'd been an undergraduate there! Why make if more difficult to be approached by students? Wasn't being thirty-two years old distance enough?

"Can I wear ordinary clothes?" I asked.

"No, Sister Michelle. As a Holy Cross sister you are required to dress in the habit. What's the point of being a nun if you don't look like one?"

Yes, but there were occasions where my wearing the habit would be inappropriate. For example, we had to dramatise a literary work. I was the shadow side of both Macbeth and Lady Macbeth. Gladly I wore a cloak and removed my veil. This is theatre and art overrides all else! Riding was another example. One of my friends rode horses. One afternoon four of us students drove off to a stable to ride. Naturally I preferred not to clamber on a horse in my habit. Sandra brought along some jeans and a T-shirt. Bless her.

I was comfortable with my new friends — that's what I missed in the convent — buddies! Someone to go have a cup of coffee with, to talk about everyday things, to share lives. The increased freedom sat well with me. It wasn't necessary to be tied to lectures all day. I could play a bit, read, talk to people, hang out. The flow of a less-structured life lured me.

Then there was the teaching practice. I had to go into public schools and take a class for a number of weeks. For many children this was their first encounter with "A Nun". "Any friend of Batman's is a friend of mine," they'd chortle. Armed with new and many techniques to add to my natural ability to hold an audience and my genuine interest in the students, I was a hit, a very palpable hit. One period of teaching was in a Mondeor school not far from the convent. To increase the understanding of the teenagers I took my classes on a tour of our house. Having come from Soweto and now being in white schools, I could bring a perspective into the classroom that the students might not otherwise have been exposed to.

A whole lot a shakin' was going on in my life. It was as if for eight years I'd been glued together, inside and out. Now the inside had become unstuck. Love, university and teaching practice shook me like a shaker. "Loosen up, girl! Get a life!"

At the close of the year I was asked to teach at Victory Park and not return to Soweto. Disappointed at the loss of Diepkloof I trusted this was the best place for me in God's eyes. I believed that the decision reflected God's will in my life. Belief and trust in myself and in God were to be strongly tried in the year ahead.

School was a short walk away from the convent — about a three-minute walk. Each afternoon I began the return in a spirit of elation, fresh from invigorating interaction with the students. The closer I got to the side door of the convent, the more my spirit sank, the more bottled up I began to feel. After a tight teaching schedule I needed to flop down, take off my clothes, relax, meet a friend, have lunch, hang out. Somewhat like the tempo at Wits. Instead I would be going into structured afternoon and evening that began with lunch. Although the sisters were all very nice people, I was not close to anyone in particular. Sister Gwen, newly arrived from Ireland and brilliant, became a major assistance to me as it began to dawn on me that something was wrong.

Unlike most of the sisters to whom the day-by-day consistent timetable was reassuring and comfortable, I was bringing with me a year of exhilaration and a lifetime of intensity. I needed more excitement and more personal attention. Yes, I had to learn to accept people as they were, and I was not doing that. I wanted them to be other, to be like me. "I am not like you!" I would think. "Why am I here?"

The mealtimes became particularly burdensome. Conversation wasn't easy. I began to feel institutionalised, like I was a patient. Swallowing the food was an effort for me. I didn't want to feed myself so that I could continue to be contained in a world that was squeezing the life out of me.

Recreation was another source of stress. We'd meet to relax and chat. I didn't find it relaxing to have to sit for an hour and force conversation. Sewing or knitting did not rejuvenate me. I'd rather go for a walk or listen to music. My individuality was invaded by forced times of "lets be happy together".

I never felt safe enough to tell another sister how I felt. I kept so much hidden inside and for much of the time I didn't even know I was doing that. It was as if Michelle was in hiding. Now I could no longer hide. The Michelle that had grown through Rio's love and the friends at Wits was bursting to come out as a real person. I felt like a Great Dane in a baby's jumpsuit. The fit was at fault.

I grew thin and depressed. Was I ill? No. Was I lovesick? No. Maybe. Did I not want to teach? No. What then? I didn't know for sure, but I wanted to find out. This malaise was not a spiritual problem; I was not going through some kind of purification or spiritual darkness. Something on the human level was askew. I decided I needed a psychologist. I didn't know anyone, but had heard about a Sister Georgina who worked with priests and sisters. I asked my superior if I could make an appointment to see her, having only the vaguest idea of what I'd say: "I think I have a problem!"

I didn't like Sister Georgina at all. She was coolly professional and distant. She suggested I tell her the story of my life and she'd write it down. I began, tentatively at first and then with more enjoyment. Four hours later I left. As I drove back to Victory Park I felt some tingling of elation; something was happening, something was moving within me, like a catch unclasps.

The following week I saw her again. This time I did the Rorschach tests, describing what inkblots on paper appeared to be. She also asked me to compose a story, in the first person, from a few photographs. One was of a darkened room with the small window ajar. Light beckoned beyond the window. "I am held in this room. It is a cell. It is dark and cold and I am lonely and depressed. But there is a window and there is light. I want to be in the light, I want to be outside where the sun is. The window is high, too high for me to climb the walls. How can I get out?" The darkened room was the convent, the window was life, real life. I didn't know what lay beyond the window, but as a plant moves naturally towards the sun, I moved towards that sheet of light. What lay beyond it didn't matter. Movement mattered, not stagnation.

On my return trip to the convent after my weekly sessions, I felt a sense of expansion and possibility. I did not yet know what all this was leading to, but I was beginning to get a sense of release. As I drove closer to home, I began to feel like a ship being pushed into a bottle, sucked into a small space. Once inside, I felt as though the corridors contained me tightly, irrevocably, tunnelled me in captivity. Gwen was a tower of strength for me.

"Michelle," she asked as we walked, "what's worrying you?"

At what point does a thought reach the conscious mind? It was as if all the hidden subconscious gnawing had somehow sent out invitations to each other and *voila*, the combined gathering produced the one clear question: "Am I going to leave?"

Like birds who peck on the ground in a scattered bunch suddenly shift into flight in formation the thought crystallised, the question was there. Dare I face it? So fixated on being a nun was I that the idea of living another style of life was like asking a fish to live on land. I knew how miserable I was. I realised all indications pointed to the strong possibility that I was in the wrong place, in the wrong role. I felt like a statue, fixed in position, staring and set yet holding a thought which questioned that existence. If I looked at this thought, no longer denied it, responded to it positively, I would have to turn around, face a different direction, go another way. I may even no longer remain a statue!

The terror struck at night when I couldn't run away. "You're betraying God," it accused, "you're denying your vocation." Is this the devil? I wondered. Am I evil? What is the will of God for me? Am I so bad that now God abandons me? Am I abandoning Him? What will I do? How will I live? Where will I go? What will I tell everyone? I'm scared! If I'm not a nun, what am I? Who am I? Curled in the foetal position, I lay fretting, my stomach knotted, by mind raving. Was I having a breakdown? Yes, I was breaking down the image of myself I had found difficult getting used to. The nun, Sister Michelle and her future, Sister Superior Michelle followed after death by Saint Michelle. This was not going to happen. The reflection of myself I had shaped lay in shattered pieces of glass at my feet. What was there to replace it? A space, a possibility.

At first there was only fear, fear of doing the wrong thing, of making a decision I would regret for the rest of my life. Did God want me to leave? How could this be? I had been so busy planning my life that now that I was being challenged to allow another possibility to enter, I freaked out. I had to have control, I had to know exactly minute by minute what was in store for me. Being a nun was so neat, so all tied up with a ribbon and a little note. "I did the will of God in my life. Amen." As a nun I didn't have to concern myself with ordinary things like cooking or shopping or paying the rent, hairdressers, dry cleaners or insurance. No, I was relieved of all the everyday things. Other people made decisions for me, all I had to do was say yes and do it. Safe. Now the safety net was cut. Standing on the trapeze bar I had to jump. Who would be waiting on the other side to catch me? From where I was standing I couldn't see a safety net.

Gwen walked me though it. She was the wall at which I threw my panic, my "what ifs". She didn't try to make it better; she didn't brush my terror aside, she listened, caught the craziness I felt as my world began to dissolve. She was there for me, a strong presence. I was being helped towards a new life.

At this moment of crisis, I had to remember that I was not alone. I was led into the convent by an inner compulsion. I trusted that I was in the hands of a loving power. This power was familiar to me, close to me, with me all the way. Why should it leave me now? The immediate panic was intense, its roar drowned out the insistent, gentle, consistent silence of peace and purpose. In an attempt to still the fear, to go beyond it, I sat in the empty chapel, reassured by the twitter of birds, warmed by the colour of the sun lying on the pews. As I allowed the stillness to penetrate, I could hear: "Yes, Michelle, there is a way, a direction to your life. I led you here, to hold you in my arms for a while in a place of safety, to let you find much of who you are. I want you to continue to become yourself. To do this, you have to move on. Take one step at a time. As you take one step, the next will be clear. I am with you."

The more I allowed myself to trust, the more I began to see a whole new vista opening out. Wow! Music! Dance! Movies! People! Restaurants! Clothes! Life!

Sister Georgina gave me the results of our meetings. "Your personality does not lend itself to the religious life. You desire to be intimate with a man, you want a partner. You need to shape and form your own life. I suggest you ask for a leave of absence for a year in which time you can decide what you wish to do."

"What's a leave of absence?"

"You'll still be under your vows, but you'll be a lay person."

"You mean I'll live under poverty and celibacy as usual, just that I'll look different and not live with other religious?"

"Something like that," she nodded.

It sounded perfectly horrible to me. I'd be neither fish nor fowl. No, that wasn't my preference. If I go, I go with no holds. All or nothing.

I asked to see Mother Provincial, the head of our order. She was expecting me. Alongside her I wept. There were no words. What could I say? It's been great? What were the tears saying? "I wanted so much to be a nun. I wanted to serve God in the way I thought He wanted me to. Thank you for your love of me. I have known all along how concerned you personally have been for me. I've seen it in your eyes, I've heard it when you spoke to me. I shall miss the sisters. I'm being separated from a life I've got used to. I'll miss the silence and the feast days, the quiet morning prayer, the being part of something that is bigger than me. I am so sorry I couldn't make it. I wish it could have been different. Thank you for all the lectures I received, all the guidance, the tuition. You put my life together, you gave me myself. I'm stronger now because of you and I am so, so sorry. Please forgive me. Have I disappointed you? It's a loss for you and a loss for me, but I have no words now, only tears."

She sat alongside me, acutely sensitive to my anguish. Her face held her acceptance of my grief. It was as if we were keening at a death, bewailing a future that could not be, lamenting the safety I was losing, weeping the end of a dream. Yet somewhere in that deluge was the relief that, yes, I could live, I could be happy and the best was yet to come. I returned to Victory Park exhausted and released.

The decision had been spoken, I had applied to our Mother House in Menzingen, Switzerland, to be released from my vows and I broke the news to Sister Fides. She knew my struggle well. I remember her telling me how she had always found men to have feet of clay. Maybe their feet were clay, but other parts of their bodies were more malleable and responsive, I thought to myself. "Men, ah, yes ..."

Sister Fides and I went shopping. "See anything you like?" she'd ask good-naturedly. I was excited. "Don't let on they're for you," she whispered. I picked out a jersey, a pair of jeans, a couple of shirts. She bought me an iron, curtaining material and bits and pieces I'd need. I was re-entering "The World". When I had left "The World" I had given Sister Laetitia a small basket containing many colours of yarn and thread.

"You don't need all these colours now, do you?" she'd said, laughing.

"What's the problem with colour?"

"Colour draws attention." She looked at me, surprised I'd even asked the question. Sisters wore black or white. Now I was returning to a world of colour. Thank God. Why did that mean so much to me?

The part of me that I could not yet contact had driven me into the convent as a "bad girl". I was sure I could become a "good girl". It was an either-or existence. There were no greys. It would take time for me to understand that we are neither black nor white, but coloured. Within us are blues, greens, yellows, purples and vermilions of our strengths, weaknesses, attitudes, feelings, wounds. As we recognise the positives and so-called "negatives" inside us, accept and integrate them, our colours blend and we radiate beauty. If the colours we wear externally could be a reflection of the harmony and brilliance of our inner life we would certainly draw attention — not to the frail and foolish ego but to the essence we all share. Nature does this effortlessly, unselfconsciously and we applaud her. If we choose not to explore and reflect our selves it's like saying to our creator, "Here, take back your gift, I don't want it. I don't want to be beautiful, I don't want to explode into a dazzling blaze of colour. Pass me my subdued shades and let me hide."

I had agreed to finish the year and leave at the close of 1978. Teaching as Sister Michelle was more difficult now. Something had happened inside me now that I had decided to leave. It was as though I were a married woman who had decided to divorce my husband but I continued to live with him. No, it wouldn't work. I was wearing the habit outside, but inside I had taken it off. I asked to be let go immediately. I couldn't pretend. Inside I was no longer a nun.

"Would you consider remaining on at the school and still teaching but no longer as a Sister, Michelle?"

"Absolutely."

It was mid-term. The principal assembled the school for the final meeting.

"I have some bad news and some good news."

They waited, not knowing what to expect.

"The bad news is that Sister Michelle is leaving."

"Oh no!" A wave of disappointment rumbled through the assembly. The girls looked at each other, frowning.

"But she will be returning to us after the break, as Miss Friedman."

"Yaaaay!" the hall erupted with enthusiasm. Excitement sped along the rows as this news penetrated. "Wow! She's leaving!"

As soon as assembly was dismissed, the girls came pouring out. "It's fabulous," they jumped around me. "We're so glad! Where will you live? How will you wear your hair? How do you feel? What's it like? Aren't you happy?" I was.

Now that the sisters knew and the girls knew, it was time to tell my father. My mother had seen it coming. In Cape Town, she had seen how tortured I was. Back in Johannesburg I had seemed more settled. When Rio and I had met at her apartment in Sandton she knew I was hesitating. What could she say? It was my life.

Tuesday twilight, close to the end of June. Winter-wafted wind tugged playfully at my veil as I dropped twenty cents into a parking meter outside the Hotel Quirinale in Hillbrow where my Dad still lived. Making sure the convent car was locked I strode up the steps into the lobby and upstairs to room number 809.

"Kalinka!" Dad smiled as he opened the door. He never knew when to expect me, but this time I had called to let him know I was permitted to spend an evening with him. Wits University was a short walk down the hill from Hillbrow. I had been a more frequent visitor while I was a student. His daughter, the nun; his daughter, nonetheless.

He shuffled back a few steps to allow me to enter. Planting a peck of a kiss on his cheek, I walked through the short entrance hall into his bedroom and sat on the edge of the bed which faced the balcony windows. He lowered himself carefully into his chair opposite me and we began chit-chatting.

How are you? What's the market doing? Are you well?

I can't wait any longer. I must tell him now, I thought.

"I have something to tell you, Dad."

"Yes?" he responded hesitatingly, not sure whether to lean forward to hear better or to rest against the back of the chair to shield himself against the blow, should there be one.

"I'm leaving the convent." I said it slowly, gently.

"You're what?" He shook his head, as if he hadn't heard.

"I'm leaving, Dad, I'm not going to be a nun any more."

I felt a heat in my throat as if I were going to cry.

He stared at me, uncomprehendingly.

I remembered the pain on his face when I told him, ten years ago, of my decision to enter. He had sat stunned, a defenceless seal clubbed on the ice. Flashes of bewilderment flicked across his eighty-two-year-old face as he struggled with this reversal now. It was another blow, but more like the slap on a new-born bum. As the sun suddenly breaks through cloud, his face lit up, his eyes filled with tears. He reached across, fumbling for my hand, his own shaking tremulously.

"My Kalinka! My baby is coming back to me!"

There was victory in his voice.

We looked into each other's eyes in silence.

Unable to contain the joy that began to swell out of him, he bounced off the bed, grabbed his cane, and tottered ahead of me as fast as his weakened legs could carry him down the corridor, to tell his sister, Selma and her husband, Jack.

"You're leaving?" they gasped, "We're getting you back?"

"On, thank God, thank God." Selma held her face in her hands and rocked forward.

"Jack, look at Jumbo, he's like a child. Michelle, you've given him back his life! You're staying for supper. We must eat!" I was smothered in hugs and kisses.

Much water had flowed under the bridge since I had lived with Selma and Jack.

Tonight we were celebrating a return to the family. I had a lot more space now to be myself. Selma and Jack were ageing. They were tired of pushing; they wanted peace. I was a nun, I wasn't a nun. Let's eat!

I said my goodbyes to the community one by one. The sisters came up to my room, some with a little gift. They wished me every joy and happiness. As I'd still be on the staff the leaving was less traumatic because of this.

The day of departure dawned. Still wearing the habit, I drove with Sister Fides to my Mom's flat, where she was waiting — kettle whistling. After tea I took off my habit and veil, put on a pair of slacks, returned the clothes to Fides and we hugged. As she left I closed the door on almost ten years of my life. It had all happened. I was no longer a nun. I had a home for the time being, I had a job. I had part of a wardrobe. I had ten years of belonging behind me. What lay ahead? "Hey Mom, I'm back! Start praying again!"

my life

steps to heal the heart

Are you celibate?

Within the religious community of the Catholic church, to be celibate means that your primary relationship is with God. As a result you are free to serve all people equally. You have no favourites and there is no sexual relationship with anyone. Today some people choose to be celibate — that is not to have sex — because of the danger of HIV and AIDS.

Have you chosen this? For what period of time? What made you decide? If you choose to stop being celibate, on what grounds will you make that decision? What are the pros and cons of being celibate?

Fatal attraction

Do you hold the view that there is one special person for you? Have you met this person?

Do you think we are attracted to certain people so that we can work out unresolved childhood (or for some people, past life) experiences? Do we choose people who, in some major way, reflect the parts of ourselves we have still to develop? Or are they our undeveloped negative side we refuse to accept? What do you think?

Being sexy

How important is sex to you? What do you need from a lover? What do you think makes you a good lover? Is sex a simple or complicated factor in your life? If you don't perform to your own or your partner's satisfaction, do you feel like a failure? Who do you talk to about these issues?

What turns me on

Some of us feel ashamed about what turns us on. We sneak into sex shops and guiltily grab a sex tool or a video. There are many taboos about sex and little open discussion. If you have cravings you wished you didn't is there a person you trust who will listen and not judge you? A blank page is excellent for receiving your thoughts and concerns. And it won't answer back.

Mirror, mirror on the wall

How do you feel about your body? Take some play-doh and sculpt your body. Notice your thoughts and feelings about yourself as you do this. If you had to change any aspects of your body, what would you change? Make these changes on your sculpture. How does that feel? Write a letter to your body, telling it everything you want to. Answer your letter by writing back to yourself as your body.

Love me or leave me

Do you think Rio and I did the best thing for both of us? We had a few choices. We could have become lovers and hidden that for the rest of our religious lives. We could have continued to meet secretly for as long as our love lasted. Or we could both have left the religious life and married. As a lay couple we could still have been of service to many people. I chose to leave and he chose to stay. How about you? Have you had a

my life

relationship with a Catholic priest or are you currently in a relationship with a priest? Describe the dynamics, the complexity and the issues you are dealing with. Are you a priest who has experienced celibacy and sex? How did your relationship add value to your ministry? Did you ever have to say goodbye?

The devil made me do it

In trying to come to a decision about leaving the convent I worried that I might be under a negative influence. What do you think about the devil and evil? Do you believe in sin? What is sin? What does sin look like? Is sin male or female? If sin has a voice is it a male or female voice? Is it high-pitched or low? Clear or foggy? What does sin smell like? If you could touch sin, what would it feel like in your hand? Is sin outside us or inside us? If inside us, how did sin get there? Can we escape sin by covering our bodies with material so no-one gets a lusty thought? Can we escape?

Making it work

Do you know someone who chose to stay either with a partner in an unfulfilling relationship in the hope that it could improve or who remained a dedicated monk/nun of any religion in spite of the fact that it wasn't working for her/him. Maybe you did this? What led to your decision? How do you view that decision today? What have you learnt from making it? Did you ever tell the other person in detail what the gains or the losses were as a result of your decision? Want to write a draft of a letter that would do that now?

Part 3

Ms Michelle Friedman

Chapter 1 *Popularity and Problems*

'Whatever happened to Sister Michelle?"

"Well, as far as I know she left the convent and continued teaching for a few years. From there she managed an art and antique furniture shop for about six months. I think she was taking another degree at that time, an English degree."

"Whatever for?"

"She always wanted to teach poetry. Anyway, then I heard she joined the staff of the university's business communication department as a tutor. After three years she began her own business as a trainer in business communication. Did very well. Is she still in the country?"

Every time I made a significant change in my life, I invited the apparent emergence of a new set of problems. But that which came to the surface now had been waiting patiently to do so. It could only arise when I had the strength to face the issues. Accompanying the strength were the people to support me through it. In the play *Macbeth* the witches make their brew of newts and lizards' legs, "wool of bat and adder's fork", all particularly revolting ingredients. Within me, swimming and squirming, lay aspects of myself I would rather not admit to. The truth is that if I did not peek into the pot, plunge my hand in, grab the wriggling "yukkies" and begin to look at them, they would emerge uninvited and usually in a public place. All that I was suppressing needed to come out so that I could be healed and made whole. Glenn High School was the arena where my "blindworm's sting and owlet's wing" would glint in the light. The world of intimacy in relationships contained creepy-crawlies which had lain fairly subdued over the years. Now was their time.

Dizzy with delight, I viewed the spectrum of life ahead of me. So overwhelming was the sensory barrage of noise and smells, tastes and textures that shopping for simple needs spun me in a vortex of exhaustion. I was a thirty-three-year-old new arrival on planet earth. I looked like a human being, I talked like one, but there was a huge gap between myself and my counterpart who had left school, married, had a career and children. I would never catch up. At the very least I had to catch on. The lay staff at the convent were interested in my re-entry, hoping it would be smooth and sure for me.

One of the teachers gave my number to a psychologist she was seeing. Mervyn, divorced with two small children, lived in Hyde Park. Jewish, respectable, sensitive, he was all the "right things". Had I been longer in the field, I might have been ready to recognise a possibility of a relationship. But I wasn't nearly ready for Mervyn. So much of me was still in hiding. He couldn't know where he stood with me. Still finding my feet, still dizzy with the novelty of release, I was in flux.

Bedazzled by a pair of steel blue eyes eight months later, I met Brian at a dance. Intellectual, sexy and emotionally frozen, he was the blueprint of a pattern that would take me years to recognise. Our relationship centred around sex, avoided intimacy and was basically abusive. It made me helplessly angry that I was unable to make him change. Not for a moment did I consider why he was important to me. I was acting from a hidden abusive past that was surfacing, warning me, trying to catch my attention. Kind men like Mervyn I shied away from; they made me feel uncomfortable. I preferred emotionally distant, abusive men.

Another pattern was I'd select men who were unattainable in the long run. They were either married or too young. There was no danger of my being betrayed, left or hurt because it was a dead-end anyway. I was neatly safe. The relationship had to be terminated and I tended to do this sooner rather than later. I decided to withdraw from the game of love. Pushing my discomfort and anger into my pants like a long shirt, I zipped up my fly, determined to carry on without them — men. "Aha," the dismissed feelings and fears sniggered, "Ignore us will you? Pretend we're not here, huh? If you insist on rejecting us, we'll appear in a way you'd never dream of." With gales of glee, smirks of satisfaction, the suppressed demons hollered their laughter down the corridors of the future, facing me in the form of one of my students, Scott Crew.

The voice of my conscience puts me on trial.

"There will be silence in the court. All stand."

A shuffling of feet.

"Does the defendant plead guilty or not guilty?"

"Guilty. I found him overwhelmingly attractive."

"Please define 'overwhelming'. Are you insinuating that you had no choice?"

"Try to understand the background, Your Honour!"

"Background?"

"Yes, I didn't have much of a private life. Scott was 19. He was in my class. He was very sexy."

"So you said."

"Sorry."

"Are you aware that you speak of him as a sexual object?"

"He had laughing eyes, a magnificent singing voice and ..."

"So you said."

"Sorry."

A silence settles on the court.

"He was clearly attracted to me too."

"How do you know?"

"He'd stay after school to talk to me about his family and his life. I listened."

"Did you touch him?"

"Once. It was at play-rehearsal, Scott swaggered in proudly. He'd just got his driver's license. Gilbert called out to me at the top of his voice. Hey Miss, Scott's got his licence, he deserves a kiss. Scott was standing in front of me, waiting. Actually now that I think of it I wonder if those two hadn't set me up?"

"Can you please answer the question."

"I pecked him."

"Where?"

"On his mouth! It was a peck! A three-second landing! And in public."

"The length of the kiss is irrelevant."

"Have you any idea what it feels like to be strongly attracted to someone and not in a position to act on it?"

"It is not I who am on trial. Try to keep that in mind."

"Sorry."

The court room is silent.

"Let me tell you how he inveigled his way into my apartment."

"Proceed please."

"He offered to clean my car."

"He could've done that in the school grounds."

"Exactly, but he offered to do it on the weekend at my place."

"That was your second mistake."

"What?"

"Agreeing."

"But if you knew how … "

"Not again."

"Sorry."

"Would you continue please?"

"I offered him tea. Just tea. Scott sat on the couch — on the opposite couch and told me, almost in tears, how he had never made love to a woman and how destroyed he was because of that, how he knew nothing. He struggled for breath and I quite forgot he was an accomplished actor with a reputation for lying. I felt suitably sorry for the poor mite. What could I do to alleviate his incredible suffering? My heart pounded with anguish. I broke my biscuit into crumbs. I twisted the napkin into shreds. My hands trembled as I attempted to pour a cup of now-cold tea. How could I leave him in his moment of anguish to get boiling water? Allowing my resistance to weaken and my conscience to remain on hold, I came to the quick conclusion that the only charitable thing to do under these circumstances would be to, well, to oblige."

Silence reigns in the courtroom. The judge clears his throat.

"Did you consider the effect of your actions on his young mind?"

"Not exactly. I considered the effect of his actions on my young body."

"So yours was a selfish action?"

"It could be seen that way."

"What did you discover as a result of your actions?"

"Scott knew exactly what he was doing. He'd spun me a yarn to get me under the sheets."

"So you came to your senses and stopped?"

"Not quite. It wasn't that simple. We continued to see each other after school."

"Weren't you worried he'd tell the other students?"

"No, I believed it was between the two of us."

"Were you not aware of the moral implications of your action?"

"Yes. I felt awkward and disappointed in myself, but I couldn't stop."

Silence.

"I guess this is a far cry from anything you've ever come across, Your Honour?"

"I'm not here to judge."

"You're not? So why am I telling you?"

"I'm here to help you understand your behaviour. What was the main feeling you experienced that allowed you to continue with Scott for a year?"

"Comfort. He was a comfort to me."

"Please explain."

"I can't really. I just felt safe. Or cared for. I needed him."

"My recommendation is that you see a psychologist."

"Am I guilty or not guilty, Your Honour?"

"It is for you to be the judge of that."

Clearly, I had to talk to somebody about my behaviour. Here I was, a gifted teacher whom the students trusted and liked, and I was overstepping the boundary line between us, veering into forbidden territory. I could lose my job, destroy my reputation. Didn't I know this was inadmissible? Hadn't I learned anything about appropriate behaviour? Why was I acting as if I didn't know right from wrong? I had a problem.

In my sessions with a woman psychologist, I discovered how desperately I needed someone to listen. Just the fact that someone was there for me for an hour was a huge relief. It was as if all my life I had been out at first base with no-one following me, no-one routing for me. I had to be big and brave and do it all alone. In this supportive and unconditional environment I was able to explore. So much had to surface before the deepest sore was unearthed ten years later.

On one level, Scott represented myself. He came from an acutely dysfunctional family of alcoholism, divorce, betrayal. I would save him. In saving him, I would be rescuing myself somehow. Instead of caring for myself, I cared for him. Why was it necessary to have sex with him? Because underneath my compassion was the abused child. This child, accustomed to abuse, would want to continue to be abused. She would seek out men like Brian, or she would become the abuser, seeking out a relationship involving power and trust and abuse it. As a teacher I had power. I had won Scott's trust. Now I used both to satisfy my needs. A willing accomplice, Scott wanted love, craved attention. Highly sexed, he and I spun towards each other irrevocably. Subconsciously I chose Scott because he could never commit to me. Far too young to satisfy me emotionally, Scott represented another dead-end lover. I was safe from real intimacy in a relationship that was like a pregnancy in the fallopian tubes. It could never be. Consciously, I didn't grasp why I was doing this. Guilty, awkward, embarrassed, I was driven. The students covered-up for me; were on my side. Nothing was said openly. Slowly I began to be aware that everybody either knew or suspected.

I decided in December 1981 it would be better for me to leave the school. Why not consider an alternative to teaching? Why not try business? I wanted to get into a world of adults; I wanted to grow up. The witches' ladle had scooped up a brew, the taste of which lingered. Would my moving out of school clean my palate permanently? Or was this a mere morsel of what was yet to be served up to my conscious mind?

my life

Steps to heal the heart

Helping another to help oneself

"On one level Scott represented myself. In saving him I would be rescuing myself somehow." Sometimes we try to help someone without knowing why. We think it has everything to do with the other person. Often it has everything to do with ourselves. Think about this. Is there a person in your life you want to help? Do you know why? Does that person remind you of yourself in any way? In which ways do you feel you need "rescuing"? How can you rescue yourself as well as somebody else?

Abusing instead of helping

My relationship with Scott was not healthy. I could have been a friend and supported him. Instead, I used him. Sometimes we use people without being aware of it. We phone a friend we don't really like all that much because we know he or she will readily agree to go out and we want to go out. We use people who we know will lend us money or feed us. Not all the time, of course. Sometimes we use people to give us emotional support and get so used to their being there for us that we seldom think how we can be there for them. Often we use our parents, and particularly our mother, to fill this role. We expect her to be the pillar of strength and forget she also needs to be listened to, to be made coffee for. There's a line between friendship and abuse. Look at all your relationships and see what side of the line you are on. If you are being misused by anyone you know, how are you going to set a boundary? Have you been abused yourself as a child or at any stage? Is this beginning to be a pattern in your life? If you are misusing anyone in your life how can you correct this?

Change and the healing cycle

When you decide to take on a new job, or have a family or move house, the soil of the soul stirs. You dislodge aspects of yourself that may be in hiding; they now have a chance to surface. A shock can also do this. Many people revisit their priorities in the light of a traumatic event. "What's important?" takes precedence. Often we don't know what's really important in our lives until we are on the verge of losing what we love, be it a person, a career, our health, our livelihood. What event made a significant change in your life? What rose to the surface for you?

None so blind as those who will not see

At many times in my life I was blind to aspects of myself, yet I longed to know myself. I drew into my life a person or a situation that would bring out in me that which I was unaware of. This can be true not only of an individual, but also of a family or a nation or the world. When an event happens, it is necessary to ask what it is that I need to know about myself, our nation or our world. What is it that I am blind to? Both the question and the answer arrive as a response to a heart unafraid of being honest, of facing the truth.

Think about your life, about the people in it and about the turning points. Think about this in terms of your family, your group or tribe, your nation. Do you have the whole picture? What is it that attracts you to a person or a group? What is it that repels you? Is it possible that both the positives and negatives are reflections of yourself? Take what you admire and whittle it down to an aspect of that which you can recognize. Do the

my life

same with someone you disdain or hate. To a lesser or greater degree we reflect one another. If you find there is one particular person you are having difficulty with, take note. S/he may well be there for you as a guide or teacher. Without her or him you may not discover what it is you need to know to become whole. This process is about learning to love ourselves, all of ourselves.

The shadow

Many of us have been under social pressure to behave in a certain way. Anything that doesn't fit we ignore. At least we attempt to ignore it. Ever noticed how a preacher has a so-called "wayward" child? Or an atheist spawns a religious boy? A parent denies the fact that she is gay and then her child is gay. It is often our inability to integrate both what we consider to be "good" and what we consider to be "bad" that unbalances us. Are you in touch with your positive or negative shadow?

What thoughts do you have that you are ashamed of? What have you done that you hope no-one ever finds out? It is healthier to face all of who you are. Talk to the parts you are afraid of. Invite them to come into the light. Tell them how you feel about them, one by one. Answer as they would. If you prefer to write, go ahead.

Only that which we suppress grows to have power over us. Whatever is hiding that you perceive is negative may well be a result of pain inflicted on you. Before that pain can go away, it needs to be felt by you. Better to feel it than to act by either trying to dull the pain or by hurting someone else in an effort to transfer the pain. Once you have felt it, it leaves. It only wants your full attention for a short time. Be as gentle as possible with yourself as you release your shadow and integrate it into your whole being.

The same goes for the gift or talent that we are terrified of. Maybe your parents didn't want you to be a stockbroker, for example, or a professional swimmer, or whatever it is that haunts you. You're at university studying for a profession you loathe. You want to do stand-up comedy. Start now. Sometimes we're taught that joy is not a full-time occupation. We learn from watching others that work must be dull and that fun only happens after hours. If we put off expressing our talent or gifts or that which brings us joy, we might find that we never do it. Do you remember somebody telling you that you can't do something? The choice to accept that criticism or ignore it is in your hands now.

Sizing up a situation

Do you remember a situation where you saw two people behaving in a way that you thought was wrong? What did you do? What did you think? Using this as a creative exercise, write a conversation in which you tell one or both people what you think of them, and what you think they ought to do. Then respond as one or both of the transgressors in writing to yourself.

Inappropriate relationships

Have you ever had a relationship that you knew was inappropriate? Write about it. If you never managed to have closure on the relationship, do it now, in writing.

How do you feel about forgiving yourself? It is unlikely that you deliberately set out to use the person. Even if you did, you can still forgive yourself. I know how hard this is. I recommend a book to you that is useful. It is written by Stephen Levine and is called *A Gradual Awakening*. He helps us understand how the mind works and how to learn to love ourselves and forgive ourselves.

Chapter 2 *Progress and Possibilities*

*I*t was time to leave teaching. I had left the convent, why couldn't I leave teaching? Go off into the unknown? I was hesitant but what was my alternative? To watch the seniors plan their careers, take charge of their lives and leave me sitting in a classroom for the rest of my life? I couldn't live vicariously. There had to be something else I could do.

Once I made the decision, doors opened for me. The move from school — teacher to manager of an art and antique furniture shop — was smooth and easy. After a few months I was offered a teaching post in business communication at a university. I viewed this as a possible short-cut to the English department, where I really wanted to be. I knew nothing about business communication. My ex-drama teacher Charles Stodel was in a senior position and he encouraged me to apply. He primed me for the interview. Oblivious of what the course was about, I spouted answers to the polite enquiries of the department head, hoping I was making some sense to him. On all systems go, my adrenaline served me well for, hardly an hour later, I emerged with a position as a tutor in business communication at the prestigious University of the Witwatersrand.

"What am I supposed to do?" I wailed to Charles.

"Here, take these books, read them, and be in for a staff meeting first Tuesday of term. Lunch with Mother, must run. Bye now!"

I sniffed around the staffroom. Mundane messages, outdated, hung pinned like the crucified on the wall. In the sometime wind that mischievously crawled in under an inch-open window, they flapped, vainly attempting to tear free. Aware that they had long not been glanced at and were now left to curl at their corners, they fluttered weakly, dying, ignored and yellow. Colourless corridors with their wooden backs turned, hardly enticed enthusiasm. I was uneasy. What world was I entering?

I had left teaching, or so I thought, and here I was back again in a musty staffroom with tutors who, for the most part, looked very much like the teachers I had left behind. Did I see myself in frumpy clothes and sandals complaining about the politics of the politely murderous world of academia, splitting hairs about minute details, scrambling for security under the title "tenure" and rotting away for the rest of my life? Why was I here?

Only my ability to be inventive and at least a half-page ahead of the students enabled me to flit across the tightrope between fake and fantastic. After one year of this teetering, I found a balance and some breathing space. The three years at Wits were the foundation for a career in which I would become more aware of my need for healing within the context of South Africa. It would give me tools to earn money in the competitive world of training in commerce and industry and it would introduce me to the art of public speaking. The seed of my future lay here, hidden to me.

It didn't take me long at Wits to understand that my future didn't lie in becoming part of it. As I tutored students, taught them how to write business letters, I realised that they'd be in managerial positions possibly within five years and I'd be in the same office, correcting papers. Why not use my abilities in a more lucrative environment? Business communication needed to be in business, not in school. How could I get into business? Around this time I met a communication consultant from London who invited me to attend one of his courses in Wales. In order to make this happen I needed a sponsor and found not only a sponsor, but part-time employment with one of the most powerful companies in South Africa — ABM.

I remember as a nun reading a card: "God also writes straight on crooked lines." A woman who was hardly a balanced individual had placed a book on Padre Pio in my hands. That had led me to my sojourn in the convent. Frank Newton would now open the doors for me into the training and development arena of the business world. His encouragement would be the fulcrum levering me to form my own consultancy and, in the process, open myself and others to healing the wounds of being South African.

my life

steps to heal the heart

Shifts

There's a baseball saying: "You can't reach second with your foot still on first." Have you ever been or are you now in a position where you know you need to make a move? Perhaps it's in connection with a relationship or a career but staying where you are is no longer an option. Are you ready to let go of what you have that's not working for you for something you have no idea of? Dare you take a job that is completely out of your previous experience or go without a relationship? Can you launch into the void? What does it feel like? What are you most afraid of? Keep a journal and record all of your doubts, fears, hesitations, expectations. Stay with your feelings — be aware of them and let them be.

A person who keeps appearing

Charles was my good-luck charm. He'd always turn up just when I needed him. It was Charles who got me work on my return to South Africa from America. It was he who recommended me for speaking engagements. Again and again he emerged like an angel. We used to have quiet and memorable *Shabbat* evening meals together. That's when he'd tell me about his spiritual journeys. Is there a person in your life who performs a similar role? Who just happens to be there either to bridge a gap or to place you on your path? Write a description of her or him in as much detail as you can. What do you still need to say?

Understanding the picture

Sometimes it isn't possible to go from A to B in a straight line. I didn't understand why I should work in an antique furniture shop, yet it was a bridge for me. It gave me time to consider what I really wanted to do. Nothing is a waste of time, depending how you perceive it. What happened in your life that you think was a "mistake"? How long did you stay in the "mistake"? What came out of it that was positive?

The staffroom at Wits put me off teaching there, but it was essential that I learn the skills that would equip me for the business world. If I had acted on that feeling, I might not be writing today. Have you ever made a decision based on one moment that affected your life? What were the circumstances? What was the decision? What was the result of that decision?

Chapter 3 *Prejudice and Preparation*

*F*rank was in his fifties. He'd run from Zimbabwe; a "retread" he called himself. After hearing what I did, he readily agreed to send me to Wales if I would design and run courses for the ABM Graduate Institute, assist in the selection procedure and the needs analysis. This would be a part-time position and could be sandwiched between the classes at Wits

Once black students graduated from colleges reserved for one race only, they had to start again and jostle to enter the predominantly white business world. Here they would be in a highly competitive environment. Black students had been subjected to education through the Bantu Education department followed by so-called "advanced" education. They were often unaware of the know-how of boxing in the business ring. Sophisticated weapons of golf-course swings and drinks at the bar were not part of their training or background. Nor were those places of entry. That belonged to the exclusively white, wealthy world. The ladder of success was built on rungs relegated invisible to black eyes. The Graduate Institute was an attempt to bridge gaps. Later the word "bridging" became pejorative; it implied an inferior African culture and a superior Western culture. I was responsible for presentation skills, body language, listening skills, business meetings and telephone techniques.

For many graduates their climb had already been so steep and tortuous that now, at a summit with a degree in their hands, they hadn't the heart to look up and see summit after summit of a career. Dazzled by their success thus far, some needed to rest at the first peak. The constant beginning again came as a shocking reality.

Companies could no longer afford not to hire black graduates and develop them as managers. There was an increasing unavailability of white managers and a one-forty ratio of white managers to employees. In addition, major multi-national companies were pummelled into recruiting black staff by the Sullivan Principles. Reverend Sullivan, an African-American, had introduced a scheme whereby a number of changes had to be in operation by due date or the company lost American or British funding. A competition between companies to gain the most points ensued. Canteens had to be desegregated and toilets made multi-racial. Positions had to be open to black employees and a certain number of black managers had to be operative by set dates. Certainly, if the South African economy wished to continue, this had to be the route to follow. Goodwill alone was too thin to offer opportunities to black South Africans; only the pressure of losing money could dynamite the mines of resistance to change.

Once I began moonlighting for ABM, other opportunities opened up. Citibank phoned Frank to ask for advice on a programme they wished to run for black school-leavers. Unilever followed closely behind, as did NCR and Colgate Palmolive. Through an old friend I made contact with BP. I had five major clients.

The NCR and Citibank courses offered me the opportunity to work with black students in their early twenties or late teens. Shining with eagerness and enthusiasm in spite of the harrowing climb to make it through a gruelling selection process over three days with hundreds of applicants, the twelve successful applicants had every right to consider themselves deserving of a brilliant future. Neither Citibank nor NCR guaranteed employment after the free three-month course run by an industrial psychologist, a commerce teacher and me — a business communication consultant. One or two lucky students were absorbed into the companies. Flung back to Soweto, the remaining impeccably-attired, promising business people tried to find employment elsewhere. It wasn't easy. Many failed. Aware of this dilemma, those responsible for the courses felt the courses and the experience would be beneficial to the students in spite of the fact that most wouldn't be able to find work. The company would score brownie points and the students would linger in frustration.

For nearly all the students, meeting me was their first encounter with a white woman at such close and consistent quarters. I chose to design the programme to facilitate personal growth. For a major portion of the course the students presented talks and reports to the class. Here they were taken seriously and listened to. Here they could speak their anger, demand change and have to substantiate their opinions and arguments. Here they were applauded and praised.

In preparing them for job interviews I'd encourage each student to be frank about his or her qualities and talk about them first to the class then to the strangers I'd bring in who provided them with practice at facing an unknown white employer.

We lived in a world of harmony and possibility that lasted all day. I'd drive home to my apartment in the white suburbs and the students would disappear into the teems of commuters boarding the trains and buses hurtling into Soweto. We got used to each other. Soon the students would find it natural to stand close to me, or brush alongside me, tap my shoulder, grasp my hand, or throw their arm around my shoulder. Crossing the chasm of touch, we became friends.

Apart from these courses and multi-racial presentation courses I also had the opportunity to run inter-cultural courses — "What it means to me to be who I am in South Africa today". In an environment of trust and over a period of days, frank feelings, gems of revelation came to the surface. I knew I was experiencing moments of intense beauty and possibility. Here in this room we were, for a brief space, the nucleus of what a new South Africa could be. Underneath our skin and in our hearts we found frustration, pain, guilt, anguish, fear, resentment and a daring to hope. We listened and healed one another; we went out into the streets together and allowed the stares and frowns to fall on us and felt exalted. We knew our lives could never be the same; we could never look at a person of another race without remembering. Was it too good to be true?

At BP I had the opportunity to train not only a multi-racial group of fast-lane graduates, but men and women who were not in this fast lane. I met people who had walked their shoes thin trying to find employment; men whose stories often had us in tears; people of quiet courage who persisted in believing in tomorrow. People like Marty Webster who invited me to his home in Cape Town. There I met his family and friends and we all went to a nightclub. I was on the other side again and this time without the habit. I found that I could just be myself. I no longer had to take responsibility for conversations, or break awkward silences. Just because I was white didn't mean I had to initiate interaction. Just because I was white didn't mean I had to always talk and never listen; and just because I was white didn't mean my ideas were necessarily the best ones, nor that I was exempt from being criticised, nor that I never needed to apologise.

During this time I had one close female friend, Xoliswa Ndlovu. She taught written communication for ABM and it was there we met. Xoliswa was abundantly energetic, always busy. We naturally liked each other but we also wanted to be friends. We'd meet for lunch at Mike's Kitchen to talk and share. It wasn't easy for her. Long past the mould of a subservient woman who lived for her husband, Xoliswa found it difficult to meet men who were not threatened by her. She lived with her ailing mother and was parenting a child not her own. At the same time she was independent and wanted to be free of many of the restrictions imposed upon her by being Zulu. She fell between the two culture cracks. I was never invited to her home.

One afternoon Xoliswa came to visit me in the townhouse I was renting. I was in number three. I had lived in number one but had moved two doors down. The afternoon of her visit was gloriously clear and warm. I had bought cake, laid the table and sat waiting. No Xoliswa. "Well, she's on her way," I told myself. In Africa whites think that only they have a sense of time. I was not going to think like this. "Something's come up" I reassured myself as 3.30pm stared out at me from the kitchen clock. "She'd definitely phone me once she could get to a telephone." That in itself would be a major problem. She could be stuck on the road. She could be arrested. She might have had an accident. Her mother could be ill. I knew how businesslike she was; I also knew she knew how whites thought!

"Where is she?" I wondered, now becoming slightly annoyed. "Did I say today? Yes." At 4.30 it hit me. I darted out the front door to see Larry watering his lawn.

"Larry?"

"Yes?"

"Did you see a woman looking for me? I forgot to tell her I moved."

"Yes," he answered, "She was sitting outside number one. I thought she was waiting for the Spencers. I didn't want to be rude and ask her if I could help her in case she thought I might be insinuating she had no right to be here on a Saturday."

"So?"

"So she left."

I dashed to the phone. I knew it would take her at least an hour to get from Sandton through town and out to Soweto.

"Xoliswa?"

"Michelle! Where were you? Didn't we plan to meet today? I was there! I waited for you for almost two hours. Where were you?"

"I was waiting for you in number three! Did I tell you that I had moved?"

"Oh my God, of course, and there was I thinking if I were a white friend Michelle would never do this and trying not to think that!"

"Larry was on his lawn."

"Yes, I saw this man watering his lawn and I didn't ask him. I've been told that whites can live next door to people for years and never know their neighbours. So I thought he wouldn't know you! Can you believe this shit? And you, I know what you were thinking, African time ... right?"

Xoliswa came up with the name Khula-Zulu — for growth — for my business; it was she who helped me move from my apartment in Parktown to the flat I bought in Yeoville, and it was she who encouraged me to act on my attraction to one of the men at the Graduate Institute — Ben Mlaba.

Ben had been to school in New York. He was more or less my height, slimly built, with a small beard. I see him in a hat, cigarette dangling from his lips, leaning against a lamp-post: "Hi Babe, doing anything tonight?" I found him very sexy. He was also very angry. Ben would talk to me a lot, stand near me, demand a lot of attention in the class. The group respected and liked him. He came from a different place. He'd lived in America and was somewhat of a hero. He was also more verbal with his frustration and criticism, less afraid.

The day the institute closed for summer all the graduates went into town to celebrate at one of the international hotels. I went home. Ben phoned me from the hotel. Would

I join him? He was saying, "I want to see you and I want you to see me in public but in a safe place." At this time in South Africa we could have been arrested even on suspicion of our being lovers. I was nervous to go. It would mean making a statement. "Yes, I am interested in Ben." Other graduates would be there — what would this message mean to them? I was also nervous of being picked up by the police.

The hotel was going-as-respectable but it was run-down. Ben and I sat outside on the deck. I had a beer. He was a little drunk. I felt uneasy, uncomfortable, embarrassed. Half of me was saying: "What are you doing here?" The other half said: "Just relax, hang loose, see where this goes." It went back to my apartment and Ben stayed the night. What did I expect? Would it be different? When Ben and I made love we were two children clinging to each other. Underneath his anger was fear. His teeth chattered in his sleep. Underneath my veneer of having it all together was the fear of abandonment. "You didn't call, you didn't come," I wept into his arms one evening after I had waited and waited. Instinctively Ben got to the nub of it. "Don't worry," he soothed, "I won't abandon you." How did he know? My being responded to his being. Children in a storm. We couldn't talk about this; we never celebrated it, but it was there.

From this point of emotional nakedness Ben and I could have built up a relationship. But I wanted him to be other than he was. I was also trying to convince myself and the world that I had overcome prejudice. "See, I have a black lover!" However, when I took him to a private party in a restaurant with many of my theatre friends, Ben got drunk and became belligerent. Instead of confronting him with how I felt about his drinking I seethed in embarrassment hoping he was not behaving too badly. I wanted someone with all the social graces, someone who could move easily from one culture into another. It was okay for Ben to come into my area, but I was very uncomfortable in his. I was also using him to confront other whites. "See, here is a black man. See how nice he is?" Somewhere inside me I was still patronising. It's so subtle you don't even know it's there. It's like a tiny needle lying in cotton wool. If by some mistake the needle point emerges from its hideaway, the serpent stings, pierces, cuts, scratches, draws blood, bursts the dishonesty.

Ben and I were scared of being arrested. I bought a long black wig. We were always looking behind us. At other times we had to send the situation up or we'd freeze into anxiety. We'd shop in a supermarket and this game arrived. I'd be the Madam, he the Boy.

"Did you wash the swimming pool today?" I'd ask loudly.

"Yes, sir, ma'am I did too. Hey Madam, don't you need this special sauce for those fancy friends of yours tomorrow night?"

"My boy, you know I don't have fancy friends."

"Well those friends who sit with me and smoke those cigarettes that make us all feel funny and look worse."

Ears prick.

"I don't know what you're talking about Ben."

"Why sure you do, Madam. You and I smoked one of those last month on your sister's birthday when you took all your clothes off and dived into the pool I just cleaned. Don't you remember?"

Faces frown.

"Boy, I will send you back to Bophuthatswana if you go on with these tales."

"Say what? You gonna send me to that godforsaken hole? You pay me just enough to live here. What would I do back there? Besides which, who would wake you up in the morning with a nice cup of black coffee and a .... "

135

"Ben! *Dis nou genoeg!*"

People shift away, throwing sidelong glances at us.

At the check-out, our conversation continues. I pile everything on Ben and he mumbles and grumbles. I ignore it all and strut to the car. He gets in and drives off, leaving me screaming in the parking lot with all the groceries at my feet.

Drawn to one another, Ben and I grew to like each other, to play with each other, and I believe the seeds of love were there. Had we known how to tend them, I might have been writing a different story. Ben died in a car accident in 1991.

It's a long road to peel off the onion of apartheid, to let go, layer by layer, the subtle skins of prejudice. I wasn't aware that the feeling of not being good enough fuels prejudice in a person. Frank Newton had opened a door which led to my forming my own business. He hoped that door would include him in a long-term committed relationship. It wasn't too likely. Frank had been an orphan. He'd grown up in foster families. He was deeply prejudiced.

What about me? Was I going to remain in South Africa? I realised how attitudes were hardening on both sides. Was I making things better or worse by staying? There was a call within me for my own life. I was burning out. Had I done as much as I could? I'd grown freer, learnt a lot but I was still ashamed of my country. A number of events occurred which began a domino effect propelling me out of Africa and into a past which would become my future. The death of my father was the pressure point releasing new energy, new direction, and a new life.

steps to heal the heart

Making an effort

When I met Ben and Xoliswa I was at a certain stage of development. The incidents I have written about may seem quite superficial — Xoliswa and I waiting for one another; Ben and I in a supermarket. In both these relationships I wanted to cross the racial divide in a way that was as real as I could make it. How do we become real? We do what we can with what we've got at that time — at our level of awareness. It takes time to become real. What about you? If you were born in South Africa or in a country where there is racial discrimination, write about your first attempts to cross the racial divide. What happened? What did you learn about yourself and about the other person?

Prejudice

Although time has passed since South Africa shed apartheid, many of us are still hurting. What about you? Take the opportunity now to express what it has been like for you to be who you are in the context of South African legalised racism. Sometimes it is easier to paint this. If you think you can't paint, so much the better. Let the brushes lead you. Or write it. Tell your story. Remember when you first realised you were of a particular race group and what that meant. What did you do about it? How do you feel now about yourself and about other South Africans? What still resides in you? How far have you come? How have you rewarded yourself for your achievements?

Negative attitudes

South Africa is still working with the aftermath of apartheid. What are your fears about our country now? Write them down. What do you feel resentful about? Write this down. Do you think your being here is a mistake? What is the particular contribution you and only you can bring to this country? Do you see how important you are to the whole? What is it about the situation now that presents an opportunity to you for growth? And to others for their development? "Be still and know that I am God," says the Psalmist. Be still and listen. You will be guided to use your gift in the best way possible.

Doing the "right" things for the "wrong" reasons

I was attracted to Ben and I wanted to have sex with him. Of course part of it was to experience sex with a black man. So in that way I was using him. Maybe he was using me too. Having sex with a person from another race group is no big deal. What is more important is who the person is. Ben was fighting his life and I was discovering mine. I was using Ben to heal me, to grow me. Subconsciously, as a white woman who was part of the system, I was using a black man who was a victim to heal me from my racism. Listening to oppressed people talk about their experiences, their lives, their hurt does build understanding, but as a white, straight, abled person I believe I have to take responsibility and heal myself first from my prejudices around colour, sexual orientation and disability. And any other oppression. What is your opinion on this?

I'm not a racist!

As an abused child I had a natural compassion for people who were abused or who were victims of injustice. That was okay although I didn't know at the time that I had a

my life

history of abuse. It is also complex in that, once I have healed myself from abuse and injustice, does that mean I do not have a place in my heart for people who are powerless? At the same time there can be no denying that living in South Africa made it inevitable that I would harbour prejudice. This prejudice operates at various gross and subtle levels. In taking Ben to a nightclub I was doing two things: proving that "I'm not like everyone else — that is, white people" to him and proving "I am better than you" to the white people at the club. I needed acceptance from Ben and I needed to be special to be okay to myself.

As a white person I think the road to release is long partly because we tend not to be aware that we are "white". A book that helped me to realise this is called *Uprooting Racism. How White People can Work for Racial Justice* by Paul Kivel published by New Society Publishers, Canada. What is your opinion of this? What has your experience been?

Chapter 4 *Paths and Parting*

Activity affords us escape. "I'm so busy I haven't time to think about myself." Good. Time on my hands would push me back on myself and then I'd be miserable. My life was my work. There was nothing else. When the courses end the music stops and you realise you've been dancing alone. You feel a little awkward, gawky. You look around embarrassed by the silence. You watch couples saunter off the floor, hand in hand, arm-in-arm. You sidle back to the chair on which your jersey hangs, lift both it and your handbag in one movement and you're out the door. Alone. Empty.

In flexing my business communication muscles, I joined Toastmasters to hone my speaking skills. When I heard it was possible to write an eight-minute speech and win a trip to America, I decided I would do that. It was more a knowing than a decision. It had to be. And it was. I became the first woman to win the South African national public speaking competition with a speech: *The Question of Existence.* The finals were held three days following the death of my father.

Dad still lived in the Quirinale Hotel in Hillbrow. Our meetings were infrequent. I'd pass the hotel on my way to Wits and drop in to see him. Sometimes I'd stay for a meal. On Sundays, Paddy (my brother now back from America), Dad and I would drive to the Wanderers Club to watch hockey, and eat scones and jam with tea.

Some Sundays we'd all go over to my sister's house. Margot was divorced and lived with her two children in Dunkeld. I thought Dad was only interested in my work, in how much money I was making and if I was thinking of getting married. There was a waiting between us. I'd wait, thinking, "What can I tell him? What can we talk about?" He'd hold the silence, waiting. He'd sit out at the swimming pool waiting for Margot to get out of bed on Sunday morning. Margot rambled on about her work as a theatrical agent, all her clients and their idiosyncrasies. Vastly entertaining, she was also an excellent hostess. But before she came downstairs on Sundays, Dad would sit in the early morning sun, head dropping towards his chest, waiting. But this Sunday, Selma and Jack brought Dad to have a meal with me at my flat in Yeoville. Dad and I decided we'd drive to the deli and choose all his favourite food.

My car was parked up the street. I hurried off to bring it closer to the kerb so Dad could get in easily. He waited on the sidewalk for a minute then stepped off the pavement into the road to wait for me. Seconds later he changed his mind, turned and tried to mount the small ridge onto the pavement. He fell on his back into the street. Like a beetle he lay splayed, his legs jerking in the air. His cane had fallen out of his hand and lay in the road alongside him. Two passers-by hurried to help him to his feet as I leapt out of the car.

"I'm all right," he repeated, "I'm fine."

A heaviness sank into my bones as if my heart had dropped anchor. A dread descended. "Oh my God," I whispered frantically, "please let me get him to a doctor!" He sat in the passenger seat staring ahead. "It's my fault. Had I been ready this would never have happened; had I not left him alone at the kerb he would not have fallen." Stab, stab, stab.

Back in his room we called the doctor who pronounced he was just shocked, bruised and prescribed rest. From that moment I grew closer to my father. I felt responsible for his fall. I wanted to make up for that and for neglecting him so much. As much as I tried to feel close to him, it had never happened. Now it was beginning to. I came to understand that it wasn't necessary to entertain him, to shower him with talk. It was enough just to be there, to sit in the chair by the window and read as he slept. It was all right not to be a visitor, to be a daughter, to be taken for granted.

The bruises came and went but one remained. Dad had knocked his foot prior to his fall and there was a sore that hadn't healed. The doctor told him to keep his foot raised. Dad forgot to do this and the sore got worse. Emily Badela became his full-time nurse. She fed him, washed him, argued with him and finally she dressed him for the hospital. The morning before he left he passed a huge stool. Emily said to me: "Miss Michelle, I think your father is going over. So often before people go over, they pass everything out of their bodies. I think your father is ready to go."

Dad was slipped into a small green room. It was like a cell, horrid, with a tiny window. Dad was fully conscious but he wasn't making sense. "Kalinka they're taking my money," he'd grab my hand, pleadingly, "they won't give me my things." I was distressed and asked Emily what was happening. "It's his time," she said, "he's becoming senile." His foot turned gangrenous. The poison seeped up into his calf, past his knee. It kept moving. We had to make a decision. Either he was sedated with morphine, or his leg had to be amputated under his knee. We didn't want to see him die in agony or drugged to death; neither could I bear the thought of his leg being amputated. Was there no alternative?

On May 11th, 1985, Dad was operated on. He came out of the theatre hazy and incoherent. He stayed like that, waving his hand in the air to people we could not see. "Dad? Can you hear me?" No sound, just a gentle wave of his hand.

On May 14th I was home, tutoring. The phone rang. "Miss Friedman, please come down to the hospital. Your father's not doing well." In an instant the students were gone and I was on the road. Was he still alive? Could I see him? Could I be with him at the moment of his passing? It was too late. He had already breathed his last breath before the call was made. His body was covered in a sheet. He never returned to consciousness. Only his faithful friend Emily had been with him at his end. My aunt had already called the necessary people to administer the Jewish rite of preparing the dead for burial.

Gone. He was gone. There is no grabbing back the dead. They go irretrievably, leaving us with all our unfinished business, our untied ends, unspoken words and forgiveness unheard. Extinguished, quenched, erased, removed, silent. "Dad, come back, I haven't finished; there's so much I want to say, want to know, want to hear, want to hold you, want to make you happy again." Gone, quite.

When he was laid in the ground and blobs of earth fell on his coffin, I exploded like a burst-pipe, doubling over in loud unrestrained sobs. I stood to one side as if to spare the grievers my anguish. A small figure slipped through the crowd and an arm went around my shoulder. I turned. "Mom!" It was Emma Harrington. I fell into her arms. She was exactly who I needed.

Why was I so hard hit? Was I weeping for a father I never had? For an opportunity that could never be? The man who lay under the earth had been my father. He may not have been the father who gets it right all the time, but he was my father, and now he was wrenched away from me and lying in the ground.

Something buried in me would now begin to rise with his death. Because Dad was no longer harnessed by his physical form he was in a place where he could see and understand. Now he would be able to influence my life; he could help me to be happy. But first I had to shift my awareness.

In a room at the hotel, family and friends gathered to pray for Dad. We did not sit

Shiva — that is to stay home and allow ourselves to grieve while friends bring us food. I did not know what sitting *Shiva* was at that time. I was a newcomer to grieving. I didn't know where to put it, how to integrate it, so I pushed it somewhere behind me and carried on.

It was back to everyday life and the preparations for the Toastmaster's competition. The excitement mounted as local, then area, then regional competition passed and I was still in the running for national. As I watched the other speakers at the finals in Port Elizabeth a week after my Dad's death, I knew it was in the bag. "Thank you," I whispered to myself, tight with pre-performance readiness. All through the stages of planning and preparation I had kept in mind that I needed spiritual help in this. I leaned on God, clinging to my inner source of creative energy, relying on it to come through for me, to calm my nerves, to steady my hands, to open my mouth and to help me remember what I had to say! It was as if I were watching the divine in action. I won the award.

Then my head began to grow. Imperceptibly at first. As it gained in size, thoughts of my reliance on a finer thread of power wafted out the window, like a breeze catches a dandelion head on and whoosh — all gone! I had only eight weeks to write another speech for the International in Ohio — which I was going to win, again, of course. Since my fare to America was paid I decided to have a holiday and visit a number of places. My hour had come. Oh Dad, if you could see me now!

Although there were a number of South African attendees at the conference, and although I had invited a past student, who happened to be black and living in America, as my guest, I had no family member, no close friend beside me. In fact, I had no private life. I didn't think that would matter. I'd handle everything. On the morning of the competition I saw a woman sitting serenely eating breakfast with a man — her partner, husband, lover? They seemed close — a unit. I wanted someone there, someone to hold me, to reassure me. I was scared and I'd forgotten my inner guide. I was doing this alone. The breakfast woman won the international. I couldn't believe it. Yes, I agreed she had prepared a fitting speech, but mine had been poetry, mine had been profound, mine had been earth-shattering. What was the matter with the judges? Wasn't this America where individuality and uniqueness counted? My dream plummeted, hit the ground head first and splattered, splaying widely to the winds. The party was over. Turn off the music, empty the ashtrays, pick up the glasses, scrape the plates, fill the dishwasher, rearrange the furniture, switch off the few remaining lights and trundle to bed. Think about who hadn't come and why and sleep with the thought of eating the leftovers tomorrow. It was all over.

At the same time I felt as if a rock had been lifted off my back. I was free of the burden of having to be great. I also remembered I had forgotten God. What had happened to my relationship? It was a piece of paper I had scrunched up, tossed haphazardly into a basket and missed. It lay on the floor. I hungered for that intimacy, for the stillness, the silence, the peace pocket inside me.

"Where were you?" I asked.

"I was there," It answered, "where were you?"

"I was busy becoming famous."

What would I have done had I won the international? I'd have evaporated on the bubble of acclaim.

It was in a spirit of soberness that I left Ohio to continue touring America. I was searching inside myself for content as a speaker. One of the founding members of the National Speakers Association, Michael Aun, insisted I consider becoming a professional speaker, but what would I say, what was my message? I didn't have one. So I was a nun, so what? Hundreds of women entered and left the convent. I had nothing to say. I wanted to meet someone who did. New Orleans gave me that opportunity.

Tadd was a street musician, a guitarist in a wheelchair. In his final year before college, Tadd was acknowledged as "Person of the Year". On the brink of a college career he looked ahead to the striving, the competition, all that would be necessary for him to continue his success. It was too much. He jumped off the top of the football stadium roof and landed on the field, alive. Twelve hours later he was rushed to hospital. He would be in a wheelchair the rest of his life. But he could use his hands, use his head; he was still a person. After grappling with all this meant, Tadd began to write music and songs. He won a talent competition. The prize? A two-week vacation in New Orleans. He never left.

Tadd sang about inner discovery. What kept him going was that which he discovered about himself, inside himself. The music was haunting, full of a painful joy, a lightness that grew from the dark. It wasn't easy listening. I sat alongside as he played in the dusk, glad that the growing night could wrap my tears in its full folds. A longing, an insatiable hunger, haunted me. Tadd touched my soul, helped me meet my yearning. It was freedom I craved, a freedom of spirit, a flying. Tadd's values were floodlights in a sea of fire-crackers. He lived simply and humbly; he was alive to life. That's what I wanted.

On my return to South Africa, my head was still bigger than my body. I relapsed into the hurly-burly of course upon course and began to forget about Tadd and his message. I forgot the clarity of my perceptions in the French Quarter. I also began to forget about God again. Grief over Dad still lay folded in a hidden drawer and from my ball-of-wool centre threads unravelled arbitrarily, loosely lying anywhere.

One afternoon around four, as I unlocked the safety doors Mom insisted I get, my two cats sped past me to play on the stairs. "Let them go," I thought, "I'll dump these groceries and then fetch them." I left both the safety door and the front door open as I dashed to get the phone. It was one of the Citibank students, Isaac. We talked for a while. I replaced the receiver, walked back down the passage from my office towards the front door to close it.

As I passed the entrance to my bedroom on my left, I was aware of a shape framing the door. Two strong arms grabbed me. One hand clapped over my mouth, the other hugged my waist. I spun round. We did a mad dance for a few seconds. He was dressed in khaki; a stocking covered his face, gloves, his hands. My mind raced. Who is this idiot? What fool friend would pull a trick like this? It's not funny! "Shut up," he said. I must have been screaming. I looked to my left. He held a knife against my neck. "Shut up or I'll use this." My God, I'm being attacked.

He pushed me down to my knees in the passage, tied my wrists together, bound a piece of cloth over my mouth and ordered me to lie on my back. He darted into the bedroom returning with a pillow which he placed under my hips. I was wearing a pair of beige slacks and a black T-shirt I had bought in New York. I had a period.

"Do you live alone?" he asked, as he knelt between my legs, pushed them open and began to undo the button on my slacks. I thought about the answer as the fear enveloped me furiously. If I said yes, he might stay. If I said no and no-one came, he might kill me.

"Sometimes."

"You're lovely. I've watched you for a long time."

Where does he live so he can watch me?

My slacks were off and he was pulling down my panties.

"I'm wearing a tampax."

He found the thread and pulled it out.

Maybe this will stop him, I thought. It didn't.

"You've got a problem, can I help you?"

He didn't answer. He pulled my T-shirt over my head and began to paw at my breasts.

"I can't breathe," I complained.

"You will," he replied, with almost a laugh in his voice.

When I spoke to him some instinct told me to end every sentence with "sir".

In my terror I began to pray. I muttered the Hail Mary as loudly and as clearly as I could. "Hail Mary, full of grace, the lord is with thee, blessed art thou amongst women and blessed is the fruit of thy womb, Jesus. Holy Mary, mother of God, pray for us sinners, now and at the hour of our death, Amen." I meant every word. He laid himself on top of me. I closed my eyes and turned my face away. He stayed there for about ten seconds. He pulled back onto his haunches and untied his belt. "Holy Mary, mother of God," I continued. This is it, I thought. But I was wrong.

Nothing happened. He knelt there. I realised he had no erection. He couldn't rape me. A rush of relief surged through me, then panic again. "What will he do now?"

"Turn over."

"Yes, sir".

"I'm going to untie your hands and tie your feet. I don't want you to follow me."

He was going to go! I'm saved! Was he going? Maybe it was a terrible trick and he'd hide only to pounce back? I stopped breathing as he untied my hands and tied my feet. He stood up, stumbled past me and out one of the doors.

I lay for a second or two, hardly daring to believe he'd gone. Rolling over I sat up, untied my feet and with my slacks curled around my ankles, hobbled to the front door, locked it, got dressed and ran to the phone, dialled 999. Shaking I looked in the mirror to see my face cut, blood on my mouth. In shock I was aware I'd escaped. Who or what did I have to thank for this?

My attacker was a first-timer. His hands shook, he was anxious. That was a factor. I'd swung the power around by questioning him, confronting him with his problem, taking back control. I had called on a spiritual power to be there with me. In those moments of prayer I lay in complete resignation and reliance upon God. And God was a woman for me, because only a woman could understand me then.

A man I was close to at that time took me to the police station and tried to comfort me as much as he could. Another male friend gave me a gun. My brother wasn't prepared for me to go to his house because he didn't want the children to know. My mother spoke her concern but she didn't come to Johannesburg. I had to deal with this alone.

I left that apartment never to return. I had taken over the bond from the university with money my father had left me. I rented it out and moved to Sandton. I had to wade through waves of guilt, shame, blame, anger, hostility towards men, fear and weakness. I couldn't allow any of this to surface immediately. I had a job to do, a course to complete. I was so relieved that my attacker wasn't a black man. It was bad enough I'd been the victim of an attempted rape, but I worked in the black community and I had to go to work the next day. I had to be all right. Or so I thought. I could've cancelled the class; called in ill and allowed myself time. I thought about the class, not about my shock, my need. I was in denial.

As soon as I had found another place to live, I flew to Cape Town to rest. There my mother made an appointment for me to see a massage therapist. Gillian, a slender slip

144

of a woman, smoothed oils over my body — an aromatherapy treatment. It was mild but the results were the opposite. All the tension, the horror, the trauma held in my body now let go. A crane opening its jaws in mid-air, my body released its load. Its cargo removed, my body lay inert, feverish. I couldn't eat, could hardly sip water. My life force slunk away. Yes, I had been violated. Didn't my body remember how this had happened when I was a small child? Wasn't that fear now reinforced, bobbing up on the surface like a corpse surfacing in a river? I knew nothing about this past; it had not yet skimmed the surface of my consciousness, but my body held it. I had to regain strength and then find my path once more. I decided to try a homeopathic cure, move to gentler treatments, take care of my body in a non-intrusive, supportive way.

Why had this happened to me? Had I attracted it in some way? Was I being warned? Where was my direction? I had none. My relationship with God was used in emergencies. I no longer went to Mass. I went to a few spiritualist church sessions in an attempt to find out where my father was and how I could get in touch with him but, by and large, I was drifting. Working for the sake of it, I was working far too hard. I still had no centre and I wanted one. I wanted there to be a core inside me, a core of me, or a core of something. What was it?

Shortly after the attempted rape I met an Afrikaans man and developed a co-dependent relationship immediately. When we broke up I felt as if I had ripped out my solar plexus and not replaced it with anything. There was a huge hole inside me; without him there was no me. I panicked. The symptoms of my post-attack period returned. I was feverish, unable to eat, terrified. Jan immediately returned to his ex-girlfriend and that made me crazier still. I'd phone him at all hours. Once I sat huddled outside his apartment in the early hours of the morning waiting for him. I couldn't stop myself. I wept as if I were losing a lifetime friend, or lover, husband or child. But whom had I lost? I had given Michelle to Jan. Now, with Jan gone, Michelle was gone too. I felt that it was impossible to enjoy anything, to be with anyone, to do anything, to go on living. It was as if all the blood had been drained out of me. He held my life-force. I had given it away. Now I had to take it back, to find it, to reclaim my self. But where was that self?

I was alone with the emptiness once more. My work could not fill the vacuum; a man could not fill the vacuum; an audience could not fill the vacuum; cats and a dog could not fill the vacuum. I could not face the vacuum, hold it, confront it, embrace it. I tried to replace it, but the replacements were unsuccessful grafts. Busy looking outside myself I was unable to see how I was missing myself, how I failed to give attention to myself. I had to fix everyone else, or be there for everyone else, but I was never there for me.

Tired, listless, hungry, my body dragged. Where could I begin to take care of myself? A friend and actor from our days in children's theatre, Magda van Streepen, reappeared. She had cancer and was attempting to cure it by eating certain foods. Would I like to attend a cooking class? It was as simple as that. That cooking class would be the linchpin drawing me back into myself, and then beyond to my soul.

What had I accomplished over the past five years since I left the convent? I'd accumulated money; had bought an apartment and all the mod-cons necessary to be part of the twentieth century; I'd gained a reputation as a fine trainer, a gifted and mesmerising speaker. Much healing had been exchanged between the people on my courses and myself; I'd given life and had received. I'd lost my father, survived an attempted-rape and severed an unhealthy relationship. I was still bleeding internally from these three.

Their combination pushed me into a new sphere. Why did I have a crisis? With the loss of my father, my heart opened, my soul stirred. My failure to become World Toastmaster prepared me to look into my heart; it opened me to listen to Tadd; it caused me to look for direction and substance in my life. The attack in my home, in my place of safety, loosened deep memories held by my body, memories that the death of my father had awakened. The loss of a lover exposed me to my dependency, my emptiness. It urged me to find the path to fill that gap. What the path was I didn't know. I was being readied for a swerve in a new and true direction that would take me to Switzerland, Israel and America. A new cycle of healing and growth was initiated. And food was the key.

steps to heal the heart

Workaholic?

On a scale from one to one hundred, how important is your work to you? Do you have a life outside of your work? Or do you work so as not to think or not to be alone? Is there a gap inside you that work fills? When do you get in touch with that gap? Can you stay there and write what it feels like, or draw the gap?

Father

What thoughts immediately come to you with this word? Write them down.

Do you know your father, or did you know him?

Did he know you? Does he know you now?

What do you remember most about him? What would you most like to forget?

If you grew up without a father being present, how do you feel now?

Write a letter to the man who fathered you. Tell him everything you want to. Seal the letter and then decide what you want to do with it. Keep it or tear it up or send it?

Wait a while, you will know how long, then, one day, reply to yourself as your father.

Victory and defeat

Stephen Covey writes: "Our private victories must preceed our public victories."

In my competitive climb with Toastmasters, I had no private victory. I needed external acclaim. I wasn't able to celebrate with myself first. I gave little or no thought to failure. When I lost I was thrown back on myself in relief and it felt like a homecoming.

It was as if I'd been away from myself for a long time.

Does anything in your life sound like this?

Did you ever want something or someone really badly and then when you weren't successful, what happened? How did you feel?

How did you get over it? That is, if you are over it.

If you are not over it, can to talk to someone about your feelings?

Can you celebrate your victories, small, medium and large with yourself first?

Rape

What does rape mean to you?

Have you been raped?

Have you found people to help you through your experience?

Or have you kept it to yourself and the memory gnaws away at you?

I know people — men and women — who haven't told anyone what happened to them as a child. Now they are adults and they are in unloving relationships. Only now are they beginning to see how their experience of rape has affected them. They thought they could put it away and it would go away. Many adults who have been raped also keep the secret buried. Maybe it's time to let go.

Writing about your experience will do two things. It will resurface pain, fear, anger.

It could make you feel insecure, vulnerable, hurt. As you keep writing you will get all your feelings out. Stay with them and take care of yourself. Be very kind and gentle to yourself. If you need to be quiet and alone, do that. Try not to run away from the

my life

uncomfortable feelings. Cry. It will help you. Eat food that nourishes you. Be warm.

Give yourself time. Let people know that you prefer to stay with yourself for a while. Don't expect yourself to be upbeat. It is "Handle with Care" time for yourself.

Keep writing. Slowly you will sense a feeling of lightness as if you can begin to let the past dim. This will not happen at once. You may do a lot of writing. Drawing also helps. It gets the experience out of you and onto paper. That's the first step to releasing it.

You might want to share this with a close friend. You will know when and who.

When you are ready, write to the man or men who raped you. Tell them everything you want them to know. Include what you think their punishment should be. Don't censor yourself. Just let it out. It doesn't have to be nice. It doesn't have to be proper. It gives you the chance to say all the horrible things you want to without judgement. Forget what everyone has told you about suppressing your emotions and give it stick until you are through.

Write it and leave it. It isn't necessary to edit it or even have it make sense. It's a rush of words. When you have written the letter, burn it or listen inside to what you must do with it. Once the feelings are expressed, you'll be able to move on to another level over time. You can't miss this step though.

Write to others who could have protected you, who could have prevented the rape or abuse. Tell them everything you want to. Get it out.

If any of these people are still alive you might feel you'd like to take a further step. When the time is right, consider telling that person face to face, or sending them the letter. Talk to a person you trust before you do this and get support.

If you know a man who has committed a rape, what are you doing about it?

Find someone to tell first, someone who will assist you in taking the wisest steps.

If you are reading this and you have raped a woman or a man, or if you have ever forced a person into sex, write about it.

Write in detail what led up to that act. Go through it again. Where do you stand now? Have you changed? Were you caught? Have you served a sentence? Are you serving one now? I believe that a person must be in pain before he can do a violent act. Are you in touch with your pain? Can you express it? Can you forgive yourself?

Write a letter to yourself and answer it.

Then write a letter to the person you raped. Tell her or him everything you want to. If you could make it up to that person what would you do? What can you do now?

Co-dependent relationships

Sometimes we act on the rebound and fall in love because we're needy. That's what I did. Jan was my answer to my problems. He would take care of me. I would allow my happiness to be dependent on him. I left myself — without so much as a goodbye — and put him in my place. He did the same. I remember one afternoon he called and asked me to meet him at a café. He told me how important I was to him, how little his work meant. He was making me the reason for his existence. He began to talk about commitment.

I should have asked him: "What is it about your work that leaves you empty? What is it about your sport that doesn't fulfil you?" I should have asked myself the same questions. Neither of us was ready to look at the gap.

The result of this co-dependent relationship is that I got angry. I thought I was angry with him. I was angry that I had held myself back; that I had prostituted myself so that

149

my life

someone else could feel okay. It wasn't Jan. It was my denial of my needs, my personality, my dreams, my drive. That made me mad.

What about you? Are you in a friendship or a relationship where there's five percent of you and ninety-five percent of the other person? Where your happiness depends on his or her mood? What's the pay-off for you? What is the worst that could happen if you take yourself back? If you choose not to divorce yourself but to reconcile yourself to yourself? To come home?

Can you find your centre again by admitting your loneliness, your neediness, that you have a hard time coping by yourself but that you are brave enough to give it a try? Who will support you in this brave action? Someone you trust.

Perhaps there is some very hidden pain that you do not know about, something that happened when you were too small to realise what was going on. This might be the trigger that pushes you into co-dependent relationships. This might be causing the gap.

I didn't yet know that I was abused as a small child. All the shame and self-blame still huddled within me. I didn't know what to do with all the anger inside, all the unworthiness. What right did I have to be a person anyway? I was unlovable. How can you do things for and with yourself in a loving way? Can you start now?

Lemonade from lemons?

After the attempted rape I started to move back to a spiritual life — back to my Jewish roots. The darkness turned into light. This perception was built through my relationship with God and through our combined effort not to let that incident mess up my life, but rather to use it to redirect my life.

What about you? What happened, small or big, that could have held you back, could have stopped you from going on and making the most out of your life? Write, draw, speak about, design something that symbolises your victory. You were given a lemon and you made lemonade. Have you acknowledged your courage in doing this? How have you rewarded yourself?

Part 4

Macrobiotic Michelle

Chapter 1 *Macro-movement*

Can something so basic, so every-day like food be the turning point, the swoop into another consciousness? I was desperately tired. Rung out like an old rag — as if a cleaning lady had washed the floors of Versailles with me, then started again with the Louvre. This flatness made me consider responding to an invitation to attend a cookery class. There was nowhere else to go. I'd been neglecting both food and my spiritual life. Now they were brought together.

Since I left the convent I hadn't put much emphasis on cooking for myself. Oh no, that would mean I'd have to take care of myself and I was always waiting for my knight in shining armour to do that. I fed my body food that could hardly be called balanced. No meat, all dairy and sweets. My body had been violated physically and emotionally by the attack and I continued this by my refusal to take care of it, to respect it. Not surprisingly, it more or less stopped. A tyre refusing to carry the car, my body was flat. I needed to be healed — my body needed to be cared for, my heart needed to be focused, and my soul was laden with dust, suffocating.

In many subtle ways it's easy to say no to life. No, I don't want to live, so I'll commit suicide very slowly and smoke my life away. No, I don't want to live so I'll stay in a job I hate and die inside. No, I don't want to live so I'll remain in a relationship that stifles me because I'm already in a coffin. No, I don't want to live so I'll live in the past or hope for the future. No, I don't want to live so I'll eat fast foods, drink coffee, grow ill and it'll all be over at last!

The cooking class Magda invited me to was in a sumptuous home in a huge kitchen. Into this room glided our cook and hostess, Elaine Sher. Twenty people of both sexes sat silently entranced as she talked and explained, deftly juggling pots, ingredients, dishes. There was a hush of awe as if we were witness to a holy ritual. Hanging on every word, we listened to information about energy in food, its connection to the universe, its relation to our bodies and who we were on the scale of creation. I paid careful attention.

After two hours of waiting, the food was served. In spite of our hunger, we ate it slowly, chewing thoughtfully. It was as if I was tasting light. There wasn't that heaviness I usually felt after a large meal. There was no dip. Instead there was a taking-off, a lightness, a delicacy of spirit, a clarity of mind, a sensitivity of awareness. I drove home happier than I had been in a long time. A shift had started.

I am convinced we grow in spirals. As I complete one circuit, I shift into another and the circle continues on that plane. It seemed to me that I had shot into a new incarnation in this life. It was as if I didn't have time to waste going through the process of dying, death, the funeral and the chaos it leaves behind. No time to move over to the other side, ruminate, make decisions and return. I was Ms Michelle Friedman one day; the next I was Macrobiotic Michelle and my friends feared I had finally flipped my lid. They were right.

It wasn't easy for them to follow me in this course of madness. I understood. What could I eat now that I had become a "born-again macrobiotic"? *Kombu* and *wakame, tempeh* and *miso* were not English, I had to agree, but they were delicious, and wouldn't you like to come to lunch? Besides which, I lost a lot of weight and I hadn't much in the first place. Maybe it was all the time it took to cook! My body began to shed whatever it no longer needed. My bust sank to three sizes smaller, as did my entire body.

I could fit into tiny men's jeans. My hair left my head. It fell out slowly, as if it had some place else to go. I waited anxiously. New hair sprouted; healthy hair, shining hair, happy hair. I would not die.

I believe healing is a matter of shedding what we are holding. It's more taking off than putting on; going back more than moving forward. It's a return to what was always there, hidden under the morass of our experience. How do we get to it? Starting from the outside was my way. The body, which is also the mind, held all my memories; memories of this life, memories of others, perhaps. It had been jolted into an openness and was now receptive. It took to this untainted food, to whole grains and beans and fresh vegetables and *miso* soup, and rejoiced in no longer having to put up with sugar and dairy and white flour. A cleansing was on. Move away the debris and let's get to where the treasure is. I thought the treasure was the food, the lifestyle. It was only the titbit tempting me to follow it further.

There was something else. Elaine was Jewish. She maintained a kosher household. She didn't attend synagogue but her husband and children did. On Friday evenings at the table they lit candles, blessed the wine and broke the bread.

"You know, Michelle," Elaine remarked casually one day when we were not doing anything of particular importance, "it wouldn't surprise me if you returned to Judaism."

"What?" I asked, incredulous. It was like offering a person a coat on a hot day. "Whatever for?" I responded. Nothing could have been further from my consciousness. I was in my Japanese era now — cooking as if I'd been born into it, as if it was all so familiar, as if I'd done it before. Although the names were strange and the food was completely other, it was not entirely foreign to me. The recipes worked; the food came together under my hands. I wasn't in another country; that place was inside me. Why would I need Judaism?

Inside my body lived fibroids and I thought I'd have to have them removed. I asked Elaine and she suggested I attempt to stick to a macro-diet and see what that could do for me. Maybe they'd go away. It was worth a shot. She also suggested while I was about it, that I go to Switzerland and have a consultation with the master of macro life, Michio Kushi. In the summer of 1986 I booked to go to Lenk for the world macrobiotic conference, then to Kiental, for a spiritual seminar, followed by a six-week intensive Level One on the macrobiotic way of life.

my life

steps to heal the heart

Letting go

"I believe healing is shedding what we're holding. It's more a taking off than a putting on; going back before moving forward. It's a return to what was always there before." What is your opinion of this statement? Has there been a time in your life when you told somebody something you'd been holding in for a long time? Did you ever feel guilty about something you did, even something small, and have hidden it still? Could you tell someone now? Or perhaps there was a major incident in your life that still needs to be cleared. Can you write about this now?

Tears as an expression of release

I cried a lot in the convent. Some of it was relief, a feeling of safety. Over the years I have continued to cry. Sometimes I wondered if I'd ever stop crying. What about you? What is your relationship with tears? Do you allow yourself to cry? Or do you wait until it is "okay" to cry, like at a wedding or a funeral? As a man, what is your attitude to tears?

Being led

Was it coincidence that my friend invited me to a cooking class? I don't think so. This was a vital stage in my life. From such a small thing so much happened. Write about something that happened in your life that started innocuously. Do you think it was a coincidence?

Chapter 2 *Macro-mulch*

Summer was a shock of flower-studded mountains caressed by sparkling streams in the cocoon of Switzerland. Clear bright blue skies with breasts of snow hovered like a protective mother. Pretty paths wound their way through chambers of bent branches, leaf-laden where heavy musk dankness danced with delicate slivers of sunlight. Every opening offered another eye-feast, soul-soar. It was beauty to a point of pain. Against this backdrop I was about to question the foundations of my beliefs; extend myself by rising to meet circumstances calling for courage and action; curl into an intimate relationship and so begin the healing process of my relationship with my father and men and glimpse promises of personal peace which would lead to my spiritual home.

The conference at Lenk provided an introduction into the multi-faceted world of macrobiotics. I was naïve. In my excitement and enthusiasm I was sure that macrobiotics was "The Answer" for the world. It's a common mistake. Anything can be the answer, or part of the answer, for anybody at any time, if you're looking for answers. It may not be the answer for anyone else, may not even be in their question file. I know now that it's not so much a question-answer scenario, like turning on a tap and filling a glassful of water, but rather it's plunging into a river that swirls about you. You stop on a rock and bathe in the sun for a minute, an hour or a year; you lie on a raft and navigate rapids; you sit on the bank watching the water swirl; you glide on your back and let it take you where it will. Maybe you even build a boat and think you're on dry land for a bit. It's the river of life where questions and answers meet and melt and flow. At the right time, it's the right thing.

I was surprised by the lack of excitement at the conference. Usually the proximity of so many people results in an explosion of energy, noise, activity. This was a different kind of energy. People were calm. There was breathing space. I was stepping into another world, an underwater world where there wasn't much noise and lots of dancing movement. I took two four-hour sessions which focused on sensory awareness and opening the heart.

"Shake it up, girl, get alive, feel, smell, taste, touch, see! Say yes to being."

"Okay, half-yes. Ask me later for the other half."

My feet were in the doorway of macrobiotics. I was enthused and cautious. I realised a lot of sick people were present; people with serious illnesses. Some people just looked sick. There was a disproportionate amount of talk about food, as if that was all there was to life; as if every occurrence was somehow directly or indirectly related to what someone had eaten the day before. There had to be a balance between rigidity and indiscriminate eating. Teachers were looked upon with awe and almost adoration. They must just be people too? I was beginning to realise that, as with any system, there's a range of responses and authenticity. The good, the bad and the ugly were drawn to this as to everything else. I was a bit of each, I hoped.

Michio Kushi guided us through the four-day spiritual seminar. I was ready. It was as if he held a huge scythe and hacked away at the roots of what I thought I believed. Belief is of major importance in Christianity. "Do you believe Jesus is the son of God? Do you believe in the resurrection of the body?" As a long blade of grass I clung to the soil while simultaneously baring my neck to the blade: "Slice me, free me, or at least shake me up a little!" Room had to be made.

Michio discussed arrogance, original sin, karma, death. Together with the lectures and group discussions we meditated, chanted and ate very simply — rice and *miso* soup. What is the result? The participant in an attitude of readiness, openness. The body is given food which harmonises with it, puts no demands on it, just blends in evenly and easily so it is at rest.

The mind is fed questions, offered alternatives, jostled. The spirit sings, moves into a greater awareness, another level of lucidity, a clearer way of seeing and a shift occurs because the instrument — in this case, Michio — imparts his presence and knowledge from a place of contained and concentrated light-energy. He is a force for awareness and growth. It's like sitting in the noonday sun, but this heat is an X-ray. It pushes into the root revealing the seedbed. That which Michio imparted to me struck and sank. It would never leave me. Only a year later would it begin to surface in my conscious mind as I groped for understanding and happiness.

Questions flew. How can one be a person of true humility? For what are we to blame? What is guilt? Innocence? Purity? How can I balance my life? Is there a good and a bad? Is there just an Is? What is the purpose of my life? How can I know this surely? How can I complete my purpose? What is death? Who is death? Do I want religion? These were not seeds newly planted. They were already there but the soil had not been fertilised and there was neither light nor water. What Michio did was to activate the seeds; he provided the light and water. His words struck home. I was on the way home; I didn't know it, had no idea how I'd recognise it if I saw it.

In the evening sessions, we'd talk randomly. Since the death of my father I had hoped there was some way I could contact him, find out how and where he was. Michio told me he could see the spirit of my father on the left side of my face, hovering, still here. He suggested a ritual I might find useful in allowing the spirit of my father to go on. Michio's secretary was Jewish. She offered me her prayer book where I could say *Kaddish*, the Jewish prayer for the dead. That made a whole lot of sense to me. Dad would respond to that. I took her book to my room. As I said the prayers I felt I was doing something important, something that would help my father and help me. It also opened me to continue the relationship with my father.

Another participant, Ehud Lebowitz, was Israeli. On Friday night in the dining-room we lit candles welcoming the sabbath. I didn't question it, I just did it and it felt like that's the way it always was.

Psychologically I was still carrying the child I'd aborted at twenty-one. Michio saw her around my waist. It seems all of us who take this action carry with us in the area of our womb the spirit of the life we aborted. To the best of my understanding, I followed his advice as to how I could release her. I couldn't let her go. She would be with me for a while still. I had to continue to carry her. Still to come was the grieving and mourning; the saying of goodbye and forgiving myself. None of this could be short-circuited.

As the spiritual seminar ended, I felt full and centred. Walking in the streets of Berne, I could pass the shops without wanting anything. I had it all. What could be more than what I already had inside me?

my life

steps to heal the heart

I did it my way

When you walk into a shop to buy a dress or a suit, there are many to choose from. A kind of marriage is what we're after, a marriage between a piece of clothing and a person. The final choice will be different for each person, but the role of the garment is the same. It clothes. It contains the person. If, to our dismay, we discover our host is wearing exactly the same outfit, it will look different on her; it will smell different because of her perfume or her body. It will not be the same; it can't be.

Every genuine body of religious teaching winds like a river to the sea — the same sea. Because each of us is who we are, the way in which we reach the open sea accords with our own particular mode of being. It may be that my way to God-ness, the garment I choose to wear is called "The way of Christ". Maybe it is "The way of Buddha"; maybe it is "The Jewish way". It is what fits me best, what fits my soul, and until I find it I'll be shopping at malls, dipping into faiths or concepts for as long as necessary. That's also why there is no "right" way, because I am not you and you are not me. You take one road and I'll take another, and if our desire is genuine, we'll both get there. There's a certainty about going home.

What has your experience been in shopping around for a way, your way, soul-wise?

What are the disciplines, courses, therapies, quests, rituals you've taken part in? Where are you now? Create that which expresses your journey or where you are now.

Chapter 3 *Macro-man*

*M*y beliefs had been questioned, shaken up and sent spinning. The process was at the point of disintegration as pieces lay splayed all over the universe of my mind-soul. In time they would regroup into their original pattern assembled before time began. Now there was a waiting, an openness in which to conceive.

My heart became hungry. In the six weeks ahead I would meet circumstances demanding courageous action as I tiptoed into intimacy for the first time. The healing process of my relationship with my father and men began. It arrived in the shape of Jussi from Sweden.

Although Jussi was considerably younger than me, I sensed that our relationship had to do with that which was beyond age, beyond form. There was growing to do, either from a past neither of us knew of or for a future we couldn't imagine. Whatever the reason (and we didn't have to know), Jussi came to me like an angel — a messenger from another consciousness to help me on my journey. And I for him.

On the first evening of the Level One, Two and three intensive, all the participants gathered to hear Michio Kushi speak. At least eighty people from all over the world sat on the floor. Mainly Europeans, the students in Level One were Italian, French, Scandinavian, German, and one person was from Iceland, Ziggy. There were two Israelis, Bella and Yakov. Simon was from New York and I was South African. Michio began to talk about AIDS and Africa.

"Anybody here from Africa?" he asked.

Elaine and I raised our hands.

"You want to tell us how it is there?" he continued.

Elaine rose, stepped out in front of the group and began to explain to everyone how black people in South Africa were just "not ready". As she spoke I heard, again, all the arguments I had lived with for the years I was there. Elaine was certainly a powerful healer. Through her I had come to macrobiotics. She had opened her home to me, and her heart, and she was important in my life. As I listened I understood that her experience of Africa was very different to mine. I jumped to my feet.

"I disagree with you, Elaine. This is not how it is."

"Please take the floor," gestured Michio graciously.

Knowing that what I would say was in conflict with Elaine, and sorry this was the case, I felt compelled to share what I knew. I sketched the social and political set-up and the privileged position of the white person. I told of how difficult it was for a black person to burst through the circle of control and limitation set by the system. I explained the different education systems for black students and white students and how apart the children grew. I voiced the frustrations of black students, outlined the few opportunities open to them, gave examples of their courage and endurance. Yes, there were white people who worked against the system and many who lost their lives for a new South Africa, but the majority were asleep. I brought it down to individual responsibility and suggested each of us needs to be healed from our own prejudices no matter what form or shape they take. I shared my own journey in releasing some of my preconceptions and insecurities.

The words leapt out like a waterfall. I felt I had been given a chance to speak from my heart, from all that had been burning within it as I had listened to hundreds of stories from black South Africans struggling with the pain of apartheid. I gushed it out, and was silent. A burst of applause returned to me. I realised I was speaking to Europeans, people who were keenly anti-South Africa. Had I not jumped up they might have torn Elaine limb from limb. Our differing viewpoints only served to highlight how complex the situation was. I felt embarrassed and exhilarated that the words I had spoken made a difference.

Elaine kept away from me for a day or two, but then, in keeping with her generous nature, she recovered. In Johannesburg, on our return, she met a group of black students I was working with. It was an eye-opener for her. On another level it was good for me to realise that I wasn't just the shadow behind Elaine, that I had something to contribute. I had been somewhat overawed by her wealth, her power, her knowledge of macrobiotics. This was my weakness. I wasn't meeting her as an equal. Had she been less rich I may have felt more equal. I allowed money to be a measure of success as a person.

Jussi was in the audience. Directly afterwards he approached me as I was drinking tea in the dining room and said how he appreciated my emphasis on the individual. He was taller than me, thin, almost gangly with long brown hair, green eyes. I was in my late thirties; he was in his early twenties. Still enmeshed in what I had said, I assumed I needed to explain something. "I just wanted to thank you," he assured me. I didn't think more of it, and the next day the course began. We were just two participants. We sat through lectures on the body, macrobiotic philosophy, cooking classes, shiatsu training. It was a packed programme with little spare time.

One rare free day everyone deserted the house to do their own thing. I didn't know where to go, what to do, so I waited. Jussi arrived late for breakfast.

"What are you going to do?" he asked.

"Perhaps I'll go walking," I replied.

"Can I join you?"

"Sure."

I rushed upstairs to put on my shoes and on the way met Simon looking like the original Swiss mountaineer.

"I'm off to this little village. I've hired a car. Want to join me?"

"Jussi and I thought we'd go walking."

"Bring him."

Jussi thought that a great idea as he had slipped class and walked for hours the day before and his legs were quite sore. A friend of mine, Helene, who worked in the kitchen, popped into my room.

"What are you doing?" she asked. I told her.

"Can I come?" Then we were four.

We drove to a quaint little Swiss village, parked the car and strolled in the small, winding streets. I noticed how Jussi would stop at a flower and hold his hand around it as if to sense it. I'd never seen anyone do that before. A wedding party burst from a small church on a cliff above us. Roses, small children, a donkey, clusters of well-wishers, confetti, a bride and groom, men in suits, women in white. The avalanche swept down the narrow road towards us, where we sat drinking beer and eating ice-cream directly in their wake. They curled around us like water and continued dancing down the street leaving us tingling with exhilaration at being wedged in the flow and feeling their feverish joy.

Helene's shift in the kitchen called her back to Kiental, while we boarded a boat which drifted dreamily on the lake. I sat between Simon and Jussi savouring the fresh, light air, switching my gaze from one beautiful face to the other. Simon was blond and beautiful; he was also coping with AIDS. This was to be his last glorious holiday before he left us for another journey.

On the way back I sat in the front seat. Jussi hunched behind me, leaned forward, his hands on my shoulders. That felt good. It was also a surprise. Introverted, he held an innerness that, when tapped, became like a ball of bright thread unravelling in splendour. That blink of blaze flicked over me like a revolving searchlight, like the sun shining off a mirror onto my face. I was a reflection of him, an echo reverberating back into the nothingness from which it came. Feather-light, we began to form.

Included in the course was an experience in the mountains, not unlike that which I had seen in Lesotho, Africa. Here, however, I had to be part of it. What we were being offered was a chance to learn about ourselves in an environment where that's all we had, ourselves, and where any limitations we experienced were more in our heads than anywhere else.

The twenty-plus of us included Simon, Jussi, Ziggy and Elin, from Norway. We were driven to a spot in the forest and left with our two guides. We set off walking down the river for miles. Obstacles blocked the way and, as a group, we had to overcome them. One of them was crossing the river. We had to grab a rope and jump with it across the water. No big deal. Except for Rosalina. For her, this was impossible. She refused. Italian and vocal, she screamed her resistance till the very mountains threatened to crumble if the noise persisted.

"It's your problem," the guide threw at us. "You all cross, or we all stay here."

He sat, pulled out a book and began to read.

Something had to be done or we'd be there all day.

"You're supposed to be a communication consultant," I said to myself. "Do something." Reluctantly I asked Anna, who could speak both English and Italian, to be an interpreter.

"What are you afraid of?" I asked Rosalina.

Anna translated and Rosaline expounded vociferously.

"The water will carry her away. She had a bad experience as a child, was nearly drowned."

It was difficult to imagine her drowning in this shallow water, but to her the water was a potential killer. What could we do to change her perception of the water?

"Tell her we'll stand in the water." I suggested. "We'll form a wall to her left, so the water won't be able to carry her away. If she falls and the water pushes her from the right, we'll be there to pick her up; if she swerves, we'll be standing there to break her fall." Anna told her.

The group were standing or sitting dejectedly, as though we were in a dead-end. Our guide still appeared to be entranced by his book. How can he read at a time like this?

"She will do it," Anna beamed. I was amazed she'd agreed.

Frowning, Rosalina hunched her reluctance as she brooded on the bank.

"Let's stand in the water," I beckoned to the group, hoping she wouldn't change her mind.

"In two rows!" improvised Anna. That made a wall on both sides of Rosalina.

Knee-deep in the river we stood, forming two lines, a passageway of safety for Rosalina, who now crouched on the bank nervously clutching the rope. She was a child again, reliving her moment of terror. She seemed immobilised. I bowed my head, "Please God." I had no idea if this would work. It was in her hands now. There was silence and waiting.

Olaf, our guide, had turned his face towards us. His eyes caught mine; they were glowing. Rosalina jumped. She sailed through the lines, her face holding tension and disbelief. We held our breath, prepared our bodies for contact. In a moment she was on the other bank, safe. A huge smile shook the darkness from her face; then she howled and wept with laughter, her large body rocking with glee. Cheers of applause accompanied her courage.

Jussi came up to me. "That was a good idea."

Simon whispered: "I like you."

I felt I had done something; that my being there had made a difference. I saw the direct results of my actions, with the help of God or grace. It was a sense of being a co-operator. Without Anna it wouldn't have happened; without the group it couldn't have happened. We were all knit together in our need for and dependence on one other. I felt significant. The group's attitude towards me shifted. I had won their respect.

Had I stopped to accept what was happening here I would have realised that this incident was a manifestation in concrete form of what I had been doing most of my life. I had been inspiring people to take a leap, to jump a hurdle, overcome a barrier. This may have taken the form of expressing their needs or fears, telling their story, leaving their jobs or relationships for what they knew they had to do, or loving a little more, or a little. Only it had not been so physically obvious. Most of it had taken place on an unseen level. Through me a spirit glided through the mist of their lives, unlocking doors, opening windows, allowing light and air to enter.

Jussi was particularly at home in the natural world. He pranced through the exercises, leapt along the routes, carried the backpacks, relished being in his element. We found ourselves walking together, talking, stopping to rest; sitting on rocks and allowing the warmth to penetrate; dipping in the water, swimming about gingerly in its iciness then scrambling for the sun.

In the evening we slept out in the open in sleeping bags. I wondered where and alongside whom I would sleep. I wanted to be close to Jussi but wasn't sure if that's what he wanted. The four of us chose a spot we liked. Simon slept a little way off by himself. Jussi laid his sleeping bag down.

"I don't have one," I said.

"You can share mine." he offered. Good, I thought, very good. We'll be together.

After the meal we eventually began to settle down for the night. Jussi wandered off to the river to meditate in the quiet. I lay in my tracksuit in his sleeping bag, wondering if he'd ever return. I began to doze. It was a splendid night. The stars were out, the air was clear. It was almost an insult to sleep through it.

As I lay, half-asleep, I was aware of Jussi's body, clothed, alongside me. I felt warm inside, to have him so close, so near. On another level I wondered if I would sleep. We were like two peas in a pod. There would be no sex. This was a friendship, yet it was already something more. There was a tenderness between us, an appreciation, a lightness.

As his body moved in the small space of the material, mine met his, moving into his shape. As I shifted, he shifted. It was as though we were dancing, sensing each other and moving to accommodate each other, comfortable in the closeness. A dark sensing. The measured sound of his breathing told me Jussi was asleep.

As I lay underneath the cover, I felt a fear of this closeness, a fear of not being able to breathe, as if I were dying. Then I remembered; I remembered who I was with, alongside whose body I lay. This was a man who could never harm me; this was a gentle spirit. In those moments it came to me that I was inside the womb of Father.

It was inside a maleness that I was lying; not a femaleness. Somewhere within my

165

concept of Father was this ability to breathe, this safety, this tenderness. It was real. I could feel it. Inside the male is also the softness, the warmth, the tenderness. The male womb is there; it's just not physical. Jussi and I were one, twins, inseparable. This was a knowing, a certainty. I lay half-awake as the night lived on, breathing surely in the dark, creating a safe space around me.

I was a little anxious about what we'd be called upon to do the following day. After a long walk we had to abseil down one of the smaller mountains to a ledge bordering on a chasm. Climbing backwards supported by a rope was something I'd done before, and the descent wasn't much of a distance. Crossing the gorge was more of a feat for me. A healthy iron bar extended across the gap to a mountain on the other side, about three hundred yards away. I was harnessed by a rope around my body, my head encased in a helmet and my hands protected by gloves. To cross, I had to inch my way over pulling my body with my hands as I hung like a monkey, my back dipping into the emptiness of space, my feet clasped around the bar. I was scared. It seemed such a long way to go. Setting off was not a problem and the first few yards went quite easily. The further out I got the worse I felt and right in the middle I stopped. The strap of the helmet was tight, pressing against my throat, making it difficult for me to breathe. My hands lost their strength and refused to pull me another inch. I hung suspended, stuck. Fear froze me; I was immobile.

Where had I experienced this before? I was between two shores; had left the safety and comfort of one for the unknown other, but en route the question of my being able to continue arose. I could not move myself; some person outside of me had to exert energy to bring me to the other side. I did not know this then, but what I was experiencing was my coming into the world. My body was remembering and trying to tell me. As I moved into the birth canal it seemed as if it would be an easy journey. Half-way down my mother stopped pushing, stopped wanting me to come out, resisted my birth. I was stuck. I felt her withdrawal. My body started to shut down to protect itself. I curled into myself as my extremities grew colder. I was losing life, beginning to die, feeling abandoned, rejected, isolated, alone. That's the place I go to when I am frightened, when I can't trust, when I fear someone who is close will leave me. I isolate myself in aloneness, and die a little. It's icy; it pushes people away and protects me. Unreachable, I shut down. In Jussi I was safe, not because I was in the womb of my mother, but because it couldn't be my mother — it had to be my father. It wasn't safe for me to be inside my mother because my mother didn't want me to live. She couldn't be trusted; she was my enemy. There were a number of reasons why I was a threat to my mother and none of these may have been in her conscious mind. But my body knew. It had imprinted this knowledge to be released at a time when I could bear it — only when I was almost fifty.

As I hung over this emptiness, the wind wafted round my body like a shroud. My wrists ached. I needed to drop my feet, loosen the helmet strap and breathe. "I'm stuck, I can't move! Pull me over!" As hands over the other side hauled me across, the rope around my waist tightened. Whose hands had pulled me into life? What made my mother begin to push again? Was it someone at her bedside, urging her to continue? Or was it life itself taking over, giving me birth. Yes, I think that was it. There was a power within me that could never abandon me, would never abandon me no matter what the circumstances of my birth were, nor the circumstances in which I might find myself in life. As I scrambled onto the mountain bank I couldn't think about the symbolic meaning of what I had experienced. I felt only fear, abandonment and failure. I blamed myself and sat humiliated, licking the wounds.

One by one the group crossed the gorge and we sat resting on the grassy bank before another abseil and one final feat to accomplish. I let everyone go ahead of me, so chagrined was I that I had been such a ninny. My ego was aching. At last it was my turn, and gingerly I lowered myself down onto a ledge jutting out of a cave. There Olaf waited. Whatever this entailed I determined to do it properly.

"Michelle," he smiled kindly, "I want you to go to the edge of the cave, and jump."

"Jump?"

"Yes, jump."

I watched as he tied a rope around my waist and handed me another helmet.

"Jump?"

"Yes, and when you jump, I want you to scream. Scream for everything inside of you; scream for everything you want, anything — just let it all out."

This was my last chance. I had to do it and I wanted to do it. I walked to the edge of the cave and looked down. Nothing. A few spots of shape below me. Where were the others? How do I get down there? In front of me — just air and sky. At my back, the mountain. My hands were free, I had nothing to hold onto. All that was required of me was to leap into space; to jump into nothingness; to trust what I could not see — to bank my life on it.

I leapt. Throwing my arms wide, I sailed through the air, renting it with a wild scream, a howl of joy. Like an eagle I swooped, straddling the sky, powerful and free. Yes I will live! Yes I will be happy! Forward and back I flew, each swing slowing me, towing me to the ground. Then it was underneath my feet, and arms held me, hugged me, clapped me on the back. It was all over.

It was about to begin. That leap was symbolic of what the future held. I could stay safe on the ledge of life, on a limited ledge where I'd know the territory, where there would be few surprises, or I could put that behind me and leap into the void trusting that this space contained all I would need; that it wasn't empty, but filled with invisible strength. It was a universal safety-net encompassing the entire world. Soon I would leave South Africa, leave my home, jump into the unknown again and again. The jump was a prophecy for me.

Outward bound had been an inward bound and a bond was formed between Jussi, Ziggy, Elin and I. Back in the routine of the programme, I grew more aware of how I felt about Jussi. I wanted him to make love to me. We were already there. One morning, at a break in the cooking class, I walked up beside him as he was sitting on a chair. Crouching down so my head was lower than his, I whispered.

"Jussi?"

"Yes?"

"I want to ask you something."

"Okay." He shifted his body to look into my eyes.

"I want you to make love to me."

He nodded.

"I've been coming to this myself," he answered, "I need to think about it."

After lunch we strolled out in the sun, along the path, up the hill, into the mountains.

"I haven't made love to a woman for two years," he confided. "At home I've just met a woman and we've been growing closer. I'm torn between waiting for her and being here with you now. I'll have to tell her and I'm not sure how she'll take it. I don't want to lose her, and I also want to live now." We stood in the dusty path and held one another, breathing quietly.

He chose to live now and we became lovers. Jussi moved into my room. The fabric changed as the texture of our relationship altered. It was a quilt of patches woven together by a past we had no knowledge of. Once we had celebrated our state of intimacy and bonding through a physical medium, I became a frivolous child, laughing and light-hearted. Jussi settled into a calm centre and watched me, amused. I wondered to myself, could I live so closely with this person day after day, eating together, studying together, sleeping together? It seemed a feat. We'd moved to a place where there was little tension; in accord, we moved harmoniously through the days.

Now that there was a person who loved me, not the outside me, the inside me, it was a light almost too bright for me to bear. Because I had not yet grasped the wonder of who I was, I could be jealous and possessive. If somebody sees who I am and chooses to love me, then only my being more and consistently who I am can hold that person. If a woman who is more beautiful inside comes along, more loving, more giving, maybe he will go. Who knows? But to live in fear of losing someone is a half-life; a rejection of oneself. It is hard to understand and live the fact that ultimately we own no-one and nothing.

Jussi is now married and has a child. The fine fabric of our meeting hangs in the air like a garment of glittering gold. It stretches through time and expands over distance. In the morning, if you rise very early, you will see bits of it shining on the leaves, resting on the flowers. Soon the sun gathers it up to help him grow brighter. It's an agreement Jussi and I made with him. Every true soul bonding affects all life-forms on the planet. Each honest attempt to love adds light.

Before my departure I bathed nude in the mountain stream in the early afternoon light, committing myself and my life to the waters of life itself. I asked for freedom to complete the will of God for me in my life, and in so doing, make a contribution to the world. I was a different person as a result of Kiental — more open, ready. Yes I was enthusiastic about macrobiotics, but not sure that I could see myself as a teacher or healer in this field. Too much study and time were needed. What was the next step? Switzerland had already swept my South African feet off the ground. I was poised for flight.

steps to heal the heart

Going for growing

When a person arrives in my life, I know he or she is there for an exchange of some sort; we are going to learn from one another. As the relationship unfolds it becomes clear what it is that can be learnt and the length of time we will be together to enable that. A whole lot of growing goes on! My relationship with Jussi was a big improvement on earlier relationships. It was filled with respect and consideration. Both of us changed because of it. Above all it was thoroughly romantic. Perhaps you have had an experience of intimacy that is precious to you. It could be a relatively short episode of significance and impact. How would you describe or communicate that? Write a brief love story.

Risk in relationships

In considering your relationships, which one has helped you recognise your strengths? What are your strengths? Tell somebody.

How about your risk-taking thermometer? When did you last take a risk moving the relationship to a deeper level? What happened? What did you learn about yourself?

What did you learn about the other?

Jussi was at least fifteen years younger than me. Have you experienced a friendship/relationship that was unconventional? That disregarded social convention? What happened? What's your take on keeping to well-trodden paths in this regard?

I remember one rainy night in Johannesburg. A friend from Angola and I had been to The Bassline listening to jazz. We stepped outside the club for air and sat on a bench in the drizzling rain. A couple in a car parked at the kerb alongside us stared at us. I said to him, "I bet they're thinking: What are these two doing together? He's young and she's old enough to be his mother. Or, he's black and she's white."

"I was thinking," said my friend, "that they were thinking, why are these two sitting in the rain?" It's all a matter of perception. It depends on how you look at it. Write a description of an incident in your life where there were two very different interpretations of the same event or happening. What was the truth?

When Jussi began spending even a little time with a younger woman, I was jealous.

I knew there was "nothing in it" but it irked me. What would you describe as a major flaw in yourself when it comes to a relationship? Where do you think it stems from? What can you do about it?

From the physical to the spiritual

Have you experienced an Outward Bound or have you jumped over a cliff with only a rope around your ankle? What have you done on a physical level that somehow informed you of something spiritual in your life? Write about this experience.

Are you a physical person in that you enjoy river-rafting or mountain climbing? What does it do for you? Describe what it's like.

my life

my life

Chapter 4 ℵ *Aleph: A Call to Return*

South Africa felt different now. It hadn't changed; I had. When you enter the country, a very fine garment falls slowly, unnoticeably, around your shoulders. Day by day it tightens until it fits your body snugly. Made from the tension in the air, the vibrations of fear held by so many on guard quickly becomes a piece of familiar clothing worn close to the skin.

It might be possible to live in South Africa and not imbibe the distress, but I was unable to. You are walking in the suburbs when a Black Maria van stops. Domestic staff sitting on the sidewalk having an afternoon chat suddenly sprint off in all directions, like a glass smashing. Police jump from the van and give chase. The air heaves with cries, the thud of blows, the heavy-laden burden of silent witness. Men and women are snagged, handcuffed, tossed into the van. Their desperate faces peer through the grated window. Perhaps their passes — identity cards — were not in order; perhaps nothing special is wrong. They are black. That was usually enough.

I'd been out for a short while. I'd seen another world, felt a different vibration, loosened the coils around my ankles; turned my head in another direction. Being born here was a life sentence for so many. Was it also for me? I was desperately tired, weary with the practices of prejudice. I noticed how attitudes held by both black and white had hardened. Have I done my share, I wondered. Dare I opt for a life beyond this? What it was I had no idea, but I had turned to face a new direction without knowing what lay ahead.

Just the turning is enough to draw the future towards us. Sometimes that's all we need to do; admit that this road has reached as far as it can go. Now another one needs to open. It was the same turning as I did when I realised I would leave the convent. It's not a step, it's a turning. First the head turns. "I'm only looking!" Breathing quietly, as the eyes gaze steadily into the nothingness, there is little room for fear as the chest joins the head. Now you feel slightly awkward with half the body facing east, the other west. You turn back and immediately that odd feeling of fatigue and enclosure envelops you. Yes, it is time to move. Your feet point the new way, and your body follows. This can be done quietly.

There was another reason that I began to turn in a new direction. The intake of wholesome food had allowed my body to discharge many of the toxins held for so long. I believe the body holds our secret destiny. Deep in the DNA it lodges, pulsing with life. Often this destiny is blocked from our awareness because of pollution of some form — emotional, physical — many forms. But once the body is able to release those blocks, the soul, the real person, is able fingertip by fingertip to emerge. That glimpse of personal peace which would lead me to my spiritual home was not on the distant horizon. Intuitively I began to give away the clothes I no longer needed; return borrowed books. Something within me knew before I knew. From within I was being pushed and prodded. A blind mole, I groped towards some light somewhere. From my limited vision I suspected it would have something to do with macrobiotics, so when Elaine asked me to assist her in bringing Katriona Forrester, one of the teachers from Kiental, to South Africa, I agreed unhesitatingly.

Katriona knew macrobiotic teaching, she taught Shiatsu, offered consultations on healing and was a great cook. Her life was a round of teaching and travelling. Seemed pretty exciting. It was also very demanding. "Why aren't you out there, teaching about macrobiotics?" she asked me one evening as we sat under the stars at the Bryanston organic market. "I know so little," I confessed. It was as if the traffic light was stuck on yellow. I wanted to be involved, but hadn't felt the force of a green light yet.

The day she left I got a telegram from Ehud Lebowitz in Jerusalem. He'd been on the seminar with me in Kiental. He complained about the extent of his commitment. So much work! On my return and before September, I sent him a Jewish New Year card and implied loosely that I was ready to look beyond South Africa. He asked me to call him; gave his number.

"So," smiled Katriona, "you're going to Jerusalem."

Am I? Jerusalem? Could this be?

As I thought about Jerusalem I saw it from the point of view of being a world centre. Why not be in a world centre? A point where three major religions meet. I'll be quite at home in such an international environment, I thought. It won't be for long. I'll go and see what it's like, help out at the macrobiotic centre, return to South Africa and see what the next step is. Simple. I called Ehud.

"I need help. With the conference," he explained across the miles.

Leah, his wife, could speak English better.

"We'd like you to come and help us at the centre for a few months. You'll have your food here and we'll provide a place for you to live and we'll give you pocket money. Can you?"

The conference was in August. They wanted me there as soon as possible. June was the earliest I could make it. June, my father's birth month. What did it all mean? Why the Middle East? Why not Italy or America? "It's only for a few months. I'll store my furniture and books; it's not forever," I reasoned.

Israel. Again. I went to the Zionist Federation in the city and spoke to Joel. Tucked in my bag was my certificate of conversion from the Beth Din. As I waited in the lobby I had a couple of forms in my hand. They were applications to become an Israeli, to make *aliyah* — to go up to Israel. I began to fill in the spaces. Name, address, date of birth and then — religion. I looked at the space, and wrote "Jewish". I was Jewish. I was leaving South Africa and going to a place where I would be accepted, where I could become a citizen. I was Jewish wasn't I? I had not thought this out at all. It was a pragmatic action. I had to be Jewish. There was no alternative.

Joel informed me that I could complete all the paperwork in Johannesburg and once in Israel, if I wanted to become an Israeli, I'd make one phone call and that would make me an Israeli citizen. Easy. I hardly thought it necessary to confuse the issue by bringing up my ten years as a nun. Joel had probably had a hard day, anyway. Why make it worse? I had the certificate, I passed the medical, enough!

One weekend shortly after this, I was invited to Natal by a brave macrobiotic healer, Patty Joshua. She had set herself up as a massage therapist and beautician in a small town at a time when this was not the easiest or most acceptable action for a woman of mixed-race descent to take. Patty asked me to give a cooking class and a day of shiatsu.

On the Friday night I was unable to sleep. As my time of departure from South Africa approached I began to panic. I awoke at four, restless and worried, tiptoed into the little garden and spoke my thoughts to the silent sky.

"Am I crazy? What am I doing?"

The blackness said nothing.

"I've a thriving business which I'm throwing away. I'm off to a place I don't know, to a person I don't know. Am I completely crazy?"

My stomach was writhing and churning.

"Is this what you want me to do? How do I know?"

The bushes held their position, hardly noticing me as the gentle breeze brushed their branches briefly in passing. A slither of moon sneaked a peek at me, then pulled the curtain of cloud across her face, suggesting that if I had any manners I'd respect the sleep of the day, the shadow of the morn to come. It was a time of changing; of in-between-ness. The universe held a finger to its lips.

That evening Patty suggested we go to a movie in the one and only drive-in miles from anywhere: *The Witches of Eastwick*

On our arrival we discover *The Witches* isn't showing.

"Oh no, bummer! What's the movie then?"

"It's a foreign film?"

"It's not English? So what is it?"

"It's Hebrew!" I yell, "It's in Jerusalem, look!"

"My God, girl" exclaims Patty, "if you wanted a sign, how's this for size?"

Of all the millions of available movies, on to this screen in the heart of nowhere is projected an Israeli film, in Hebrew with English subtitles. It is about a love affair between a religious girl and a soldier. Of course it could be dismissed as coincidence but I don't believe in coincidence. I needed reassurance. Only God knew what I was going through; and God answered me in a concrete way. "Thank you!" I intoned to the beat of my heart as my eyes fixated on the screen.

I continued to make arrangements. One final Outward Bound for BP was still on my schedule. There I received a warning. As I was abseiling down a steep mountain, the rope snagged on an outcrop of rock. I couldn't move. I tried to swing the rope free but it held. The guys at the top flapped the rope from their angle and it loosened. What did this mean? I had come to recognise physical events as a sign. I had to be prepared for a temporary hitch. Sure enough, the day before I left, as I was about to sell my car, I was told I needed the original papers. These were in my filing cabinet now in storage with the rest of my furniture and possessions in a warehouse somewhere. I had the telephone number. I called, got directions to a place about 10 miles away, found the file, took out the papers, rushed back to the garage and sold the car. Whew!

What was I leaving behind? Most of my life. Most of my friends. Two animals. "It's temporary," I lied to myself, "I'll return, collect my things and my animals." I found a good home for them, not seeing a pattern in having to leave pets. As if I were repeating a scenario I had learnt from my mother. This would become clear to me in Israel. Much would become clear to me in Israel. I had no idea what was ahead of me. In a sense I was leaving Egypt, leaving a place I had thought was my home, making a crossing, a crossing from one world to another. Not merely a physical crossing. I would soon be immersed in a new life, a new awareness, a transformation.

I left behind people who loved me, particularly the woman who, in her role as domestic worker, had become a close friend and part of my life. Elizabeth was mourning my going. Ever since I left the convent she had been with me. Together we had shared our losses — her son, beaten by the police, and my dad's death. Together we had celebrated the birth of two of her children, the birth of my business and together we had moved apartments at least five times. "I'll be back," I consoled her, "it won't be long."

For many of my friends my departure was somewhat of a betrayal. "How can you leave now?" It was a hard question to answer. But I had to go. I had to follow my life, find my destiny. I was still searching, searching for my place, searching for home, searching for meaning, searching for God, searching for love. To find I had to let go, had to close the door behind me. I groped my way forward, blindfolded.

174

Any move invites a wave of growth. Leaving a country is massive and I was sliding out sideways, pretending it was only temporary. So much of me resented being a South African. The country was limited, provincial, rigid, closed, cruel. I longed to leave, but never knew how. Now a way lay before me.

I wanted to be free, but free on all levels, free of the fears that still waited inside me, unexplored, unnamed, growing; free of the anger I had repressed; free of the mistiness that now surrounded my relationship with God; free of the loneliness that held me imprisoned in isolation; free of the mistaken assumptions about my mother always on my side; free to become the person whose potential faced me at moments in workshops, in the eyes of trainees, and sometimes in a lover's face.

This was a death for me. Death as a South African, death as a Christian, death as a businesswoman. I'd be born as a Jew, born as an Israeli, born as an artist. I'd find my home, my place, my religion, my roots, my destiny. I was forty one. As I boarded the El Al flight, I was sure that if God opened the palm of his hand, I'd be sitting there — safe.

my life

steps to heal the heart

Coincidence?

Do you believe in coincidence? Was there a time when you were unsure of a decision you had made, or were under pressure to make, and you prayed for a sign? What happened? Write about it, then give it to a friend to read.

The search

Imagine you are standing inside the place where you stay and about to go out the door. See the room you are standing in. See the door handle. Turn it, open the door and move out. Close the door behind you. Hear the sound of the door closing. As you stand outside your home a beautiful angel appears. The angel takes your hand. Look into the eyes of your angel. Then together you walk forward holding hands. Write where you go and what you find.

Leaving South Africa

As a South African, have you ever wanted to leave your country? Why? Did you go or did you stay? Trace your thoughts as you struggled with this decision. What was the result of your decision? If you had to leave, but didn't want to, describe what that was like for you. How did you cope with exile? What was the best and the worst for you? Where are you now?

Freedom

Freedom is a powerful word, or maybe it's a word that has lost its meaning. What does the word mean to you? Would you describe yourself as free? Were you always free or did you become free? Free of what? Was there a price you had to pay? Were you glad to pay it? Write a story in which you describe your movement towards freedom.

Madam and Eve

If you have lived in South Africa you are well aware of the relationships that are built between women and their domestic staff. If you were a domestic worker, what was your experience? What were the positives and negatives of working for another woman in her home? Write a letter to the person you worked for, or each of the people you may have worked for, and tell them what is in your heart.

If you employed women or men as domestic staff, what was that like for you? Write a letter to the person or persons you employed and tell them what is in your heart.

Part 5

Michal Ish-Shalom

Chapter 1   ב   *Bet: My Spiritual Home*

*I*t was this sense of quiet certitude, a knowing in the not-knowing; as if someone loving had crawled into my bed in the early hours of the morning and snuggled up beside me, warming me. I felt warm. With the warmth came a feeling of relief, release. I had left behind my country, my past, my family, my friends, my success, my belongings, an identity, me. I knew one person in the place I was headed towards and I could not speak the language. But there was a stirring in my soul; a hibernation period was over. It was as if I were a tree that had first been planted in a pot. The tree grew and the pot proved too small. The gardener, wanting to preserve the tree, began to dig it out. She loosened the soil around the roots and finally hoisted it out, roots dangling in the air. I was being held in the air, en route to a more appropriate container. When a tree is transplanted, does it know right away that this is its best possible place? Or is it still in slight shock as it feels the new earth, the space, the light, the air, the freedom to grow?

When the plane landed on the tarmac in Tel Aviv I was groggy with tiredness, having chosen to stay up most of the night chatting with members of a water-polo team. Passing through customs I felt heavy but not uncomfortable. Ehud was there waving his arms. In broken English he ushered me to his car where his children — screaming and crying — were waiting to receive me. Welcome to Israel.

In the intense heat Ehud drove to Jerusalem pointing out places along the way. I struggled to respond. At his wife's workplace he disappeared into the building leaving me with his two children who were still screaming. "I'll kill them!" I thought. "No, I'll kill Ehud! How can he leave me here?" I was angry already.

"Now, now Michelle," the voice of reason interrupted, "you're a guest, remember? Be nice!"

"Nice?" I replied, fumes rising from my head. "It's bloody hot; these kids don't know me, I don't speak Hebrew, I'm hungry, tired and where the hell is he?" I tried to look innocent as people emerging from the building peered into the car. The children screamed louder: "*Abba! Abba!*" After what seemed like six months Ehud smilingly returned to the car. No Leah. She was too busy. Too busy? Michelle Friedman has arrived in Israel after a sixteen-hour journey and Leah is too busy to run down and say hello? Are these Israeli manners? I was piqued, my ego bruised, my ears sore, my temper on hold. Welcome to Israel.

So where was my apartment then? The apartment wasn't an apartment. Ehud was acting the way many Israelis act. He waited until I was there before he made any arrangements. We drove to a hostel. It looked very pleasant, but my room would not be available for a couple of hours. A couple of hours? Could I bath? Could I have something to eat? Ehud pushed some food in my hand and said I could either go for another drive with him (and the children) or study some material he had on the conference or just wait. I'll just wait, thank you.

Surprised at my easy anger I was to find out that here my volcanic anger would at last be disturbed. I'd awake like a dormant volcano. The first step to begin the process was to complain. I learnt quickly that in order to survive it is necessary to complain. Everybody complains in Israel. It's a way of life. Not complaining is like not having an opinion. You complain, they fix it, then you complain again. That's progress! Sweet little Michelle had been so nice for so long, so accepting, so decent. She wouldn't dream of raising her voice. Sweet little Michelle was going to disappear. However, learning to wait wasn't so easy. I wanted to scream, beat on my cases, kick my feet in the air, hold my breath in a tantrum until the entire staff came rushing to obey my every wish. South African white. "You need to know two words here," Ehud smiled, "the first one is *savlanut*. It means patience." I pursed my lips, breathed through my nose like a dragon, tapped my feet, clutched my return ticket and phoned my mother telling her it was all wonderful. Then I sat in the foyer and watched the time tick past. A slow fume set in. The other word Ehud kept for me until later. It was *balagan*. It means chaos. Now they tell me.

But in spite of my tiredness, my irritation, my spoilt South-Africanism, I felt in place. And precisely because I felt in place I could allow the squashed sides of me to fill their shape, assume their size like air-filled balloons. What does being in place mean? Everything around me was new, strange, different. Street signs were in Hebrew, voices spoke Hebrew, buildings were low and white, lots of new noises, plenty of colour and where was I? I was in place. Something small, something irreplaceable, something that could never go away, something so deep inside me like a compass was now at resting point. I was home.

Home. What does this word mean to me? Somewhere that offers me complete comfort because I belong there entirely. It is mine. Home is the feeling that it's safe; home is the sense that I'm understood; home is where I can be myself in every way; home is permanent. There the refrigerator holds no surprises for me; the cupboards harbour my clothes; the toilet seat imprints my bottom on it; the garden is glad for me to play in it, and everything can be re-arranged if I wish. It is a space with my name on it, and at night I can sleep with ease, breathing deeply, content at last. It is closely linked to freedom. "Free at last, free at last, thank God Almighty, I'm free at last!"

How could this be happening to me? What was happening to me? As the days passed the mayhem continued. The macrobiotic centre turned out to be a long corridor with curves for rooms. And two staff members. Jose-Maria was Spanish. He was unable to communicate although he spoke English well. He would not take orders or suggestions from a woman; he insisted on doing his own thing his own way and nothing would make him change. Ehud cared for him because Jose-Maria was also weakened by epilepsy. It was important for him to maintain a macrobiotic diet to prevent an attack. Debra the cook was full of resentment because she felt she wasn't being paid enough and because Ehud restricted her choices of what she could cook. She never complained to him, just to me and I allowed that to make me unsettled. If the people I worked with were unhappy I allowed that to affect my happiness. The centre was certainly not thriving and the likelihood of a conference of any proportion evaporated after two days. If we were to have ten people, we'd be lucky. Ehud worked like a madman, threw orders around, disappeared to heal in Tel Aviv, returned to rip the place apart and leave us all whirling in bewilderment. *Balagan*.

Nonetheless I felt an incredible peace in Jerusalem. What was it? Why was it? Who was I? Why did my feet feel as though they were stuck to the sidewalk? Why did they seem to travel down, down to the centre of the earth and there hold fast? Why did I wish to kiss every stone of every street? To pick up every paper on every corner? To lie down on the road, resting? Why did I feel so secure? How could I explain this sigh of rest which the wind carried from me in each breeze? Every sneeze sounded a release of tension trapped in time gone by and every breathing out a reminder that the next sip of air inhaled came from a place so precious that no dream of its existence could give me warning. It had everything to do with the past, the historical past of this place and everything to do with my past, the past of my ancestors and everything to do with eternity. I was finding my place in world history, finding my place in my own history, finding my place in God. I was fitting in! Yes! I fitted in! At last! Here, I was home! After forty years of looking and searching and being lonely and alone and anxious and afraid, Michelle had come to rest; she had found her place, and that place is a people, is a connection, is a stamp on the soul. It says: Jewish. Michelle, you are a Jew. Nobody can take that away from you; it's not something you can put on; it's a gift given to you eons ago, carved on your *neshama* (soul); it's deeper than DNA, its significance has to do with your relationship to God. You carry it with you forever. You may claim your birthright now. It's okay you are home at last. You have found yourself. You are Michal.

When I was converted at fourteen my Hebrew name was Michal. Now I retrieved it. Michal Friedman. It sounded strange. One word Hebrew, one English. Could I make it all Hebrew? Friedman is a German word. *Fried* means "peace". "Man of peace". What is "man" in Hebrew? *Ish*. So my name would be Ish-Shalom. *Ish* is male and *shalom* is female. Michal Ish-Shalom. My name in Hebrew encompasses the male and the female, a wholeness, a combination with both energies available.

I quickly recognised the special quality of Hebrew. At first glance Hebrew appeared so formidable. Strange shapes, awkward sounds that move from right to left, incomprehensible. Then I began to explore. At that point it takes over. There is a presence and a power in the letters that claims my heart, speaking to a part of me I was never fully in touch with. It takes me back to the past, then brings me forward into the present, before it shoots me into the void of infinity. All the while it is loving. It fills me with deep joy. Alive like a flame, it licks and touches, caresses and holds; it crawls into secret cracks healing a sore, closing a wound or soaking one's spirit in peace. Power embeds in the letters, mystery moves in the spaces between the words, awe hovers over the page. Whoever pronounces my name is speaking what I consider a holy language.

I was home. I had found my place, found my language, found my people, found my roots, found my history, found myself. This is why I came to Israel. My exploration of macrobiotics led me here. Macrobiotics was a step on the way, a means, not an end. In my end is my beginning, the poet declares. "All beginnings are difficult," says a Hebrew proverb. I was about to find that out.

Steps to heal the heart

What is home?

"Something small, something irreplaceable, something that could never go away, something inside me like a compass was now at resting point. I was home."

What does the word "home" mean to you? Is it a place? Is it a recognition? Perhaps it's a shared history? Could it be a person? What is it for you?

A spiritual home

Many of us never find it necessary to question our roots. We are born into a culture or a nation and we settle for that. Being Jewish is more than a religion or a race or a culture. It is a hybrid of many aspects. I have read many stories of people who thought they were Christian and came to recognise that their parents had hidden their roots from them.

How significant are roots? Where do yours lie? Are they challenged in any way? Do you experience yourself drifting away from your roots and being seduced by another more dominant culture perhaps? Or have you tenaciously clung to your roots? How important are roots in South Africa today? Write everything you think and feel about this.

A spiritual language

If you pray, what language do you use? At times of intimacy the language we choose is the language which is most important to us on a soul level. How many languages do you speak? Is another language now more important to you than your own? What do you think we give up when we take on another language that is not our "mother tongue"? What do you think we gain? Language is also about power. Or the perception of power. If I see my language as powerless, I will be less likely to use it. But if I see it as powerful I'll speak it more. When I learn another language I begin to understand more about the people who speak that language. That's a help. Hebrew is a special relationship for me. It's more of a mystical relationship. How would you describe your relationship with your mother tongue?

How do you identify?

Up until this part of the book I have been mainly Christian or Catholic. Now I am a Jew. What is your feeling about this? Have you experienced a major shift like the one I did? What happened to you? Write this down.

A new country

Have you gone to a place where you couldn't speak the language? What was that like? What did you learn about yourself? I realise that many of us English-speakers think that our language is the only one and everyone should speak it. This is linguistic arrogance. We also tend to think that people who do not speak our language are disabled in some way and that's negative. How do you feel when people around you speak a language you don't understand? What if you can't hear them at all? What if your hearing is impaired? What then do you notice about yourself and about them? Have you ever watched a group of people using sign-language? What did you learn?

my life

my life

Chapter 2 ג *Gimmel: Land of Milk and Honey*

*I*had found my people. What did this mean? It felt as though a long-lost family had appeared casually one morning for breakfast. This family stretched over thousands of years and spread out in all directions encompassing the globe. Here we huddled after centuries of homelessness; here we began a healing after horror; here we began to build.

The face of Israel looked at me each morning as I boarded the bus from Kiryat ha Yovel. Ehud had found me a charming, fully-furnished apartment for a couple of months. Bus number eighteen traversed almost the entire circumference of Jerusalem and everybody climbed on, shoving for space. Weary women with lined faces, their heads held in a scarf, hair tickling down their chins, sat absorbed in their conversations with themselves. Sharing the seats were females in their forties, their skin beginning to show signs of wear, still somewhat beautiful, but beauty which faded fast under the everyday struggle to survive. Young, strong girls, a shock of hair halo-ing their striking faces, tight skirts clinging to their vibrant bodies, sat proudly — sure of the future. Soldiers, guns draped over their shoulders, moved out of the way. Some wore skull-caps, evidence of their belief in the presence of God. Men of all shapes and sizes climbed on and off, some loaded with net shopping bags, some in cut-away shirts sporting sexy tanned shoulders and doused in cologne, some staring out the window far away, and those dressed in black with hats stood rather than sit next to a woman.

I was dazed, awed, horrified, fascinated, revolted, inspired by the bus-people. I wasn't used to rubbing shoulders, not used to riding buses, certainly not used to being in the midst of a whirlpool of people. "*Rega! Rega!*" someone would yell and the driver would spring open the door for a passenger to lift a pram down for a mother and everyone would wait. It was this sense of being a stranger and not being a stranger. I knew nobody, yet I felt people were accessible to me, that it was perfectly normal to strike up a conversation with anybody because we were all related. It was a bond that simply could not be broken. We can choose to pretend it isn't there; we can try to ignore or suppress it, but it is there, like the air, and like the air it is unlikely to go away. As a Jew I am bound to all Jews; as a human being I am intricately knit into the fabric of all human beings. Why is it so strange for us to discover we are all related?

When, in this scrunched-up busload of bodies, a disembodied hand would tap me on the shoulder, shove a few *shekels* into my hand with a nudge, I, as if trained, simply passed the fare on to the next hand who continued the communication until the few coins reached the driver. He pressed a small thin ticket into the closest hand. Along the corridor of heads, scarves, hats and hair this ticket found its way back to its owner.

It was impossible not to think of the holocaust when I sat in those buses. Which of these faces had seen Dachau? The woman alongside me, what had she lived through? Where did this man's mother die? And you, sir, what is your story? Hannah told me how her mother had pulled her brother and herself off the train bound for the death camps, escaped across Europe and eventually into Israel. In Kiryat Yovel the man next door was letting the upstairs apartment. I went to look at it. He showed me the book on Treblinka. "*Ich war da,*" he nodded. In the buses I swam in a human sea, a sea of survival. Every life in this bus was a life saved. Mine too. My life felt as if it had been given back to me, or given to me.

Being a Jew — a treasure immeasurably rich that would take me the remainder of my life to appreciate. I was given an inheritance of majesty and awe and also a history of unimaginable suffering. Just as I would have to probe my personal pain, connect with my anger, release it, grieve and heal, so too would I need to face our collective agony, allow that anger, face the confusion, wrestle with God. In Israel my eyes were further opened to the situation of Jews since time immemorial. For the first time I saw Christianity through Jewish eyes. What had been done in the name of Christ? What had been done? The questions were legion, the bewilderment intense as I read Primo Levi's experiences in Auschwitz; read the *Encyclopaedia of the Holocaust*, spoke to people, visited monuments, museums, and allowed the evidence in, drop by drop.

It was my family who had been savaged, my people. This realisation came as a pounding in the belly, a knocking about the ears, a reeling of the mind, a gasping for breath. Of course I knew about the Holocaust but now it was different, now it was close, on my skin, in my veins. Now it was a blood link. Knowing swept down on me like a torrent, swirling, rending me helpless and dumb. I held my head in my hands. I remembered in my Catholic days how Jews were seen as misguided, as having "made a mistake" by not recognising Jesus as the Messiah. "There will be a place for Jews in Heaven," *Vatican Two* footnoted. "My father is Jewish," I had said, "What happens to him?" I'd experienced a condescension, a contempt towards Jews. "Us Christians" had the real thing; the Jews were stuck in the *Old Testament*.

I remembered a conversation I'd had with my old school buddies in Johannesburg. Judy had made a derogatory remark about Jews, revealing both her and her father's dislike for Jews. We'd been talking about the economy.

"How can you say that?" I asked her, nervous suddenly, "My father's Jewish!"

Judy leapt into craziness.

"But Michelle, everybody knows that the Jews killed Christ."

My two other long-time buddies looked embarrassed but said nothing to oppose her statement. Did they believe it too? I wanted to belong in this group, but at that moment something changed. Quickly cold, I stayed put, lacking the courage to walk out. Couldn't I counter this ludicrous remark? Why did I sit in sudden shame? Did I believe it also? Was I ashamed of my Jewish blood? Where does this irrational prejudice and hatred come from? How can it go away? Is it here to stay? Isn't the world a nice place where people love one another and reach out to each other? What about entire countries holding these prejudices? These questions would be with me for the rest of my life. The realisation grew that I was part of a minority and life would be different because of it.

When I open the door on the Holocaust, it's as if a mighty wind surges into the room, a wind that wipes everything away before it. My mind is not large enough to cope with it; my heart sinks into the depth of the earth, seeks deeper for rest from it; my soul splits, tears from its moorings, spins dizzily in space, orphaned. Push the door closed, heave, come on, use your shoulders! There. Now there's quiet for a bit. Let's eat in peace. We'll look again another time, but only a little. Later, much later, we will attempt to understand. We may never do it in our lifetime. Now, dear, what were you saying?

Life goes on. And life is unpredictable. Especially in Israel. Once a woman had an epileptic fit on the bus. The driver stopped, ordered everyone out and drove her to hospital. Another day, as the bus was careering down a narrow road to the Old City, its course was barred by a car parked with its rear jutting onto the tarmac. The driver braked and climbed out. With the six remaining male passengers, they surrounded the car as if this were part of their everyday lives, lifted it off the road and replaced it on the sidewalk. Dusting their hands down their trousers, they climbed back onto the bus and were off again as if nothing had happened. In Tel Aviv in a traffic jam, the driver wheeled the bus into a u-turn, lurched down a side-street, wound in and out of back alleys and little known paths until he beat the road block. There was a spontaneity that left me breathless.

In Israel one has to live for today because one cannot be sure of tomorrow. Every man in the street will have been, or is in the army; each one may well have killed a person. War can break out on a large scale at any moment or a bomb can explode in the market-place. Nothing can be taken for granted here. Expect the unexpected such as a genuine question from a driver or even a passer-by who stops you to ask, "*Makera hayom?*" What's the matter today? A man hands you a rose and blows you a kiss or a taxi driver refuses to charge you. Often spontaneous discussions evolve with a group of people listening to a speaker in the street. Perhaps a road is cut off and you watch the police defuse a bomb, or you watch a piece of paper loitering at a garbage bin. When the wind comes near, it throws itself against the base, desperate for someone who knows the secret of the city to lift it into the inner sanctuary of safety, drop it into place, close the lid securely, respectful of its privacy. Once when I did this, when I picked up a piece of litter and put it into a garbage bin, a man came up to me and said thank you. Aha, the streets speak too. That unexpectedness can also be like a drop of water dripping endlessly until you scream. What is there to hold on to? To be sure of? Life tantalises with its fluidity. I was in love with Israel, particularly Jerusalem.

I found Israel musky with sensuality. Sex simmers in the streets; in the swaying hips of the dark-haired, non-smiling *sabras*; in the blatant groping of the taxi drivers; in the heavy restraint of religiously guarded eyes that dare not look; even in the wigged women hiding their hair for what one hopes will be a passionate night.

A power pervades and fear is there also. So many guns; so much tension. One day our Hebrew class went through the market Mehana Yehuda as an exercise. Many Arab students were in our class, most of them in their early twenties. Their schooling was disrupted because of the *intifada* so they came in to learn Hebrew. I watched as two Israeli female soldiers stopped the group and demanded to see their papers. Suddenly I was back in Johannesburg. There it was again. The Arab girls were scared, one student began to cry. It was her first encounter with soldiers. The Israelis were pushy, loud, aggressive, rude. The Arab men were angry. They tensed, tightened their jaws, spoke back, bristled. Crack! It was in the air. Hiss! Steam rose. Brrr! People froze.

Two Arab students from the British Council, where I began to teach English as a second language, were psychologists We'd meet in a central area for a coffee in the afternoon but as the evening entered Oman and Abdul became nervous. They wanted to get out of the crowds, and once again I felt as though I were in South Africa. But there was a complication here. It wasn't as simple for me now. I felt this land; I felt a possessiveness that surprised me. I also felt a fear that dismayed me. Where did it come from? The person who resisted apartheid is defensive here. I couldn't agree with Oman in all he said. I felt almost a traitor that I listened to him, yet I had to hear him. I had to listen to people, ask my heart, use my head, face my fears. I stood on a keg that had burst into flames millenniums ago. Shards and splinters flew in the air. The implications of that which met my eyes ran deep back into time and perhaps even beyond it. I would never unmake the muddle. If I could just see a tiny piece of it clearly I would perhaps be at a starting point. This too was part of my inheritance.

After six months in Israel I had paid my dues at the Macrobiotic Centre. I changed my status and become an Israeli. I worked as an English teacher at the British Council, moved to my own apartment in Kiryat Moshe and was adopted by a street cat called Matanah ("gift"). No longer scrambling to find my feet, well over the honeymoon period, I looked at the person who was emerging in this context. It was time again to ask the two vital questions: Who am I? Why am I here?

steps to heal the heart

If you are a Jew

What was it like for you growing up as a Jew?

What phases have you gone through in the development of (or resistance to) your Jewish identity?

What has been most difficult for you in being Jewish?

What has pleased you the most about being Jewish?

What messages did you hear or do you still hear about non-Jews? Are they true?

Anti-Semitism

A couple of times in my life I was jolted into awareness that my close Christian friends were prejudiced against Jews. What has your experience been? Write about it.

Israelis and Palestinians

As I write this in 2002, Israelis and Palestinians have been fighting one another for many months. When you read this it could all have changed yet again. In Israel I had the experience of being a Jew and being part of humanity. I still have that experience. At the same time I want justice and I want peace. I also need to understand fully what these words mean. Have you been in a situation where your loyalties were divided? What was the situation? What was the background to it? In what way were you part of the problem or the solution or both? Write about it.

In love with a city?

What do you think about this? Is it possible to be in love with a city? What's your experience? Describe a place that has a grip on you unlike any other. When did you first become aware of this? Are you living there or do you promise yourself to go one day? Do you think we need to have a place of dreams?

Buses, taxis, trains

There is both a comfort and a stress about using public transport. It's nice to have people travelling with you; it also depends on the people! Add to this one's state of mind on a particular day or a particular journey and you have a mixture that could spark off an unforgettable incident. Write about an experience in a bus, or a taxi or a train that you have never forgotten. What happened? Who were the people involved? What did you learn about yourself?

my life

my life

Chapter 3 ד *Dalet: Inner Fire*

'W ho are you?" One of millions moving through the Middle East, I guess. Yes, I'm from South Africa, I had my own business and I ... "Don't tell me what you did, what you do. Tell me who you are."

I don't know. Stripped of my past I can live only in the present, face to face with myself. There's no escape. Because you don't know me, because there's nothing to remind you of who I was, I'm under no pressure to be anything other than who you see here now.

Who emerges in this vacuum? An angry Michelle, a depressed, lonely, confused and needy Michelle. When a puppy messes on the carpet what do you do? You rub its nose in just a little, give it a small tap on its buttocks and take it outside hoping it'll get the message. I was being soaked in all the masticated, churned-about feelings I had carried inside me for so long. My nose was right in there. I had to breathe it, smell it, see it, feel it, face it. Why? Because I'd asked the question. I wanted to know myself, not just the good parts but the whole Michelle. I wanted to be of service, to be of healing to others. I was committed to life itself, and life was taking me at my word. Who is in here? How can I be truly beautiful until I know what I carry within myself? How can I be of value as a healer when I'm loaded with unknown, repressed feelings?

I was not alone. Divine action had brought me to Israel; it would not desert me now. There was a certainty, often vague, often eclipsed, that I was in transition, that this was a passage only. In moments of doubt where the tendency to forget loomed, there was always someone who believed in me when I could neither believe in myself nor find that self. A pebble, the waves of healing rolled me, threw me, drew me up, enveloped me, let me rest, then caught me again and again.

Rage emerged and I let it. It began as impatience. I'd been impatient before — with myself, with others. In Israel people often got angry. They'd express it, forget it. It was a flare-up, sudden, swift, then doused with muttering. I found it encouraging. I'd always been afraid to speak out, to express any anger. Anger's ugly, it feels uncomfortable, it may make people reject me, and I can't afford that. I have to be liked at all costs. Until the cost is my life. Here it might cost me if I didn't emote. So I pushed and shoved to get on the bus; I yelled at the taxi drivers when they attempted to grope me or overcharge me; I refused to pay duty for a parcel my family sent me from Africa and the post office clerk hurriedly gave it to me: "*Ten la!*" The rage was linked to powerlessness, a lack of control, a sense of being trapped. Will this be what it's like for the rest of my life? I was close to panic.

Angry at the religious men who shied away from me because I was a woman, I wanted to shout "Boo!" and knock their hats off. They looked so smug and self-righteous and I felt they saw me as a devil. My anger towards men bubbled onto the surface. One evening at a friend's house in the Old City my anger erupted. I'd encouraged a Yeshiva student — a man who was studying at one of the religious schools — to tell me about his life. He'd acted on impulse and run away from a broken heart in America to hide in Israel. We loosely attempted some form of sexual expression which wasn't very satisfying for either of us. This Friday evening we shared a meal with a mutual friend. In the course of a discussion I felt a fire shoot out of me towards him. It leapt from the area around my belly-button. He stopped in mid-sentence. "You're very angry with me. I can feel it. It feels like hatred. Is that right?" Yes. It was a wave of hate.

Where had it come from? Why did I release it on him? Was I a terrible person that I could feel this?

The feelings had to be let out. They were inner demons long held hostage, tightly roped, repressed, ignored. I was afraid to feel. I wanted only to feel safe emotions in limited doses. In Jerusalem I felt as though I had come home so I allowed my defences to slip. Through the crack, through the space between the curtain and the wall, part of my shackled soul began to breathe. I thought I was dying; I was only now coming to life. In the dark safety of the soil the potato grows in the night. In order for me to grow I needed to grow in the night shades of my soul. From the rubble and dirt I would re-form and rise. If I wanted to be of service I had to know my weakness, my pain, the squelchy squirming softness of the underside. Israel offered me a glimpse. At the edges of the rock a few worms crawled — the first shocking glance.

Anger turned to depression. It was easier to deal with. I'd been depressed before in Africa, so depression was a familiar friend. I'd call a friend and bleat over the phone; go next door where my neighbour would feed me with cookies and coffee; wander around the cafes writing my woes soulfully; bury my head in a book. I'd write home and worry everyone there or I'd hold on to the depression, be with it, sit with it, make no attempt to escape until, like a guest with whom one has nothing left to say, it rose, picked up its hat and left. That was a tougher route but it strengthened me. Hold it, just be there with it. Confront it by sitting. Like a piece of clothing it lay over my feet, ominous in its attempts at nonchalance. Up my body it grew, its tentacles choking life, constricting my heart. As it reached my head and still I made no attempt to fight it off, the root lifted and the air whooshed it away. Gone. My lack of resistance, my refusal to divert it or distract it, my looking it square in the face frightened it away. I felt freer.

Maybe relationships with men will make it better for me, I thought. Maybe that would remove the loneliness. So what's the course of action? Brief encounters? Short-lived sexual adventures? There were plenty of takers. I forgot my relationship with Jussi, forgot that I had moved to another level of loving. My primal need for comfort now drove me back to promiscuity. Why was I promiscuous? I didn't even acknowledge that I was, let alone seek the root cause. I was being offered an opportunity to change but I couldn't take it. I made attempts at relationships but there was always a missing part: the timing was out, or the man was older, married or in some way unattainable. Why is this happening? What am I doing wrong? I dreamed that in Israel I would find my soul mate. I clung to the idea that a man would make it alright for me. I would be rescued if I waited long enough.

While waiting I fell pregnant. Again. "Oh my God!" I sat with my head in my hands at the edge of my bed. "What do I do?" It was as if every time I attempted to leave South Africa, I was given the chance to have a child, to make my own family. In Israel it was a chance I wanted to take. My child would be an Israeli. What could be better? The father was unprepared to shoulder this kind of responsibility. I'd do it alone. I would reverse my decision of almost twenty years ago. I accepted the consequences of my actions.

My body had other plans. It could not hold the foetus. Within a couple of days it went into release and a close and loving friend, Aviva, took me to a doctor who sent me to hospital immediately. There I wept with guilt and disappointment, reliving my earlier trauma. This was a child I wanted. I was advised to make room in my womb for the possibility of falling pregnant and taking the pregnancy to term. I'd have to have an operation, have the fibroids that had grown inside me removed.

Shaking with nerves I walked up to the desk at Misgav Ladav. I was about to put my body into the hands of doctors I didn't know and who couldn't speak English in a country I was barely used to. I was about to lose the little power I had. The nurse who took my pulse could feel how anxious I was. I was so tired of being brave. I'd heard terrible stories of people in hospitals here. I immediately disliked the doctor. He was Russian, didn't speak English. My attempts at keeping a brave face were fast slipping away.

I sat waiting on a bench, the harrowing waiting prevalent in Israel. Wait for hours at the immigration offices, wait at the renting office, wait, wait, wait. Waiting makes us all equal. The poor wait more. Someone else has the power to change the light to green for go. It's humiliating and challenging at the same time. In the lines of immigrants waiting to get their papers, people would begin talking to one another and pretty quickly I'd have a picture of their attitude. I discovered that what they expected, they got. If they were full of resentment, the chances were they'd be there all day. If they were argumentative, they'd find a clerk to fight with; if they were self-pitying something disappointing would invariably present itself. There I refused to allow the negativity of those around me to define my attitude. But here, with an operation imminent, I wasn't doing so well. My encounter with macrobiotics convinced me that doctors were monsters and my body was about to be cut to pieces and loathsome drugs poured into it. The reason I'd gone into macrobiotics was to dissolve the fibroids. Macrobiotics was the reason I'd come to Israel. But the fibroids were still there. They had to go. I needed to believe that I would be okay. I had to hold on to whatever was available inside and outside of me.

It was time to abandon myself to God. And God took form. My friend Aviva stood in for a mother. She came every day. She brought food, sat by my bed, watched me like an angel. The anaesthetist, Marcel, a Frenchman, discussed the procedure with me step by step. I wanted to be awake throughout the operation because I didn't want to lose control over any decision that might be made. If the doctors discovered they had to remove my womb I wanted to be consulted. We settled on an injection into my spine which would numb the bottom half of my body but keep me alert mentally. An epidural. I'd been a patient of a French gynaecologist Jean, but because of the system in Israel there could be no guarantee that he'd operate. You got whoever worked the shift, unless you had money to pay for your own doctor. This operation wasn't costing me a cent. It was all on medical aid. As the time neared I learnt that Jean was on my shift. Finally I began to respect the Russian doctor. I saw another side of him, a gentler side. I realised how handsome he was, how strong, how sure. Yes, I was in good hands.

The day of the operation I was wheeled out of the three-bed ward. The two women in the ward encouraged me. They knew this was my first operation. As I was carried out on a trolley, a woman, a stranger to me, pressed a book of prayers into my hand. My fingers closed tightly over it. "Thank you." My eyes swelled with tears. "Who are you? This is exactly what I need. Thank you." Clutched in my other hand was a tape of classical music I wanted the operating staff to play. I knew that any conversation the doctors had would be carried to my soul; any sound would reverberate on my psyche. Yes, they would play the tape for me. I slipped the prayer book under my pillow and waited for the needle. Entranced by Bach's *Suite No 3 in D*, I watched as both men, one on either side of my body, began to cut into it, dipping their hands inside, tugging. They looked like vultures ripping their prey apart. Tug, tug, tug, I felt as though I were being pulled up from my back. "It's okay," whispered Marcel, "no hysterectomy." I smiled at him, closed my eyes and let go.

In the darkened ward after the operation I lay on my back for twenty four hours. I should've been moved. A nurse had forgotten me. In terrible pain I called for Marcel. "I can't give you any more morphine," he explained. Into the night I lay whimpering "Where's my bloody mother?"

Dizzily I stood up with help from Aviva the next day. I began to eat, smile again. In terror had I arrived, in safety had I stayed. Surrounded by people who were getting to know me; visited by friends who brought me flowers and fruit, I sensed a loss leaving. I photographed the nurses I had become friends with, "my" two doctors and returned to what was commonly called the real world. I had survived an operation in a strange language. What was next?

my life

steps to heal the heart

Do we act or are we acted upon?

"Divine action brought me to Israel."

What does this statement imply about our freedom to act?

Do you believe that what happens in your life is the result of divine action? What is divine action? Does this apply only to the good things that happen or does it include the negative things that happen? Do you think that you somehow accelerate or induce that action? Can we influence God/Spirit? Or is everything that happens to us a direct result of our own thoughts and actions?

Write about a time in your life when you were convinced that you were being led by a positive spiritual force.

Search for self

If you want to "find yourself" leave the place and people familiar to you and start again in a foreign country where you know only one or two people. A friend of mine was sent to France for a year. He didn't know the language, he lived alone, he had to adapt to his new job. It was a huge challenge for him. In that year he got to know himself. If our lives are comparatively settled, we do a lot by habit and we are surrounded by people who do not rock our boat, we may never find out more about who we really are. On the other hand, if our life is a struggle on many levels, going somewhere else may only make that worse. For me, leaving everything I knew behind, everything I associated with myself allowed me to look at what was hiding underneath. What do you understand as "finding yourself"?

"I'm not angry!"

Many people don't allow themselves to feel their anger. They suppress it.

Can you identify with the anger I felt in Jerusalem? Where do you feel your anger? In what part of your body do you feel it? Can you sit with it, let it rise so you feel it fully?

If you're a woman, what were the early messages you got about anger, and being angry and about the way to deal with your anger?

If you're a man, what were the early messages you got about anger about being angry and about the way to deal with that anger?

Write about a time when you were angry. What provoked your anger? How did you handle the situation? Who was involved? Are you angry now? Often under anger is pain. Write about your feelings.

The cycles of healing

Can you identify with the concept of cycles of healing? Have you worked on one issue, and then later it comes up again but at a different level and you work through it again? My experience is that an issue operates at a number of levels. The stronger we get, the greater our sense of self-worth, the more we are able to tackle the pain or hurt we grew up with. This continues until they are just a flicker on the surface of our consciousness. Like a familiar scar that needs no further attention. We let it go. Can you give some examples of this process in your life? Can you share that with a friend?

my life

Losing a baby

As a man, has a woman you loved had a miscarriage? Was it your child? How did you feel about the child you never knew? Would you prefer not to have known she was pregnant? What do you do (or did you do) with your feelings? Can you describe them in some artistic way — in writing, or in a painting or in clay?

Losing a child

I lost two children. One through an abortion and one through a miscarriage. Since then I have met parents who have lost children. I cannot begin to imagine what this must be like. I am aware that this wound may never heal. Even though the children I could have had were never born, I still remember them with a sense of loss. I ask you to take a few minutes to think about your child, and in the creative silence may a message of love and tender holding rest in your heart.

The attraction of a medical man

Have you, straight or gay, ever fallen for your doctor? What is it about The Doctor that carries an aura? Is it her or his power? The mystery of healing perhaps? Or is it a form of gratitude? Perhaps your experience was negative. Has a doctor ever taken advantage of you? Has a doctor harmed you more than healed you? I have a friend whose doctor made a mistake in surgery and my friend's life was ruined. Because of the laws protecting doctors in this country, that doctor was never made to pay for his negligence. What about you? What is your experience of the medical man or woman? Write about it.

Hospitals

Not many of us escape the experience of being in a hospital, being powerless. Write a description of a time you were ill in hospital or someone you cared about was ill. What do you remember most? Tell the story.

Friend power

"In moments of doubt there was always someone who believed in me when I could no longer believe in myself nor find that self." Talk about a particular person in your life who took you out of an inner darkness or who sat with you in the confusion. Perhaps you might like to write to that person. Perhaps you'd prefer a portrait in words or in crayon.

Perhaps you were that person for someone else. Have you acknowledged your part in her or his growth? What do you think it is about you that enables someone to lean on you in time of pain or trouble? How do you reward yourself for your compassion?

Chapter 4 ה *Hay: Inner Peace*

A space had been cleared; room was made inside me for newness. "Now, go have a baby quickly!" laughed Doctor Jean as we parted. Yes, a pregnancy would now occur, an expectancy of life but it would not be the life of another soul; it would be life of my own soul, it would be me I could now bear. The growths in my body may have been the result of harboured rage, resentment, fear. Layer upon layer of repressed feelings firmed to form shape, size and volume. Only when I began to loosen up, to let go, to let out, could this bundle of withholding unravel and be ripped out. The action was severe, yes. It unlocked a process that would continue for the remainder of my life — the recognition, acceptance and appropriate expression of my feelings.

"Is there anybody there?" I asked of the waiting inside me, the gap. "Who are you?" I asked of the surround of nothingness, the empty space in my centre. "Stay with it," came the reply. "Stay with it long enough and it will reveal itself." I began to face my self, to walk with my self, to eat with my self, to live with my self in peace. I was no longer trying to escape by distracting myself with work or movies or the newspapers. "Get away, lose yourself, do something, anything!" No, now I'd wake to the awareness that I was here and I'd be here all day. I began to go for walks fully aware of the houses, the streets, my feelings, being there. I'd eat meals at restaurants I liked and laze in the sun sensing the harmony, appreciating the flowers, hearing the music, honouring my self. I began to give myself the recognition I had always hoped would come from others. I gave myself time, attention and respect.

I felt most comfortable with artists, people who created, sculptors, weavers, musicians, painters. I met them — in cafes, in small shops, at a friend's, on the street. "I'm an artist too." I'd play my guitar, sit on the porch, listen to the sounds of the late afternoon, drink in the full silence that came like a cat and curled into my lap, offering me a completeness.

Each morning I thanked God for the day. Through gritted teeth, often. Bitterly cold in winter, the Jerusalem wind whipped my legs and the rain attacked sideways. My apartment in the German Colony was small, sufficient, simply furnished and freezing. "Thank you for my life," I'd mutter, "Thank you for my job," as I jumped off the bus and crossed the street before Misrad Hachutz (the Department of Foreign Affairs); "Thank you that I have food to eat," as I'd buy a falafel on the street en route to the British Council for the evening shift of English teaching. "Thank you that I have clothes to wear," as I'd put on again the skirt I'd been wearing forever. The more I expressed a gratitude, the better I felt. It seemed to lift the fog of heaviness. Like magic it worked. My spirit lightened. Gratitude — a rope — pulled me out of the well of self-pity and reproach. I met people who introduced me to Louise Hay, *A Course in Miracles*, Carlos Castenada, Lazaris. Welcome to the new age. It was not enough.

Who are you?

I'm an Israeli. I live and work in Jerusalem.

So? This is just the surface.

I am a Jew.

So?

So, let me discover what it means to be Jewish.

How are you going to do that?

I didn't have to worry too much. Just being in Jerusalem was already prodding me.

200

The space inside me was holding two answers, twins. The one was that I am present inside myself and I am great to be with as a human being; the second, now emerging, was that my self-with-God was engraved in Hebrew, the name on my soul was Michal, four letters of the Hebrew alphabet that housed sacred space. Having come into contact with myself, I was now in the process of finding my soul, the deeper ground of my being. The Sabbath was the starting point.

I was warned that Fridays and Saturdays were different in Israel. Friday morning at the market was the Middle East at its best. As I entered under the tin roofs, I was sucked into the human rapids that swirled through, breaking into small circles where a body stopped to haggle and to buy. Smells assailed me from freshly baked biscuits to fish still flapping, gasping for breath, desperate to be decapitated. Spice sacks, burnt-orange blotches, squatted on their haunches like well-thighed women comfortably nudging one another. "Fresh parsley," a veiled Arab woman would offer in Hebrew, waving the green bunch towards me. "*Shekel Echad*," she'd plead. "*Shekel Esrim*," another voice would boom from behind a vegetable stall offering every conceivable array of produce all neatly stacked in rows. "*Peyrot peresh*," a competitor cackled well above the din, proud of the fresh fruit splayed before him. Buffeted by bodies bent with bags, I'd sidle into a cafe "*Shachor*," I'd order, sinking to rest, sipping the sweet black brew.

The market mazed for miles, sometimes under a low smelting tin roof, sometimes bursting into the open air where clothes, shoes, tapes, hardware, groceries sprung up unexpectedly. Round surged the people, pushing, pressing, delving into pockets or purses, braking briskly to gossip, sampling an olive, swallowing a grape, stuffing their plastic bags full. A human river, relentless in its eagerness, unquenchable in its vitality, deafening in its roar.

Not far from this maelstrom a very different Friday morning was underway on Ben Yehuda, a street closed to traffic. Here the pace was languid and leisurely. Cafes birthed their chairs and tables onto the cobblestone streets, where avid readers grabbed them and gobbled up the weekend news from one to five newspapers. Armed with delicate cups of espresso, men lounged in the sun, a cigarette smoking in their fingers, their eyes flicking lazily over the women swaying past as they spouted their opinions on the state of affairs in Israel and anywhere else that might affect her. Lovers strolling by lingered at jewellery-shop windows; they'd eye a ring and then each other, laugh, hug and wander on. Soldiers, home for the weekend, stood talking loudly, basking in the bright air, rifles slung across their backs, eyes alert for action of another, softer, more sensual kind. The streets carried friends who'd meet to catch up on the week and watch the crowds juggle by like corn, hotly popping, falling over one another playfully. A harpist caressing her strings stilled those restless saunterers, some even stopped to drop a coin into her case. Surrounded by open-mouthed children, a clown blew life into a balloon then curled it into a dog that barked.

The hours passed until mid-afternoon when the frenzied shoppers scurried home to add the final touches to the Friday evening meal. The laidback Ben Yehuda bourgeoisie, having filled their eyes, minds, stomachs and lungs, petered off to nap before the siren sounded. Shops slammed shut self-righteously. Buses pummelled the fast emptying streets scrambling for their bay of rest to sleep until Saturday night when, one by one, they'd lethargically lumber out of line, still yawning, reproachfully switch on their lights and awake begrudgingly, to work again. Until then the city fell under a spell. The market became a vacant shelter, the frenetic bus station a shell and the streets were struck silent as a magic wand of stillness started *Shabbat*, the day of rest.

Not everyone adhered rigorously to *Shabbat* in its pristine sense. Many Israelis still chose to drive their cars and watch television. There were even a few places open in holy Jerusalem if you knew where. Friday night however, remained a time you spent with people important and dear to you. It was the family night. But on the other hand it was an entrance into twenty four hours of as blissful a life as one could imagine on earth. Ideally it could be a time where time no longer existed. Nothing mattered now. Not the news, not the stock market, not plans for the future, not regret about the past. There was only now and the joy of being with people you loved. Mystically you allowed yourself to be carried in the arms of God.

One moved into another consciousness on *Shabbat*. All the food for the day was already prepared. In the best of circumstances the man would lay the food on the table, take over the daily tasks if the woman usually performed them. She too, was entitled to rest. Lightness and light characterised *Shabbat*. From the glow of the blessed candles came the release of care, the expression of joy, the delight of eating, the blessing of the children, the sharing of insights about God, the singing of songs, the night-lamp lingering, making love and sleeping securely, knowing that the next day offered a continuation of this floating on a wave of peace. Peace in Israel was also to stop complaining!

For me, *Shabbat* was a dual personality: one face bliss; one face battleground. Of course I wanted the splendour of all it could be, but as I was single and not part of a family I often felt pinched and lonely on Shabbat. Perhaps it would be a happier day for me if I were out in nature, on a hike. Being close to the earth and the trees centred me, reminded me of my place in the larger scheme, lifted my spirit. So I'd do that too. Sometimes I was invited to other people's homes and that could be pleasant or a bit tedious. Being a guest three times in one day became cumbersome. A family of secular Israelis "adopted" me and to them I could always go, no matter what was happening in their lives. It made a big difference. Occasionally I'd be in Haifa with my friend, Yehudit, and we'd go to the beach. I was always torn between "keeping" and "not keeping" Shabbat. It was a wrestling match that would continue.

Underneath was the awareness that this tradition came from a history of which I was part, a relationship with God that was offered to me too. It was vital that I explore this. Jerusalem teemed with lectures, schools and seminars. Scanning *The Jerusalem Post* I read of a series of lectures offered by a Rabbi David Zeller on "Kabbalah and Meditation" at the Israel Centre. He was telling a story of a king looking for a princess. Having scoured all the main roads the king got side-tracked and slipped down a dirt road. That path led him to his love. As he talked I listened with an attention that gripped me unyieldingly. I got it. My trip to Israel was not to preach macrobiotics but to find my heritage, to find myself as a Jew.

How do I do this? I made an appointment to speak to David Zeller and he recommended a school in the Old City. I hesitated, waiting and praying for guidance. One afternoon while meandering down King George Street, I passed a pizza shop where a notice board was smothered with flyers and bits of miscellaneous information.

"Come to Israel," read one, "and meet someone you would like to know. Yourself." It was the same course David Zeller had suggested. It ran from May 7 to June 13. May 7 was my birthday and June 13 was my father's. Dad definitely had something to do with this. It was as if since his death he'd been planning assiduously on the other side for my return to Judaism. He wanted me to be happy, to find peace. What better way?

Steps to heal the heart

Time in

It seems to me that our lives are very externally focused. They are about doing. About being busy. Business has become positive. But business can distract us to such an extent that when we find we have a minute to ourselves we feel anxious and lost. Or we feel a vague emptiness that we rush to fill with another task or distraction or "important business".

Women are socialised to take care of everyone else first. Often there is no time left for ourselves. Or we think we are no longer important. Finding ourselves again is a slow process.

Men are socialised into taking the pressure, winning, being strong, providing and protecting. They are almost not allowed an inner life. When events occur that require an emotional response, many men cannot access those emotions. This makes them feel isolated and stuck.

Do you make time to spend with yourself? It is something that has to be created. We need to choose this time. When you take this time, what do you do? Besides watching television — which is another distraction and a filling of a void. What do you do with yourself? For instance, do you go out for a meal? Do you visit an art gallery? Do you listen to music? Perhaps you play a game of golf? Treat yourself to a tennis class? Or just make a cup of tea and sit and do nothing? During these times what do you notice about yourself? How does it feel at first? When you get used to spending quality time with yourself what's it like? Do you notice a difference in yourself when you spend time alone and when you don't? What is that difference? Do other people notice anything about you as a result of your taking time for yourself?

A day of rest

Are you familiar with this concept? If you are a Christian what do Sundays mean to you? If you are a Jew how is your relationship with Shabbat? And if you are Jewish, single, and female, does this make a difference in any way? Do you consider "holy days" useful or burdensome? Write about a day of obligation where you were able to enter fully into what it represented or where you struggled with the tampering of your inner spiritual cycle and resisted going through the external rituals which were demanded of you.

Prayer and meditation

There's finding yourself and there's finding your Self. The first self is the person in all aspects — sex, religion, sexual orientation, race, class, ability and so on. That self is connected to The Self — the all-encompassing being-ness we share. We leave behind the little self and move into the big self when we pray or meditate, or at other times that we recognise. Whether we reach our inner being-ness by saying words, or by watching the mind, or by speaking to God from our heart, or by twirling in a dance, or by any other means, what we are doing is essential to being human. It reminds us who we really are.

my life

my life

Chapter 5 ו *Vav: Beginning again*

*I*was always excited when the bus stopped outside the Old City and I'd cross the street heading determinedly for Jaffa Cafe. Yes I was going inside! Along the narrow entrance road I'd breathe deeply, aware that a heightened sense of energy and activity existed here. It felt like I was walking on mines that could explode at any second.

Arab vendors lined the sides of the street surveying the possibilities. Tourists, clutching their bags, peered into shop windows and were wooed inside; students with knapsacks swung in as though they had lived here all their lives; young couples on honeymoon clutched their maps and each other as they peered gingerly around them; groups of pilgrims with loud-voiced guides stopped, blocking the traffic; Greek Orthodox priests in their long black robes, Arabs gliding in full-length white garments, religious Jews with wide-brimmed hats and peyot mingled with pastors in dog-collars and shorts.

The throng at the entrance then split into two streams. One flowed past the King David Museum towards the Armenian Quarter, the other cascaded in steps through the market place disappearing into the bowels of the Old City. Take your pick. I was taught to cling to the wall which tunnelled before the Armenian quarter and then to disappear through an archway which immediately became a cobbled street. Keep walking. The street burgeoned into what might have been a square. Turn right. This was always a quiet part. It couldn't have been more than a hundred yards. Seldom occupied, this ledge of street caught time. History hung in the air here, suspended in space. It was empty and it was full. I'd stop and honour the silence. Often I waited to see a figure emerge from the walls, from the stones. They were all there; I just couldn't see them. The street went on but I'd duck to the left where I'd soon be led into the Jewish Quarter. Made it!

An alternative route was to enter through the Arab Market when it was open. That could be slower as I'd stop to look at the jewellery, the scarves, the dresses, the plates — wares that warranted attention. Invitations to buy would come thick and fast and I'd have to make some excuse. I looked like a tourist and often acted like one. Towards the end of the market, on the right, a fabric store bore into the wall. This was the one. You had to be able to recognise it. A handsome Arab vendor always stood outside. "Hello!" I'd smile as I passed him. Into the depths of the shop I'd dart, my senses swooning with the seductive smell of Turkish coffee, the lush texture of puce-stained, sensual silks and Persian carpets curtaining the walls. It was womb in colour. "Coffee?" he'd ask, emerging from yet another recess. It was so inviting! "*Lo, hayom,*" I'd refuse, shaking my head. Up three steps to the left. Now I was in a street bordering on the Arab and Jewish Quarters. Arab children squatted on the square stones playing with marbles. Halfway along this road and a right turn — the last lap into the Jewish Quarter. This street took me just above the Cardo. No matter which route I took, the journey into the Old City was always mysterious, dangerous, intoxicatingly invigorating.

Inside, the city exploded with a dense past, a bristling present and an uncertain future. In the cocooned enclave of the Jewish Quarter, many religious Jews lived and studied. It was like a campus for Judaism. Alongside this intensity, artists, sculptors, creators of many fashions found their foothold. Burrowed in small apartments thickly strewn along the maze of streets, inhabitants guarded their privileged position tenaciously. It was a rare honour to live in the Old City.

My course was here, held in an apartment adjacent to Rechov Ha-Shofar. Fourteen participants were to spend six weeks together. The majority were young Americans in their early twenties. I chose to live in my own apartment and come in daily. The rest of the group shared two apartments in the Old City.

What was there for me to learn? I entered the course with some apprehension. Modern Orthodox. The Modern part was okay; the Orthodox part made me slightly queasy. I was wary of substituting one rigid system for another. Ten years in the convent had offered me a highly disciplined life, set times for prayer, certainly a separation, a clamping down on sexuality, a "we-they" attitude, a striving for perfection that inhibited expression, a male-dominated hierarchy and plenty of rules. On the other hand, it led me to realise that once past a certain point one could arrive at a place where God was touchable. Teresa of Avila, Therese of Lisieux, John of the Cross, Friar Lawrence, the Curé of Ars, Martin de Porres had got there. Plus thousands of other Catholics who didn't make it through the Vatican Selection Committee for Saints. You got there because you followed the way for you, your individual path, whether or not it was part of an institutionalised religion.

I came to the course with a respect for my Catholic past, knowing that it had taken me only so far. I felt an eagerness to explore and embrace the way that my soul sought. Could I grasp this in six weeks? After the course will it all be clear, my struggle over? A hornet's nest now stirred as I began to wrestle with characters, concepts, traditions, interpretations, patriarchy, mind-sets, language, history, relationship, communication, revelation, and books upon books to both baffle and bombard me with information, explanation, inspiration. It was only a nibble I'd get, an aperitif.

Perhaps the weaving, winding, somewhat scary entrance into the Old City is symbolic of the way to the heart of Judaism. It's a circuitous route. The point of entry makes a difference; you bring yourself into the Old City, into Judaism. It's not all laid out as if "this is the way it is and it's the same for all of us". It cannot possibly be that because each of us approaches as a unique self. Where we have come from, the people whom we bring with us, all of our experiences come face to face with the Torah, with the words of the prophets, with the psalmists. This is what makes it alive. Not that it's been handed down in stone for thousands of years, but that people over the thousands of years have interacted with it. It has to be a blend of who I am and Itself. This continues its existence. There needs to be a respect for the tradition and a respect for the person. We are not blank slates onto which our fathers and mothers, be they spiritual or physical, stamp their names. No, we have our own names carried within us from time immemorial and it is the duty of our parents to sit back and honour our names as we both discover what they are, and who we are. I cannot abdicate responsibility for my own progress by blindly accepting whatever I am told and negating the imperative work of delving into myself and discovering myself. As I approach the Torah, that blast of power must send me reeling back into myself. From there I boomerang back and so it continues. For me, it's an authentic interaction between the individual and the tradition.

I came to the course with fear and prejudice, hope and expectations. What I received and how I integrated this reflected where I was within myself. I felt comfortable with the idea of the relationship with God being open-ended. There was a dynamism to it I hadn't found before. Judaism encourages questioning. To argue is to show respect. "Don't just sit there, dumbly accepting everything, challenge!" I felt as if the ceiling had slipped away quietly without my noticing and fresh air streamed in with the light.

There is no concept of original sin. We are made in the image of God and this is good. The huge, unyielding questions of suffering and evil cannot be simply addressed.

Judaism catches me in my every-day-ness and shoots me into the stars. It combines the earth and the sky. It freezes the actions of my life — rising, washing, eating, loving, dancing, working, sleeping — like an instant photo-flash where at any point I can meet God, I can pass into God. I hadn't known that this mystical element was available in Judaism. It was available to me as a nun but in a restrained way. We were taught to convert every moment into an awareness of God. Here it was so okay to be human. We didn't have to repress anything. That was my understanding. Eating, making love — all part of an awareness of the presence of God. Particularly the concept of God being in the home — in the family. Like you couldn't miss God.

The weakness and flaws of biblical characters was consoling. Nothing was covered up to make them look like angels. Just human beings in a wrestling match with God. In fact they had so many faults one sometimes wondered why God spent so much time with them! I didn't have to be perfect. That is not Jewish. It was also a huge relief.

I was impressed by a tradition that had continued for so many thousands of years and was so diverse and rich in its resources. The written tradition, the *Tenach* which includes the five books of Moses (*Torah*), the Prophets and the Writings, was familiar to me. The oral tradition, the *Talmud* consisting of *Mishna* and *Gemarah*, was a world unknown, as was *Halacha*. *Midrash* — imaginative stories illustrating the *Halacha* and the moral ideals of the Jewish faith. *Kabbalah* — the mystical aspect of Judaism became a powerful attraction. Judaism is a smorgasbord, replete with everything necessary to feed the spiritual seeker for a full and meaningful lifetime. Why hadn't I picked this up years ago?

I had problems too. Where were the women sages? I'd stand at the Western Wall, impressed of course, but then I'd measure how small the women's section was. In one of the most highly respected schools, I saw how the women were squashed upstairs at one of the functions. What's the matter with being a woman? I was fascinated by the array of wigs I sat behind on buses. A religious woman kept her hair for her husband. What was left of it. After being under that wig all day I wondered how healthy the hair could be. I know, I used to wear a veil! Not being allowed to sing in the presence of men threw me into what could only have been short of an apoplexy. Women's voices were said to rouse the sexual desire of men. All women's voices? Some of the women I've heard sing sent me screaming for ear plugs. So what if men got aroused? They can deal with that. It's called honesty. A man dare not sit next to me on the bus in case I'm menstruating; nor can he shake my hand for the same reason. There was a consuming passion to suppress and repress sex and sexuality. (*Déja-vu?*) That seemed to be at odds with the generous celebration of life. The men had to be protected from women. There it was again, evil Eve. Did the beliefs work? Some couples seemed very happy; three orthodox couples I knew personally, divorced. Nothing is magic. The aspect of women's status in Orthodoxy angered me. Part of that anger was justified and part was linked to a hidden hurt soon to surface. It was the same anger when three Catholic nuns were in attendance to one bishop and where Catholic priests depended heavily on the service of sisters to keep them alive.

I'd met fundamentalism before and what saddens me is a "we-they" attitude; that "we" have the "truth" and everyone else is running around mistaken. I think there is a violence in dogmatism. In the name of truth many have died and will die. Anyone who claims to have The Truth scares the shit out of me. Whatever The Truth is, I don't want it. Please don't drop it into my lap. I pass. I prefer to live my way sensing and sifting and maybe never knowing anything, really, and trying to be patient with others who claim they do.

I believe that at the end of each route and along each route, the same light streams. Finding my path and following it is the key. The continued experience of God (whatever God is conceived to be); the day-to-day focus on living that experience and awareness, the refining that accompanies this is part of each soul's journey whichever religion or path that person sincerely follows. It's not necessary for me to try to alter anyone's route. Her way is sacred to her and calls for my respect. Side-tracking by comparing religions or faiths is such a waste of time, in my opinion. I prefer to concentrate on what I have. If I compare my friend's cake to mine, and we sit there comparing ingredients and recipes, we'll never eat! Besides which, her taste buds respond differently to mine. What tastes good to her may not taste as delicious to me. "Taste and see that the Lord is sweet," sings the psalmist. To each her own. If the person is a Jew, I would invite her to explore her Jewish opportunities for peace.

On the whole, the course was powerful, demanding, enthralling, annoying. Six weeks later I reeled away drunkenly and put it all down for a few months. I needed to allow it to rest within me. What was crucial would remain. Over time I could explore a vast world. My hunger would be met. I would find my place within the vista. *Savlanut* —patience. There was plenty of time, wasn't there?

my life

steps to heal the heart

Return to roots

My return to Judaism was powerful. Since then, 1992, I have continued to sift, weigh, absorb, compare and integrate my Catholic experience into my Jewish soul. It is very difficult to put into words an experience of this nature. Possibly it is impossible.

Have you had an experience or a transformation that was profound? Did you, too, grope for words or ways to express it so that someone else could appreciate what happened to you? Perhaps a poem or an art form could do this well?

Many of us who grow up in one religion take it for granted. If you grew up in a particular faith and you are still practising, take one ritual or aspect of your faith that is very beautiful and meaningful to you. Describe it in words or create it in an art form and share it with a person or persons from another religious belief-system. Perhaps they'd like to do the same with you?

Whose truth is it?

As I began to share my experience of moving back to my Jewish roots I noticed how some Christians responded. They felt as though I had made a mistake; that I had "back-tracked". They assured me they would pray for me. My soul was in danger. It wasn't possible for them to accept that Judaism is a way with God just as Christianity is. Because of their religious education they were sure that Judaism was "old and limited" and Christianity was "the truth and unlimited". They had made no effort to find out what Judaism was about, nor about the depth and breadth of Jewish teachings. I found this attitude patronising and self-righteous. I found it even with some of the Catholic sisters and priests I talked to. What is your opinion on this? Have you had an experience where someone from a different faith tried to convince you that you were making a horrible mistake by continuing on your path? Write the dialogue and your thoughts in between the conversation.

Catholic apologies

On my return to Johannesburg, I passed through Auschwitz for a conference on reconciliation. A Jesuit priest spoke about the role of the Catholic Church in fostering anti-Semitism. He apologised for the verses in the Bible that were clearly against Jews and for all the teaching down the ages about the Jews having killed Christ and other similar prejudicial teachings. In St Louis I met a Catholic writer, Harry James Cargas, who gave me a copy of his book *Shadows of Auschwitz: A Christian Response to the Holocaust* published by The Crossroad Publishing Company, New York, in which he traces the history of Christian persecution of the Jews.

What is your response to the above? Do you know about the Holocaust? Have you studied the Bible to find where it continues to teach prejudice against the Jews? How does the knowledge of this, or lack of it, impact on relationships between Christians and Jews?

Chapter 6 ז *Zayin: A call to go forth*

Where to now? Do I continue teaching English at the British Council for the remainder of my life? Do I immerse myself in a long-term course on Jewish studies? If so, how do I pay for this? Perhaps I could trade by cooking for the course? If so, why not go to Sweden to learn how to cook first? What to do? I swung around, vacillating from one idea to another. A friend called Michael sensed my unease. Teaching English was not challenging me. I found it repetitive and limiting. Studying would be interesting, but did I want to be confined to an Orthodox setting? Where to go? This way? No, this way!

"Call this friend of mine in London," he said, one evening, "she's a psychic. I always call her when I've reached a wall."

"A psychic?"

"Why not?"

So I called.

"How can I help you?"

"I don't know," I answered, abashed. "I don't know what to do with my life."

"What are you doing now?"

"I'm teaching English and I hate it."

"What are you doing teaching English? You're a spiritual teacher. That's what you're supposed to be doing. I see you travelling and speaking to many people. Soon. You need to realise who you are and be open to that."

Me a spiritual teacher? Travelling? On whose bank balance? Impossible!

I always find that if there's a decision to be made between two alternatives and neither seems the right one, it means that there's a third option. What I have to do when I'm getting nowhere trying to decide is to do nothing. Wait. Help is on the way. Something is working its way into my life and my job is to be there when it pops up.

One June morning at six o'clock the phone rings. It's Rabbi Simcha — only he's not in Jerusalem but in the USA.

"Michal, would you like to come to work for us from St Louis?"

"St Louis? What's that?"

"I can't tell you much, but a couple here are interested in offering you a position where you'd promote our *yeshiva*."

"In America?"

"Yes. You'll receive a call from a Kathleen Walston. She'll interview you. It may be just for the summer or it could be longer. Good luck!" He was gone. I crashed the phone back into its cradle and shot into a level of excitement that prevented me from remembering my name.

"America? Do I want to go to America? How could I leave Israel? How could anyone ask me to tear myself away from my soul-spot? Never! I'd be crazy to go! America? Malls? Television? Fast-food? English? Well, almost. Me? They want me? Why me? Are they mad? Is this a movie? Is this somewhere over the rainbow? Is this a rags-to-riches saga? Do I have time to make some tea? Me?"

And the phone rang again.

"Michal?" came a female tone from thousands of miles away.

"This is she!" I replied in my most Oxford of accents.

"Hello! I'm Kathleen Walston. Can you tell me about yourself?"

Off I shot about my communication business and training and public-speaking skills. All the while I'm thinking, "Do I want to do all that again?" Just get the offer then decide. We talked for almost an hour. I was glad I wasn't paying. Kathleen sounded very pleasant.

"I'll call you back in two days. I need to discuss this with the board and make a decision. Bye now!" I knew I was going to America. It was absolutely clear. Why I was going I didn't know. I began to pack, to throw away, give away, resign, clear out, phone my friends, speak American. Locate St Louis on the map. Two days later the phone rang. It had an American ring to it.

"Hello Michal? This is Kathleen! We'd love to have you come help us for the summer. If you like us and we like you, we can apply for you to stay. We need assistance to get the school better known here. We need some organising and education. We figure you can be based in St Louis and travel. Now please book your ticket as soon as you can. We'll send you the money, plus whatever you need to release yourself from your rental contract. I'll phone you again or you can phone me."

That was it. Confirmation. I, great illustrious Michal Ish-Shalom, had been discovered by a rich and influential business in America (in the mid-west, but we'll leave that out) and I was to be a key figure in the expansion of this special school in Jerusalem. "It was roses, roses, all the way and myrtle mixed in my feet like mad." I conveniently forgot the last verse of the poem which tells of the turnabout of the crowd and the death of the hero. All I knew — and this was enough for me — was that I needed a couple of suitcases. Have case, will travel.

The family responsible for my good fortune had been students of this school. Now they wanted to do something for Rabbi Simcha, like take the school over and design a five-year plan. My background in communications, my experience at the school, would place me in the position of being able to contribute. First I would fly to London to see my brother, then to Scotland to see my mother and her husband and then, to the strains of the *Star Spangled Banner*, I'd fly on to the Land of Opportunity whence came Abe Lincoln, Martin Luther King and all the movie stars I'd grown up on. I'm going to have a nervous breakdown!

You may say my feet were somewhat suspended from their normal position of feeling the ground underneath them. I was on such a high I couldn't pause to consider whether there was anything I hadn't thought of before consenting. I was leaving, again. In a rush, again. It took me a week to pack and put everything in order. Convinced that this was part of the grand scheme for me, I knew God would make it all happen as quickly as necessary. "Watch God Work," I muttered to myself as I walked into the towering electricity building, where, after waiting only for one hour instead of all day, I was given a cheque, a repayment on my electricity. This was unheard of. Money poured in from my work, from St Louis, from my mother, from friends. I was being moved forward at a pace.

On the 13th of June the call had come. That was my dad's birthday. On 19th June two years previously I had arrived in Israel. On the same date, I left Israel for America. How could I possibly know what lay ahead? Somebody was going to make it all happen for me, the husband, the fame, the money. In that couple of weeks between continents I was in a state of euphoria. It was the "and they lived happily ever after" moment that has no sell-by date.

This was to be another beginning. I was coming to America as a Jew this time, not as a Christian. Coming to a Jewish community, to a position I believed in. What could go wrong? It was the start of another spiral. Only this kind or rush could have ripped me out of Jerusalem. Enveloped in this frenzy of activity and enthusiasm I didn't know what I was doing. My impulsiveness would pay off but not in the way I thought. There was more growing to do and I needed another environment in which to do it.

Jerusalem had given me the pillow underneath my head, the magnet under my feet. I could never forget her. "If I forget you Jerusalem, may my right hand wither." Jerusalem I carried inside me, always pregnant with her. I had to uncover more aspects within myself that had lain low for so long. Under the loving awareness of Israel's caresses I had summoned the courage to face myself. In America my personal archaeological dig was about to unearth artefacts more deeply hidden even than those Jerusalem had revealed. The two people who were responsible for my relocating would provide me with a scenario so hostile that I'd survive it only by understanding why I chose it. America would give me the opportunity to focus on my destiny. It had the people, the tools, the awareness to push me in the direction towards personal integration.

steps to heal the heart

Dead can dance

Do you believe that family members who are dead can still influence our actions? That our ancestors care about us and take an active role in directing our lives? How would you explain the influence of my father on my life at this time? Have you experienced something similar? Write about it or talk to someone about it.

Numerology

The dates that I began and finished my course in Judaism were highly relevant. What do you think about this? Do you think numerology is useful or not? Are there significant dates in your life? What happened on those dates or how are they linked?

Intuition

This is the scenario. You and a friend or two are all set for a journey. Money has been saved. Tickets have been bought. People have been notified. It all looks set to happen, when you get this nagging feeling that you should not go. Sound familiar? What do you do? If you stay, what happens that confirms your intuition? If you go what happens that confirms your intuition? Or is there something I'm missing? Write about it.

Impulse

Remember when you acted on impulse? What was the impulse? Where were you? What happened? Or did someone who was responsible for you in some way act on impulse with serious consequences for the rest of your life? Please write about it.

A time frame

I'd done a lot of inner work in Israel. I thought I'd live there forever. I couldn't see into the future. Has there been a time in your life when you were sure you were going to stay put, either in a relationship, a career, a country? Something unexpected happened to change that. What? Why was it best for you that your life took a different turn? Or was it best?

Sudden parting

I loved Jerusalem as though she were a person. Write the final dialogue you had between yourself and someone or something you loved. It can be a person, an animal, a country. You have to leave. You are sad to leave and it is difficult for you. Even though the one you love may be inanimate in that she doesn't talk, in this imaginative exercise she talks back.

my life

_____
_____
_____
_____
_____
_____
_____
_____
_____
_____
_____
_____
_____
_____
_____
_____
_____
_____
_____
_____
_____
_____
_____
_____
_____
_____
_____
_____
_____
_____
_____

my life

Part 6

Michelle Ish-Shalom Friedman

Chapter 1 *St Louis*

*I*flew to America on the wings of a great bird whose name was Success. Everyone had congratulated me on my new job; my mother was as proud as punch. I felt like a celebrity. Here I was, one day a nobody and the next flying to St Louis to take up a powerful position representing the institute where I had studied. Big shot. But why be surprised? Isn't this the great American dream after all? Rags to riches overnight? I'd be successful, secure, marry an American and live happily ever after.

Kathleen was late. My mood minutes earlier registering about ninety-eight percent deliriously happy dropped about fifty percent immediately. Okay, I thought, let's get my suitcase. While I was walking to the baggage-claim a pretty-blonde-slim-blue-eyed-small-cute-turned-up-nose-all-American girl ran up to me. "Hello, I'm Kathleen, sorry I'm late." She stopped. "Oh, you looked so much fatter on the video!" Great start. The institute had made a video of the students expressing their experience of the course. What could I say? "My car's parked outside," she continued and in a few moments we were in the thick of the St Louis June heat that clung onto me like a sauna with no shower afterwards. Heavy and hard it sat on my head in front of my mouth. Even my breath was scorched.

Kathleen drove on the wrong side of the road and so did everyone else. She talked all the way to the restaurant — an upmarket place with three glasses per place, murals on the walls and waiters serving with an alacrity that startled me. I tried to behave as if I did this every day. What a shock after Jerusalem, after the small cafes, the limited choice, the lack of sophistication. All through dinner Kathleen chatted about the job I'd be doing. I listened, dazzled and bewildered. I understood nothing. She then drove me back to a house where I'd stay for a week or two until she got me an apartment. She hadn't asked me one question.

The house was one of many similar-looking houses, all with neat front lawns. The air-conditioning didn't work so I lost a couple of pounds that first week. When Kathleen appeared the next morning to take me to breakfast, I was lolling around in the oldest and shabbiest of my clothes — and most of them fitted this description. "Shall I change?" I asked her. "Don't bother," she replied, and promptly took me to the most expensive hotel in St Louis. While I tried to pretend I was one of those eccentric millionaires who wore ragged clothes, she chatted away once again, but this time she had loads of files to prove her seriousness. I was still not sure what I was to do, but it sounded as though I'd be fund-raising. Fund-raising? I knew nothing about raising money and had little desire to. But Monday would arrive and I'd go to the premises of the large pharmaceutical company out of which I would work and all would be well.

My office was indeed large and at the end of a long corridor of offices. I looked out onto the back of a brick building. This was where I would work from nine until five every day. I was startled. An office? But I hate offices! "Yes, and you'll travel, and write grants (grants?) and speak to people about donating large sums of money ..." And she was off again at a great rate. Into a boardroom we zoomed to see the completed video. I wanted to be back in Israel with my friends, with the culture I had become a part of. Tears streamed down my face. The love I had for Jerusalem overwhelmed me. Kathleen was taken by surprise. She put her hand out and touched my shoulder with her fingertips. "You miss your friends," she said. Then she stood up, opened the door and summoned me to follow her. I did, like a sheep. She then introduced me to her partner, the man whose father had established the company. My eyes were red and I was still engaged with my past. I mumbled something to him and moved off as quickly as I could. "How could you introduce me to Mendel when I was so upset?" I heard myself say to Kathleen. She had nothing to say.

These few signs were telling me something. I ignored them. They told me that Kathleen had her plans worked out and I was to fit in with them no matter who I was; that there would be no time for emotional adjustments; that the show must go on. I could be bought. I was given a car. A stunningly beautiful apartment with a swimming pool became mine. Whatever I needed I could buy and I would be reimbursed. I arrived in America with $300. I couldn't get a salary because I wasn't legal. I was a tourist and my benefactors would apply for me to be allowed to stay on the grounds that I was the only person in America who could do the job. I'd be tied to them for five years.

St Louis was huge. On July 4th I drove downtown to the fireworks where the full force of efficient America hit me with stalls and loud music, well-behaved crowds, a variety of food, organised traffic. I was intrigued. Everyone was so polite. Nobody hooted like in Jerusalem. People were friendly and then they cut off abruptly as if there was an invisible boundary. America, indeed the land of plenty — supermarkets and malls. Where did everyone put all their things? Houses were large and grand. How many people lived in those mansions? How many families?

One of my expectations was that all African-Americans would be just as well-off as white Americans; that the neighbourhoods would be integrated, that it would be easy for me to make friends with anyone. Wrong. I soon discovered the colour-bar but it wasn't obvious. The neighbourhood I stayed in, the U-district, was mixed and it looked as though younger folks were more integrated. Although there were black families on our street, the majority of black people were over in East St Louis — the Soweto of St Louis. Segregation was certainly alive and well. I was shocked. Shocked at the wealth of the many and alongside this, the slums of East St Louis, the inadequate schooling of East St Louis, the unsanitary conditions, the refuse dump of the mid-west. Welcome to the real America.

The "things bug" bit me badly. I wanted clothes and a television set, pretty writing paper, couches and chairs, lamps, kitchenware — after all I was setting up from scratch. "Just write down what you need and how much it costs and we'll reimburse you." I was a child again, spending my parents' money. But it had a price. I was to raise millions.

Where to begin? I began to write letters and read as much as I could. Kathleen worked with me; she told me how to plan a year ahead, and what to do and how to do it. "I'm grooming you to be an executive," she smiled. I wasn't sure I wanted to be an executive. I was to go to New York to bring back the loot. Sure. Off I flew, delighted to be going on a mission. After all, we were going to save all the wayward Jews by bringing them back to Orthodox Judaism. A noble task.

So, in high heels and in the heat of New York August, I schlepped from firm to firm, from foundation to foundation. I hated pounding the pavements but I loved being in New York. It felt a little bit like Jerusalem with a broad American accent. People were aggressive and that felt familiar. It was a whole lot more exciting than St Louis. Couldn't I set up an office in New York? Have a life? I returned to St Louis with no donations and somewhat more sombre about the task allotted to me. It wasn't going to be a piece of cake.

My hosts tried to make me welcome. They invited me to their home over the weekend for *Shabbat*. I went a couple of times but I never felt comfortable. I just couldn't relax with them. Somewhere I did not trust them. I felt I had to bring in results and I wasn't qualified to do this. How on earth was I to raise large sums of money? What had I got myself into? As the days and the months went by I realised with gnawing dismay that I wasn't going to be able to crack this. I was frustrated, isolated, and caught up in somebody else's dreams. I was to make their dreams come true. Their dreams, not mine. I felt restrained by having to write down every penny I needed. I felt thwarted that I didn't find it easy to communicate with either benefactor. I felt I was expected to produce miracles but had not been given the magic password or the super-glue. I was drowning.

In order to reassure myself I joined the local Toastmaster's Club and began speaking. That was more like it. I talked about being single and the joy of it. One of the club members asked me to repeat the talk to some of her friends at her home. I did so. Following my talk, we discussed divorce. Every Monday night for six weeks after that we continued to meet. I had created a workshop. Couldn't I do this instead of raising money?

I began to make friends at work. That was a mistake. People told me how miserable they were and passed on company gossip about my benefactors. Their input unsettled me more. I drew pictures of how I felt — my hands tied with a rope, me behind bars. Sold to the highest bidder. I felt mildly dead. Who could I turn to?

I asked Kathleen if I could see a psychologist. It might have been a lot simpler if I'd talked to her but I couldn't. I spent time with a woman therapist who saw immediately that I'd given myself away — rather like the novitiate situation. I'd given up my power. And there was something else that I couldn't put my finger on, something nagging me. What was it? That itch I couldn't quite scratch. Where had I felt this before? In the convent when I was in the encounter group. What was it? My therapist and I decided I would remain with the company until I had an alternative. Patience was called for. A virtue I had little of.

Ten months into the job and my enthusiasm was low. Although I appreciated much of Orthodox Judaism it was becoming increasingly clear that I felt constrained rather than freed by it. I preferred the Conservative route. That allowed me as a woman to have a voice, to make a contribution. Could I continue to ask for support for an institute that I could no longer fully endorse? It was just before Passover and I took very seriously the passing-out from Egypt into the Promised Land. I wanted to be free. If God could release the Jews from Egypt my release could be carried out with one hand tied behind his or her back. I asked to see Mendel. He was busy, but then he was "The Most Important Man in the Business" and I should know my place. I didn't know it. I nagged him to fit me in. I explained that I didn't feel I could carry on with the job. It was a question of integrity. It was as if he didn't hear me. His face was pained. I was letting him down. He had dreams of providing this institute with a clear and strong future, of hundreds of American Jews regaining their heritage and I was pivotal to this. I didn't know how to negotiate or compromise. I had to leave because I couldn't put my heart into the job.

"Yes," he agreed finally, "you will leave as soon as possible and you will return to Israel or South Africa."

"No," I responded, "I want to remain in America."

I felt I was fighting for my life. Kathleen was as cold as hot ice and Mendel shut his door. What to do? I left the building, got dropped off at my apartment with one month's rent paid and not a penny more. I was on my own.

I waited upon God. Not a listless, ho-humming kind of post office waiting, but a sure waiting that out of the impossible the possible would arrive. I had an appointment with the Creator. I was a cat who sat at the door, my face towards the handle, waiting. Who would not get up from her cosy chair and open the door? Who could ignore my resolute back? I was holding the space, moment by moment. On the one hand I was an inch away from being homeless, on the street, and not even a familiar street. On the other hand I was in an adventurous space. A friend suggested I read *The Path of Least Resistance* by Robert Fritz. The book showed me how to concentrate on what I wanted; to be clear about the present situation and then to use the tension between what was now and what I wanted to take steps towards it, without knowing how. How could I get a car? How could I work in America? How could I pay for my apartment?

Each morning I'd meditate and take long, slow walks. In the silence I felt whole; in the silence I was touched by another kind of knowing. All the voices telling me how crazy I was and pointing out the ferocious possibilities faded as I drank deeply. Along the tree-lined streets I'd move slowly in the early mornings. The slower I walked the more I was able to receive the spirit of the trees. The hush of the new day enveloped me in its softness; spider-webs dangled before my now-quiet eyes. Taken out of my own concerns into the marvels I saw around me, it was impossible not to know that the spirit who hovered there was fully aware of my existence and my circumstances. In the stillness of the street I was given courage.

I thought a lot about money and would stare at the sign on the dollar bill. "In God we trust." God and money. How were they related? I wondered why I felt more secure, more of a person when I had money in the bank. Was this my security then? And am I no-one when I have no money? Is my identity so flimsy? I saw how I tied up my worth as a person to paper. I forgot that my trust lies in that which lasts, in the eternal. It was a matter of refocusing. I focused on a workshop being run in my apartment. Sure enough after I gave a couple of talks six women sat in my lounge and we were off on a "Whole in One" seminar. And they paid for it. One of the women, Harriet, became a good friend.   I still needed a car. I wanted a red Toyota. I saw the very one in a second-hand dealer's showroom. A saleswoman asked if I'd like to drive it. Sure, why not? And yes, I'd take it. I had two hundred dollars. So I sat in an office and a very charming man asked me for my credentials.

"How long at your present address?"

"Ten months."

"How much do you earn a month?"

"I don't know yet; I've just begun my own business."

"Do you own anything?"

"Not really.'

"What do you mean not really?"

"Well I guess I don't own anything."

"Did you ever own anything?"

"Oh yes. I owned a flat."

"Where?"

"In South Africa."

"Okay, let's write that down. Social security number? "

"It's coming," I lied only for the moment. After all the number was on my wish-list.

"How much do you want to put down?"

"Two hundred dollars."

"We have a problem. Think about it and come back to me."

Later in the week I met Harriet. I told her my problem. "No problem," she says, perky as ever. "I'll sign security for you and you'll have the car. I have plenty of money."

I hot-footed it back to the dealer. I signed the papers. He phoned the bank. All clear.

"Oh, by the way, Michelle, what's the number of your driver's licence?"

"Driver's licence? I don't have one."

"Don't tell me that!" he whispered between gritted teeth as he leaned over his desk and peered into my startled eyes, "Go away and get your licence and come back to me!"

Swiftly I drove away in my own car. In debt, I was now an American.

But I couldn't yet work. I'd applied for my visitors' visa to be extended and heard nothing. I had to have a social security number. A large building in St Louis was the place to apply. Nervous, I walked in. I'd been told it was possible to get a social security number if you wanted a driver's licence. I showed my passport — my Israeli passport — and said I was a visitor and I wanted to drive. I'd have to wait a couple of weeks and then I'd get my social security number. On the back of the social security card would be stamped: "Not permitted to work in the USA". Three weeks passed and no card. Back I went. This time an African-American woman sat at the desk. I explained that I'd applied for a social security number a couple of weeks back and nothing had arrived. "Let me do that for you now," she replied and pressed a number of keys on her computer. She looked up at me and smiled.

"It'll be with you within a week. Have a nice day. "

"Thank you very much"

I was thrilled and began to walk out. At the front door I stopped. Shouldn't I make sure she knew that I was a tourist? I walked back to the desk. There was no-one there. I stood around for a minute and a voice inside said to me: Get out of here, now. I left. Five days later an envelope appeared in my mailbox. It was my social security number. I turned the card over. No stamp on the back. No restrictions applied. For some inexplicable reason I had half of what I needed to work in the USA. Once I had my driver's licence I'd have the other half. It was a miracle.

Two women who had been friends with me in Jerusalem were now in the States. They were happy to send me some financial aid to tide me over this rocky patch. I gave presentations at singles clubs and attracted people to my workshops. I was making ends meet — just. The nagging itch continued. This unseen thorn in my flesh was pushing to the surface. I asked my therapist if she knew a good hypnotherapist. She advised me to see Gable Storm.

We wasted no time. I wanted to find out what was niggling me so far under the surface that it couldn't be reached by ordinary therapy. I didn't believe I could be hypnotised. Gable was gentle and understanding. He was also an African-American. Under his guidance I went back to my childhood. I was about five. A man, a huge man with glasses and a moustache hit me across the face. His hands touched my body, my clitoris. A large fleshy object was in my mouth. I wanted to scream and I couldn't.

I left his consulting rooms amazed. Could this be true? Was I abused as a child? By whom? It couldn't have been my father. It was someone under whose care I was; an older man. Could it have been my grandfather on my mother's side? Her stepfather? Who had access to me as a child? How could I find out? Gable warned me that the emotions suppressed over time would emerge. I began to draw and my drawings helped me to objectify what had happened. I went through a variety of emotions. I cried a lot; felt depressed, got into bed and stayed there for days.

Looking back over my life from this perspective, I was able to make sense of it. Now I began to understand why I had such a poor self-image. I could see why I had been so promiscuous, why I was so wary of intimacy. Real intimacy was something I'd never experienced as a child. Physical intimacy I knew, but in a warped way. The people who were closest to me in my family, were the most dangerous. In order for me to be aroused I had to not want to have sex; or it had to be with men who were only sexual objects. It was a hard, rasping act, neither tender nor loving. And I always tensed, tensed so much in order not to have an orgasm that that became the only way I could have one. The child in me knew that what was happening was not okay. She tried to stop her body from reacting, but the body was a physical organism and responded naturally in an unnatural situation. So I felt guilty. I felt ashamed. I felt I was a bad girl. And sex became a bad thing.

Later, under the guise of a helper, I slept with younger men. I was trying to help myself as the child, trying to love myself by loving another. Why then did it have to include sex? Because often the child who is abused becomes the abuser. I was repeating the pattern I'd known. I now understood the overwhelming rage I felt in Jerusalem at the younger male friend I had. He epitomised all the men who took me, who used me. I became the victim — the conscious victim. I gave permission to be used. That anger was upon me again and it roared in my ears and I could feel it in my throat, wanting to come out. How could I get it out?

I returned to Gable. I told him there was something stuck in my throat. He put his hand over my throat and slowly coaxed the sound up. Deep within the bowels of my sub-conscious a scream had settled and cemented. It couldn't come out. Over forty years the wail waited, turning green with age, crusted over with secrecy. Now the volcano was erupting and it was dislodged. Inch by inch Gable's fingers let it know it could come out. I didn't know what was going to happen. Out like an unchained monster it sprang. A creature in filth, in rags, caked with dry sores, crumbs of crusted blood tangled in its sticky beard; wild eyes staring in a red haze; feet dragging dust, a tongue lolling uncontrollably, hairy hands groping the air, yellowed finger-nails under which tiny life forms teemed. It lurched to its feet as the clink of the keys unlocked. Into the room it leapt, holding the entire space, roaring in pain. A bark — the bark of a wounded animal, a large wounded animal. It was low and gruff yet round and echoing. I had held this anguish all these years. It was the concentration of hours of silent screams: screams of betrayal, loneliness, shame, guilt, abandonment and terror. No-one had come to save me. The hardness of anger gave it its velocity. As the sound vanished I was left shaking. Was it gone?

A week later I was exercising with a friend in the park. Energetically he was showing me some yoga-aerobic exercises and I was attempting to follow him. I couldn't. My body was rebelling. It was feeling like I had felt in aerobic classes with my benefactors. I was being forced to do something physical I didn't want to. At the close of each class I wondered why I felt so angry. There was this resistance again, but this time I recognised it. I turned away and bent over as the sound emerged again. My friend came up to me and held me in his arms. I cried for a long time.

In the days, weeks, months that followed I took care of myself. I spent time with myself, nurturing the child who was in pain. Moods sometimes swept me away but I knew I had to allow the healing to take its course. And part of that course was being a victim. I began to understand my benefactors more clearly. I had wanted somebody to save me from life that held me in a painful grip. These two beautiful people would be the parents I had always wanted. They would take care of me, provide for me, love and nurture me. But they couldn't. They had come into my life to re-enact the parents who couldn't be there for me. Kathleen was beautiful physically but she couldn't empathise, she couldn't care for me. Ring a bell? Mendel was full of lofty aspirations and dreams but he was a distant man emotionally. Like my father. Neither of my parents could parent me when I was a child. So I was neglected. And neither of them came to save me. I continued to yearn for one who could and would save me. I thought it might have

225

been Jesus Christ. The convent gave me the place to begin the healing process. No-one would save me. It had to be me who saved me, the adult Michelle who could now take care of the child. I had to nurse myself, love myself, protect myself.

I returned to Gable. He took me inside myself one more time. I told him that now that the sound had come out I didn't know what there was inside anymore. Was it all gone? So down we went. And there was nothing. Not a nothing that means that all is well, but a nothingness, an emptiness. It was as if I had stood at the edge of a cliff and looked out to see only space. No-one was there. I left his rooms.

It was the period between Rosh Hashana (New Year) and Yom Kippur (the Day of Atonement). I sat alone in my apartment feeling this nothingness. I waited. Inspired after a while to pick up a book I was reading about this period in the Jewish calendar, my eyes fell upon the psalm that is prayed on the days between the two major holy days. "The Lord is my light and my salvation, whom shall I fear?" it asked me. "The Lord is the source of my life's strength, of whom, then, shall I be afraid?" it continued. The words flew out at me, a presence wrapping itself around me, palpable. "If father and mother desert you, I will still be there." What was the nothingness I felt? Or was there something beyond the nothingness?

From out of the nothingness came the All, the Everything, God. I felt a tightening in my belly as if I were attached by an umbilical cord to Life itself. I am Siamese-twinned to that which Is and Its capacity to hold me is stronger than any human channel I mistakenly lean on. Beyond mother and father I am loved and sustained by this presence, every day, in every situation, now and forever. I was confirmed. This was a mystical *batmitzvah*. The experience also reinforced the essence of my meeting with Padre Pio. It told me again that no matter what I had gone through as a child, it had not been my fault. Within me was the innocent, unlimited, whole being who was good.

I'd stopped the workshops because I needed the time to recover. But I had a problem with the rent. What to do? What direction was I headed in? I knew God loved and cared for me and I knew I would continue the healing process, but how could I best serve God? What did I need to do? Perhaps I should become a rabbi? Why not go to New York and check out the seminary, just in case. My local rabbi set me up with a couple in Manhattan and I had an appointment with the head of the Conservative Seminary. Cool!

My visit to the seminary appalled me. It was a huge, dark building which reminded me of my early days at Aliwal North. The smell of an institution sent me reeling out. Besides which my Hebrew was abysmally poor and I hadn't nearly enough experience as a Jew. What was I still looking for? Two incidents in New York gave me the answer. They came to me through the Arts.

The Secret Garden was showing on Broadway. I longed to see that. I remembered reading it as a child and the contentment and joy I experienced. I had to see it. As I stood outside the theatre counting my dollars, my heart sank slowly. It was $30 for one seat. That was a lot of money for me. Well, I thought, trying to shrug it off, maybe it's not so important. Why not cross the road and see *Phantom of the Opera*? That was just as expensive. So there I stood, debating what to do. I better go back to the apartment, I told myself. I took two steps. Lying on the pavement was a $20 note. I looked again, bent, picked it up, ran across the road and bought a ticket for *The Secret Garden*. In the third act I got the message. Wait. Winter is a time for hope, for waiting. The seeds that burst in the Spring are already planted. Darkness is a passage, not a place. Do not act. There is that which needs to grow. Allow it to do so underneath the soil. There is always a garden. It's just easier to see it in the Spring.

The second and similar message came through a Seurat exhibition. The paintings were arranged in such a way that all Seurat's darker paintings were seen first. Then, as if the sun came from out the clouds, his lighter paintings blazed into colour. I got it. From the darkness into the light. My soul needed to grope for a bit; needed to lose its way for a while, needed to hide a little in the dark before the splendour of the light blazed brilliant.

Pacified, I returned to St Louis. I knew my life was in good hands and I understood from my New York hosts — both established writers — that I should pick up a pen and pass my life on. Acting on this, I left my fancy apartment to live with an elderly and exceptionally kind woman, Lorraine Ashburn; took a job as a receptionist for a Jewish newspaper in St Louis and began to write my story.

It had dawned on me that America was indeed the land of opportunity but not the kind of opportunity I had been led to believe. The real opportunity for me was the chance to look deeper than what I saw on the surface; to realise that material assets cannot get me happiness on a long-term basis. The American dream was empty. It was an illusion. A trap. I needed to take the opportunity to go further inside myself and find out all I could about inner space. There was potential for healing in this huge country. I had to follow the yellow-brick-road of intuition, explore the edges of my frontiers, and go from nobody to somebody in my eyes only. I decided to move out of St Louis. I chose Seattle, Washington.

my life

steps to heal the heart

The dream vs the reality

I had an idea about my American job and my expectations were high. Write about a time when you had expectations, either about a person or a situation. What did you expect? What was the reality? What did you learn?

No questions asked

I was stuck in a job that was entirely inappropriate for me. Had I asked a few more questions before I left Jerusalem, I might not have gone. Are you in a job you know is unsuitable for you? How do you know? What keeps you in it? Do you believe there is no alternative? In what way do you think your belief system is holding you prisoner? In your deepest self what do you know about what you need to do? Write a letter to yourself as a good friend and give yourself the advice you know you need to hear. Then reply to yourself.

The material girl

I was vaguely surprised at my grasping for things once I got to America. Suddenly I had to have everything I had done without in Israel. What about you? How important are material things to you? Having them gives you what? Not having them makes you what? What do you think about people who "have everything"? What, to you, is "everything"? What could you live without? What could you never live without? How do you know this? Knowing that you could have every single material item you wanted, write a list of them and ask for them.

Miracles

"Out of the impossible, the possible would arrive." I believed this and it happened. I had slipped through the legal cracks in the USA but I had the documentation that verified my status. What has happened in your life that beggars explanation? What were the circumstances? Who was involved? What was the impact on your life and on the lives of others? Write the story or make one up. Write what you would like to happen.

Creative waiting

The term "waiting" has become synonymous with passivity. On a spiritual level and maybe this is from my Catholic background, surrender to God comes with a type of waiting that I call creative. It's a hope, but it's also a knowing. Sometimes it's a matter of not knowing which of two alternatives is the best one. At other times there seems to be no movement, no alternative. Do not allow yourself to be misled into thinking that God has deserted you. In both cases the soul needs to "hang in there" and do nothing. What it can do is to keep its eyes on the Beloved. Go for God. When I was considering leaving the convent, I was told to do that. Concentrate on God. Get into the presence. When the moment is ripe the best action will reveal itself. It is difficult for us as "doers" to let go and follow. This is a following routed in faith, not in fear. It takes courage. Write about an occasion in your life which demanded this type of courage or creative waiting.

my life

Survival without money

I learnt to expect money to come from unexpected sources. Having lived in Israel I was prepared for this. I learnt a great deal about my level of faith when I had little or no money. Not having money began as a constant crisis. It changed over the years. Now, when it appears that there is little money, I relax and wait for more to come. Sometimes money hides from me because I have to move into another field and the only way I can discover this is when the flow dwindles and stops. At other times it slows down because I am allowing it to have more power over me than is necessary. My relationship with money fluctuates, just like a relationship with a person. Over the years I have continued to refine and explore this relationship. What is the story of your relationship with money? Make a collage of your relationship with money. What does it teach you about your personal and spiritual growth?

Awareness of abuse

If you have been abused in any form you may recognise yourself here. You may have uncovered the abuse in a different way of course. How did your new knowledge affect you and your life? Did you have support at this time? When you looked back, did so much of your life begin to make more sense? Write or tell your story.

Gradual healing

I was led to a place and time where I could become aware of the wound of sexual abuse. I was already aware of emotional abuse. But healing of any kind of abuse doesn't happen in one day. Depending on the depth of the wound, healing oneself takes time. The body carries the scar and slowly releases the pain and the memories. Only in my late fifties did I finally uncover who it was that abused me sexually. My body gave me this knowledge when I was with that person who appeared from my childhood. I think it is essential that we take gentle care of ourselves for as long as we are alive. A quick-fix is no fix. We need to honour the more natural way of healing which is gradual and complete. We have all the time we need. Write what comes up for you now.

Being black in America

Meeting a man called Ozzie Diamond woke me up to what it was like to be black in America. I was also led to read books that reinforced that experience like *Faces at the Bottom of the Well. The Permanence of Racism* by Derrick Bell. I was starry-eyed about the States. Especially in the field of race relations. Ozzie taught me the difference between being African-American and Black American. He was relentless in my education. Has there been someone in your life who came from another group or race or religion or nation and wanted you to know the truth about his or her situation? Who was it? Where did you meet? What did you have to learn? How has this stood you in good stead over the years?

The Native-American experience

What was also valuable for me was my experience with the Native-American people. I learnt much by reading, speaking and taking part in ceremonies such as a Sweat Lodge. I developed a deeper understanding for the natural world. I saw the devastating effects of America's attempts to wipe out the Native-American population. What is your opinion of America and the values it stands for? How have American values or America impacted

my life

on your life and the lives of your friends? Do you see this as positive or negative or both?

When you are not like the majority of people where you live

I was interesting to some Americans because I came from South Africa and because of my accent. What has your experience been as a newcomer to a country?

Perhaps you are Nigerian in South Africa or you are from Angola and speak only Portuguese. Have you been welcomed by South Africans? Describe how your time here has affected you and your family. Write your history in South Africa.

If you are a local how do you feel about living with people from the rest of the continent? Is it easy or difficult for you to do? What messages have you been taught about "foreigners"? Write a story with yourself as the main character in which all your thoughts are laid bare.

A book in time saves

The book I was given in St Louis on creating my own reality helped me. Do you find that a book will arrive in your life just at the right time? Like when, for instance? What was the book? What were your circumstances? How did the book make a difference?

Knowing God

My experience around Yom Kippur when I understood how I was protected was a powerful expression of God's love for me. Often we are uneasy talking about God. That little word has many connotations. What does that word mean to you? If you have had an experience of God, express what happened to you on a mystical level and where you could feel it physically. The spiritual "highs" we can feel are just a part of it all. They come, they go. There are also the plains where life is routine and the desert where there is dryness and no sense of God's presence. But behind it all is this "loving nothingness". I think it is more of a commitment of God to us — a covenant. What's your take on it?

From majority to minority

I left Israel as a Jew, no longer a Christian. I soon became aware of the difference. As a Jew I was part of a relatively small group. When Saturday arrived I no longer did the shopping or went to a movie. I went to synagogue. When Sunday arrived it was just another day for me. The American Jewish communities I met were friendly, kind, open. Of course, we were a minority. It was a very different perspective. I began to have more of an idea of what it was like for a minority anywhere. Have you felt anything similar? From what aspect? Religious? Racial? Physical? What is it that you would like to record in writing?

Chapter 2 *Seattle*

Why Seattle? Well it reminded me of bits of my life. It rained, like in London, and since my childhood and the later years I spent in London were familiar to me, I felt comfortable in the drizzle. Then there was Mount Rainier. Woman-rock, softly splendid, she rose above the city like a huge breast, pouring milk. She reminded me of Kiental where I learned Macrobiotics; she gave me strength. Often when I was feeling overwhelmed I'd look up and there she'd be, firm, powerful, tender, urging me on. She was a mother. And all around was water. That was new. I'd lived mainly in Johannesburg and longed to be surrounded by water. Drive through the city and the silk shone in the sometimes sun and rippled under the rain. Water. The ferryboats bobbed briskly across her huge stretches; languid and available she lay as we glided along her luscious thighs, weaving our way into the tight harbours — to rest for a while.

Pike market place, a tiny taste of Jerusalem and Meghana Yehuda, the market.

Row upon row of fruits and vegetables, rings and bracelets, arts and crafts tucked under canopies, still spilled into the street. Across the cobblestones they seeped into the stores on the other side of the narrow roadway, past the woman who sang her broken heart whole, past the duo dressed in ragged trousers and skimpy shirts who raged against the status quo as they struck their cheeks, arms, thighs and sometimes the soles of their feet with spoons held like castanets. Teeming with polite north-westerners the market burrowed beehive-like underground surprising the tourist with tiny store upon store, offering everything from way-out clothes and children's toys to exotic-smelling oils and incense from a very eastern new-age corner. There were breads and baskets, cakes and canaries, restaurants and refreshments. Everyone came to see the flying fish. A customer called for a fish. One of the fishmongers would shout the order and throw a fish to another man behind the counter who would prepare it, then toss it back to the first man yelling loudly to warn anyone who got in the way. The first man rang up the price, wrapped the fish in brown paper and gave it to the customer. If he didn't throw it!

I was told Seattle rated first in the States with the highest percentage of readers. I'm not surprised with all that rain! So many writers, actors and artists lived in Seattle. What was it? Those of us who choose to live on the edge probably chose Seattle. Loud rock groups, plenty of tattooed, pierced, hair-raised, gutter-sitting teenagers, homeless hundreds, and downtown jazz. Not a bad place at all. So I thought if I take out the "a" in Seattle, I get Settle. Maybe it was about time? The murmur in my heart was that the "a" in Seattle stood for Africa. Does this mean I won't be going back?

I shared a house in Greenlake with Tess and Kelly. Tess was studying naturopathy and Kelly was a researcher. I had to find work quickly. I answered an advertisement for a telemarketer, selling theatre tickets. Agnes Parker, a warm, motherly person, trained us and soon there I was selling Intiman theatre tickets, Fifth Avenue tickets, The Group tickets over the phone — evenings five until nine. I also worked for an organisation that walked door to door canvassing to pass a bill that would protect the elderly in homes of care. It was as if I were in hiding.

I reached the point where I needed to stop doing borderline work and offer myself on the market. I had little money. How should I deal with this? A friend gave me some valuable guidance. Nat lost his wife in a divorce; then he lost his house. Then he lost his job. He recovered from those disasters to become a man who lived fully and enthusiastically in the moment. He suggested I hold onto the moment. This was a repeat of some of my Israeli experience plus the St Louis crisis. It felt worse now because I expected more of myself. I'd been in the USA for over three years. It was enough already. "Trust," he kept telling me. There it was again. I had to trust that I would be taken care of. I had to walk my talk, even if I wasn't doing much talking at the time! Nat didn't only give advice he sent me $500.

I lived in a studio apartment downtown. I'd walk over to the corner cafe, buy a yoghurt and a muffin and eat very slowly. I was determined not to run back to Citizens Action and I didn't feel I could respond with any degree of integrity to the ads I saw in the newspaper. I'd read a little, meditate and take thoughtful walks. I passed many homeless people and knew that we were closely allied. The days became crystal clear; I could see the trees and the skies as if for the first time. My awareness was heightened because I had to live and I had to see and I had to hear. I would not slip into despair.

It wasn't easy. Sometimes I would feel the terror begin to wash over me and I had to let it arrive. "Being human means feeling," Nat explained, "Only in the body can we experience the gamut of our feelings. So feel. You may not have the opportunity again. Go for it." Somehow I felt somewhere inside me that I had to wait, I had to hold on. I had to do nothing but this.

"And what's the worst that could happen?" asked Nat.

"I could die"

"Is that so bad?"

He had a point. I didn't believe that death was an end. So there was nothing to fear.

One afternoon as I sat at a downtown café, a man at a nearby table chatted to me. He was a sculptor and invited me to a party to celebrate July 4th. I went. The hostess was a key person in the art world of Seattle. We became good friends. She offered me a job for a couple of weeks "to help me out with some details" and she paid me disproportionately. Isabella moved easily around money. She looked after herself and was surrounded with beauty. She'd not had an easy life and had lost most of her friends to AIDS but she was resilient. Being around her was like standing under a bright light.

One morning in August I bought a newspaper and in the positions available column I saw an AIDS organisation offering a position for a community relations manager. The person needed experience in working with diverse communities. Yes, I'd try for that. The audition for the position went like an opening night's performance. I say audition because it was like that. I was on a high, the high of living at the very blade of the knife. Did my life depend on this interview? In a way it did. If I didn't get the job I would return to South Africa — a negative returning but a returning nonetheless. Did I know which way my life was meant to go? No. I had to give the interview all I could muster. If I didn't get the position it was certainly not meant for me. The next morning I get a call offering it to me. I was going to stay, after all. Seattle had not finished with me yet. Little did I know then that this would be my last year in Seattle, that during this year I would share deeply with my mother, learn about loving and dying and return to South Africa out of choice. It began and ended with Justin James Campbell.

Justin was twenty-nine, Scottish. Not tall. The top of his head came up to my eyebrows. He was slight. His eyes were a vibrant blue, shielded by long black lashes. His nose was perfect for photographs and his skin was like velvet. When he smiled his lips opened just the right width and when he was serious they rested in a gentle bow over his straight white teeth. Justin was beautiful. Not only because he was so handsome but because he was hungry for life. Every ounce of his being urged to live and live he would even though his body was fighting a daily battle with the AIDS virus. Justin had been HIV-positive for over seven years.

During that time he determined to carry on as normal. He kept a senior position with the firm he worked for and journeyed on through bouts of pneumonia like a robust raft across rapids. I gave a brief morning talk at his company as part of my work. Justin wanted more. This hadn't always been the way with him. Brought up in a quiet corner of Scotland he became an outsider, not finding a place where he could be accepted because he was gay. There was little alternative for him and he left with the man he loved more than anyone else. Together they lived in Europe and eventually America. And it was then that Raoul told him he had AIDS.

Justin changed. He asked more questions, deeper questions. He realised how low his self-image had always been even though he was so strikingly handsome. He didn't love himself. Now he began to. He saw life in America as superficial for the most part. There was little loving, lots of sex and lots of pretending. He wasn't bitter; he wanted to do something about it, he wanted to give. At the same time he was wary. His trust had been betrayed by Raoul. He was still very much an outsider.

He was drawn to me because he felt a spiritual bond; a bond that he couldn't share with his other friends. I was drawn to him. There was an aloofness about him and a warmth. Justin reminded me of myself. As we spent more time together it became clear to us that we were alike in many ways. I too had a fear of intimacy. We both found trust an issue. We thought the same about the States and we both saw AIDS as an opportunity for many Americans, who lived so much on the surface, to delve underneath the obvious.

At first I spent short periods with him — we'd eat together or go to a movie. He talked often about taking his own life. He wanted to go out like a light, not wither away. His had been a long, hard and often lonely road. He'd kept the news of his illness from his parents for fear they might reject him. He hadn't yet told them he was gay. His heart was hardened against them. When it became too unbearable, when he could no longer enjoy his work, or really enjoy his life, he would go. I couldn't believe him although I said I understood. This was the first time I had been close to a person who was dying. But Justin was living — he was living with passion and flair.

We began to spend longer periods of time together. This wasn't easy for me. I was nervous of extended periods with anyone. Intimacy, again. But he was so gentle, playful and imaginative. We didn't notice the hours rustling past us. Slowly Justin crawled into my heart, like a child creeps under the blankets in the early mornings and nestles close.

One afternoon we chose to attend a short course on how to give a massage to a person with AIDS. Justin was wary of touch. He was comfortable with sex because it wasn't intimate for him. So like my attitude. Sex was what he got at the Baths or maybe he took someone home but he wasn't in a relationship and hadn't the energy for one. But touching was different. He wanted me to touch him in this appropriate way and that afternoon was intensely meaningful for both of us. We sat listening; we practised on each other. Gently, reverently, we draped our arms around each other and I laid my head on his shoulder and cried a little. The tenderness of it all. I lived knowing that his presence was smoke in my hands; that his precious being would not stay. When it came to massaging our feet he said softly, "Just think Michelle where these feet of yours have been — so many places, and how good they have been to you." I'd never thought of that. He lay back as I massaged his feet and then his hands. Tears wet his cheeks. For him I was the mother who was not physically demonstrative. He said she never touched him. We were catching up on all we had missed. "I feel as if I've lived seventy years in these seven," he said in his lilting voice. "I'm old already."

He got ill suddenly. AIDS doesn't let you know what the agenda is. He'd been on steroids and that masked other possible complications. He called me over to his place on Friday night. "I've a gruelling headache." He asked me to pray with him and then to write a living will. He didn't want to be kept alive on any machines. I wasn't ready for this. It was too soon, too fast, it wasn't happening. But it was. We called his close friend Danny and the three of us took him into Swedish hospital for a spinal tap.

That was the beginning of the ten days that led to his death. I want to share a couple of moments in those days. The first has to do with his parents. Justin and I were at similar stages with our mothers. I had written a letter to my mother telling her how I had been feeling about our relationship, or lack of it, for a long time. To my intense relief she responded magnanimously asking me for time when we could open our hearts to each other. At about the same time Justin wrote to his mother telling her how he felt she had left him, abandoned him. He never heard her say she loved him. Why was that? His parents thought he had liver cancer and were coming to see him the following year in January. He was dreading their visit because he always had to hide his real life.

My mother came to visit me before Justin got ill. The three of us spent a day together. Justin's openness and freshness acted like a facilitator preparing the ground for our long talk. The following day my mother told me the story of her life. It was the first time in over seventy five years she had told anyone. Hers was an enormous gift given amidst tears and large cups of tea. She was quite faint at the end of it, as if a giant oak door had finally opened. The relief of the telling sucked all the sap out of the wood, she felt dazed, drained of energy. For us it was a beginning.

The night Justin got ill he called his parents and put me on the line. I was to become the connector. As he got worse I took it upon myself to let them know what was happening to him. They decided to come to America immediately. They still didn't know he had AIDS. Justin was taken aback at their decision to come and a mite annoyed. He wasn't ready for them; but then again maybe this was a sign? I knew a Catholic priest who was gay and who worked with men and women with AIDS. I asked Justin if he thought it a good idea for Father Morrissey to see his folks. Justin met Father Morrissey and liked him a lot. The Catholic Church had done nothing for him; if anything it had made matters worse. But he warmed to Morrissey and we set up an appointment for his parents to meet with him on their arrival.

"You know, Mishka" he said, "My mother always liked the movie about the young boy from home who goes to America and becomes rich and famous. What's she coming to now? Her son is gay and dying of AIDS. She'll be real proud of me." Who knows what a parent will do at the moment when her child is facing the journey of death? We were alone in his hospital room the night before his parents were due.

"Mishka, I'm going to phone them," and he began dialling.

"Hello, Dad? Yes, I want to talk to you before you come. Yes, I know you're coming. I want to prepare you for what you'll see. I'm ill, very ill. I can't see out of my left eye. I look awful. I have tubes in and out of me. I'm not sure how you remember me. And I'm scared. I'm scared," he began to whimper. "No, we won't talk about it when you get here. We'll talk about it now. Why won't you listen to me? Why won't you let me speak? I don't want you to tell me it'll be all right. It's not all right. I want you to be with me in my pain. Do you hear me, Dad?" He lay the receiver down on the bed. "He's gone! He's given the phone to my mother!" Then back to the phone: "Mother, where's Dad? Why won't he talk to me? Why won't he? He always does this. I'm his son and I'm dying and he refuses to talk to me!" He was sobbing. "Yes, yes I know you do. He never listens

237

to me. Why did he give you the phone? Why wouldn't he listen? He's what? Okay, okay. I'll see you tomorrow." He replaced the receiver. "Fuck. I was seven years old again!" He stretched out his arms and I leaned in to hold him.

I didn't know what to expect in his parents. But there they were, standing in the corridor outside his room looking small and vulnerable. We embraced, crying together. They were simple people, anxious, devastated, afraid. Not only of losing their son, but afraid of their son never knowing, never accepting that they truly loved him. That was what both the parents and the son had to accept — they were loved. When Justin was ready they entered the room. I will never know what words were spoken or how their love found its way out. It must have been one of the most painful and beautiful moments in a life.

When, about an hour later, the door was opened, there they were, sitting on his bed, their arms wrapped around him, their faces lighter, much lighter. Justin sat splendid, cushioned in years of love now pouring out unrestrained. Gone was the misunderstanding, gone the fear, the expectations, the assumptions. Now only clear love flowed between them. There was a sacredness surrounding that room; it was indeed a holy place — a place of transformation for many of us. A sanctuary.

Justin had a wide circle of friends. Those that were part of an inner circle I got to know a little. Each one drawn to him had grown immeasurably through the relationship. How did Justin do it? It wasn't as if he set out to heal anyone. He never lectured or preached or gave the impression he had hidden knowledge or understanding. He just was himself and that self was steeped in gentleness and kindness. Each person who I came to meet had his or her story to tell about him. Even as he lay in the hospital bed he'd be on the phone, saying goodbye, suggesting reconciliation between a pair of lovers; encouraging, thanking, kidding, consoling. He grew larger. His wisdom and insight were making him a giant. Before our eyes he was transforming, vanishing into a blaze of light.

That light was reflective. It shone on me revealing the broad spectrum of who I was. The two questions I held dear were: Who am I and why am I here? Justin was answering both of those. In the heat of those final days my closeness to him revealed both my strengths and weaknesses. At first I was in charge: dealing with doctors and medicines, taking him to hospital, taking care of him, calling in his friends as I needed them; keeping visitors at bay, keeping his parents on line, liasing with Father Morrissey — great in a crisis. Underneath it all I was terrified I was doing the wrong thing. I felt inept and clumsy, sure I'd foul everything up. I was so close to him those first few days.

Then he was admitted and suddenly I was no longer necessary, not in the same way. I realised how basically lonely I was and how his illness had given me the chance to be useful to somebody. I needed him to need me. Then there was the jealousy. I was jealous of his friends, felt ousted, felt like I was the odd person out and in a way I was. Much older, I couldn't fit in. Why did I want to so badly? I felt part of his family, as if we were married. I can't explain that. Justin felt it too and we talked about it in the hospital. He loved me immensely yet part of me couldn't trust that.

Justin was told he had mukor mykosis, which is a kind of meningitis. He had a few days left before the fungus would destroy his brain. He wasn't going to wait in hospital for that. He was going home. Danny and I sat on his bed. "If this is it, this is it," he said softly, resigned. At first he'd battled, determined to beat whatever it was. He knew his body, knew all the treatments, talked through each step with the doctors, took responsibility. When his parents arrived he wondered if this was the end of his life. Their love and care softened him. Slowly he grew to understand that he would not reach his thirtieth birthday. Then he went into action again — closing all his friendships, leaving no-one out, doing what had to be done. Now this last step.

"Mischka, give me your blessing."

"I bless you for your journey, Justin." What could I say? Two nights after he'd fallen ill I knew he was going. In the deepest darkness of that Saturday night I had woken to feel a cold wave ripple through and over my body. Justin is dying, the movement warned me. This is it. My body knew but my emotions and my head couldn't catch up with that truth.

"Now, forgive me," he asked.

"You are forgiven for anything and everything. You are completely forgiven. You are in love and ready for your new life. May you be blessed by all the angels and all those waiting to take you across."

"What will it be like, Mischka?"

"I don't know. I've only heard that you are met by people you love, people you always wanted to meet. It's a new life." We sat quietly in the dark. He asked Danny and I to go through his things with him and write down who would get what. The night was coming in fast; the main light was off and I was scribbling his words onto a sheet of paper we managed to find. He was sedated and often lapsed into a slight sleep.

That last night in the hospital was painful for me, not only because he was going but because he had gone. Something had happened between us and I didn't know what. Justin had distanced himself emotionally. He withdrew from me. Jeremy and I slept in his room that night. Jeremy was naturally attentive and a quiet presence. I felt as if I'd been hit and didn't know where the blow had come from. What was it? The next morning, Monday, Justin returned to his apartment. I had left at about six and came to him later in the day. When I entered he was sitting with Jeremy.

The feeling was still there in the room. I wasn't welcome. Justin suggested I join the others at Sally's place and I read that I was being dismissed. I said, no, that I'd come back later. I stood outside the door leading down the stairs and put my briefcase down. I don't know why I carried it anyway. What was wrong? Justin would be dead within a couple of days — was I going to let him go without sorting this out? I had to know what was wrong. I turned, went back through the inter-leading door and knocked again at his.

"Yes?" It was Jeremy.

"Can I come in for a minute?"

"Justin," my throat was dry, "may I have a word with you?"

"Sure" he responded and rose. Gone was the drip. He was dressed in his regular clothes and if you didn't know, he might have been going out for a walk.

"Let's go into the bedroom," he said graciously.

"Justin, what is it? What have I done? Something is wrong, I can feel it."

"I'm so glad you came back," he burst out, "I've missed you terribly." He put his arms around me.

"And I you," beginning to cry, "what is it?"

"Come, let's sit on the bed."

And we sat.

"It's just that when we were writing my will yesterday, it seemed to me that you were a little ..." he paused, "greedy, and that made me sad." His voice was soft. "I felt it was my things you wanted, not me."

"Things?"

"Yes," he was holding my hands, "the kitchen things."

"The kitchen things?" I repeated, "I don't understand ..."

"You said ... 'I want the kitchen things' ..."

"No Justin, I said what about the kitchen things. Those were my words."

Yes, those had been my words but what he caught was that underneath my words I wanted his kitchen things. He was right. I protested that I didn't want anything of his.

He had given me his bed, his stereo system and his parents had offered me his apartment. Wasn't that enough? No, it wasn't enough. I wanted everything, including him. I held him in a possessive grip. I had someone who I loved, someone who loved me and he was unclasping my grasp and slipping away. Terrified of abandonment, I clung to whatever I could.

"Hush," he whispered, tired. "there's no time for this now. I missed you, the Michelle I knew, the Mischka who doesn't need to do anything but just be there for me. I need you to be there for me now, today. It's not going to be easy for you. I don't think you realise just what's happening. I think it will hit you later." His eyes scanned my face. "Just be real for me today. Be real. There's nothing to organise, nothing." He paused and waited a few moments. "Now I'm going to leave you for a few minutes and I want you to think about what I said. Then I'll come back." He stood and slowly walked out.

I sat on the edge of the bed stricken, ashamed, discovered, appalled, guilty. I rose and walked to the window. Who was I? Was this me? Yes. All of who I am is me. There's no place for pretend. It was hard for me to "be real". I wasn't sure I knew how. But maybe that was it; there was no "how". I just had to be. That's what Justin and I had talked so often about — being. Being open and vulnerable and weak. Real loving in a one-on-one total relationship including sex was hugely daunting for both of us. It was what he'd always wanted. It's what we both had to learn. He came back into the room.

"Are we reconciled?" he asked, taking my hands and gazing quietly into my eyes.

"Yes," I whispered.

"Is everything all right between us?" he insisted gently.

"Yes."

He had seen me in all my colours; he saw that I was not Mother Teresa or Florence Nightingale, but a very ordinary person with some strengths, some gifts and points of pain. Wounded. Like everyone else. And I saw him in all that he was.

The next day was Justin's last day on earth.

It was as though we were waiting, waiting for 8.30 when he would leave us. Wednesday. His parents and friends came in, sat with him, went out to buy food. We lit candles and they glowed all day. Justin loved candlelight. He played all his favourite music so the apartment sounded as if there might be a gentle gathering of friends for an all-day party. And in a way that's what it was. The gentlest celebration I'd ever attended; ever been privy to. For it was so intimate. A conscious goodbye. He moved slowly about the room. Sometimes he would sit between his parents on the couch. We had all cried so much and still we would cry a bit, now and then. It was almost unreal, surreal, the feeling of that day, moment by moment dripping by. "I want to weaken my body," he told me, describing how he had stayed up all night with his buddies. He looked so small, so frail on this, his last day. "It's all worked out so much better than I could have imagined," he confided in me. "I thought I'd die alone with a plastic bag over my head, leaving a letter for my parents and friends. Instead I'm surrounded by people I love and I will be helped to leave." He lifted my hand and held it in both of his. "You know, Mischka, before I left the hospital my Dad washed me in the shower. He washed me. Can you believe that?" His eyes were shining.

"Michelle," his Dad drew me aside, "do you know what Justin said to me in the shower? He said, Dad, I want you to know, just in case you may not be sure, I want you to know that God loves me. He loves me, Dad." And his father wept.

"Am I doing the right thing?" Justin asked suddenly of Jeremy and I who were sitting alongside him. It was early afternoon.

"Come on guys, reassure me." He was scared.

"What's your alternative?" I asked.

"That I just drain away, maybe in a few days or fall unconscious, I don't know."

"What do you want?"

"To stay with you." he smiled into my eyes.

We sat in silence.

A slow, endless dying, drip by morphine drip. This way, the way he had chosen, he turns the light off. This way it's his. I stared out the window, amazed that anyone else in the street could live this day as if it were just another day. Didn't they know what was happening in this room? This holy parting? I read him a couple of lines in Hebrew. "*Be yadoh afkid ruchi, be at ishan ve-ah-irah, ve-im ru-chi ge-iyati adonai li ve-lo ir-ah.* I place my spirit in His hands, when I wake as when I sleep; God is with me, I shall not fear, body and spirit in His keep." He sighed and rested his head on my shoulder.

The light was on its way out. Fourteen of us gathered in a circle on the floor. One by one we told him, in as best as we could put it into words, what he had meant to us in our lives. This was his memorial service, one he could attend. His parents heard our stories and they saw how love surrounded him. They were so proud and so stricken. "Thank you, you've given me strength," Justin responded.

He got up to go. The morphine had been coursing through his body all day. He fell in and out of a nodding. It was time. His two friends arrived and the mood changed. Justin walked slowly to his bedroom assisted by his parents. I never said goodbye, never said the words, neither did he. He left within the hour. A great spirit passed and was gone.

I could feel him in the wind, in the moon, in the night air. "You're free, Justin, free!"

Reaching my studio apartment I switched on my answering machine to hear his voice quoting from the film *Yentle.*

"Hi love, thought you might like to hear this: 'The more I live, the more I learn, the more I learn the more I realise the less I know. Each step I take, each page I turn, each mile I travel only means the more I have to go. What's wrong with wanting more? If you can fly, then soar. With all there is, why settle for just a piece of sky?'" I believe that one of the main reasons I had to live in Seattle was so that I could engage with Justin. He taught me to be intimate and to love. He showed me myself. Still with me today, he is a bright light in my life, a sun.

And now, a year later, it's time for me to face another sun; the one rising over a newly liberated South Africa. I want to find family again. And to be free of exile. Suddenly I know this is the God-given wanting I have inwardly uncovered. Now that all these shafts of other people's lights in other people's lands have set me free: I want to go home …

my life

steps to heal the heart

Straight and gay love

If you are straight, have you ever fallen in love or deeply loved a man or woman who was gay? Write or describe your relationship — how you met, what happened.

If you are gay and love a straight woman or man, can you describe, write or draw your relationship? What did you learn from your relationship? What difficulties, if any, did you encounter? Is the friendship still alive? What keeps it going? Have you told the person you love what it is about him or her that is so important to you? Can you write that letter now?

Loving, winning and losing

I think it's hardly possible for any of us today not to know someone who is HIV-positive. This doesn't always mean that person cannot live for many years or even get to a point where he no longer needs medication — as was the case with one of my Seattle friends. But that wasn't the case with Justin. He taught me about love.

Is there a particular person in your life who came into your life to teach you about loving? How did you meet? What was it you needed to learn? How did you learn this? Did the person stay with you or not? In which ways did you win and lose in the relationship?

Living with HIV/AIDS

Write about your experience. When did you first discover you were HIV-positive? What was your immediate reaction? When did you tell someone? Or maybe you still have not told anyone. What is that like for you? If you told someone, what support did you get? Do you have access to treatment? What is that like for you? How are you coping with your status? Write in detail everything you want to get out of you.

Living with a person who is HIV-positive

Write your experience of living with a person who is HIV-positive or who has AIDS. When did you find out s/he was HIV-positive? How did you react at first? How has her or his status affected you? How has it affected your relationship? How much do you know about the disease? Do you have support from other members of your family or from friends? Write about that too. How does the community assist or resist you? How does that feel? How are you preparing yourself for possible loss? Write how your life has altered. Include the ways in which you may have grown as a result of your experience.

Taking over as a result of losing a parent to AIDS

Are you in a position where you have to step into the shoes of your mother or your father who died of AIDS? Write what that is like for you. What are the responsibilities you now carry? How are you managing to do this? Do you have support — emotional or financial?

What are you learning about yourself as you take on this role of parent? How many children are you looking after? Are you still at school or are you working? How are you dealing with your loss?

Write a letter to the parent who died and tell her or him everything you may not have

my life

been able to when s/he was alive. Then create a small ceremony for yourself and ask someone to be there with you. Pray for your parent, talk to her or him and then light the letter and burn it. Bury the ashes somewhere close to you. Continue to pray for her or him.

Living in South Africa with AIDS

Each one of us in South Africa has a contribution to make within the AIDS pandemic. In what way/s can you make a difference, even a small one? Perhaps one of the following could suggest an area where you could contribute.

- Find out everything about the disease.
- Foster or befriend a child who is HIV-positive.
- Adopt a child with AIDS.
- Be supportive to a person who is HIV-positive or who has AIDS.
- Volunteer to help at places like Cotlands Baby Sanctuary.
- Arrange to give informative talks to people who are still afraid of the disease.
- Contribute a percentage of your earnings to an organisation that is making a difference in the field of AIDS.
- Learn to be a counsellor and counsel people with AIDS· or teach others to do this.
- Send or take a basket of food on a regular basis to children who are at risk because of the danger of rape linked to a belief that sex with a young girl can cure AIDS, or because one of their parents is HIV-positive and cannot support them.
- Start a support group for parents of small children. Discuss with them their fears and concerns.
- Get involved with a project that reflects your interests, eg. Legal aid for PWAs.
- Campaign for the free distribution of anti-retrovirals which save the lives of the mother and the child.

Being gay, lesbian or straight

Write or draw your experience of being gay or lesbian or bisexual or transsexual. Share this with a friend. If you are straight, evaluate your attitude to the gay/lesbian community. Share your feelings and perceptions.

Being the parent of a gay or lesbian child

When did you realise your child was gay or lesbian? How did you help her or him to understand her/his sexual orientation? How did you find support for yourself? Many adults are unprepared for a gay or lesbian child and tend to think they have "done something wrong". There are many groups and associations that counsel parents through this misconception. How have you grown as a result of your experience?

Being in a situation you were not ready for

When Justin got ill I was very scared. I had never been responsible, even for a short period, for someone else's life. What about you? Have you ever found yourself in a situation where suddenly everyone looks to you to make the decisions and do something.

What was the situation? What did you discover about yourself — both positive and negative? How has this changed you?

my life

Facing the death of a friend or a child

I lost two people I loved — my father and Justin. What about you? Were you there when the person you loved was dying? Did you feel that same powerlessness to help? Were you aware that in a short time that person would stop breathing? How did you get through the experience? How did you deal with your grief? Are you still holding back from fully expressing your loss? Have you ever thought of writing to the person and telling her or him everything you never said when she or he was alive?

A letter to yourself

This is the second last item in the workbook. As you look back over what you have responded to and how you have responded, what does that tell you about yourself? Complete the task by writing a letter to yourself pointing out what you have discovered as a result of your response. Leave nothing out. Write the letter in tenderness and love. Or if you prefer, create a collage of yourself. Reward yourself for whatever you discover. Find a way to express your appreciation to yourself. The journey continues ...

A letter to God

This is the final item in the workbook. Write a letter to God or to whoever or whatever you conceive God to be. Now that you have worked with your life, either in a small way or in a long-term way, what do you want to say to God if God was sitting with you now and you could see and touch God? Then write a letter from God to yourself, in reply.

The journey continues ...